WHAT REVIEWERS SAY
about 100 Names *of* Mary

"The genius of Catholicism is its sacramentality—the belief that God's grace takes root again and again across history and in diverse cultures. Anthony Chiffolo's *100 Names of Mary* presents a fine overview of the ways in which Mary's faithful witness, made possible by God's grace, has blossomed and become a source of deeper faith around the globe. Chiffolo's summary of each devotion and his enhancement of traditional prayers with contemporary ones provide a wonderful resource for spiritual growth and awareness of the richness of the Catholic Marian tradition."

—Charles E. Bouchard, O.P.,
President and Associate Professor, Aquinas Institute of Theology

"Alongside a number of informative Marian studies there has been a need for contemporary devotional works that open the faithful heart to the wonder and intercession of our Blessed Mother Mary. Anthony F. Chiffolo has written a warm and attractive guide to a faith relationship to Mary in [this] intriguing book…. Its great strength is its broad sweep of history linked to a modern sensitivity. It is a work of beauty, faith and truth and will inspire all who meditate upon it."

—Rev. Alfred McBride, O. Praem.,
Professor of Homiletics, Blessed John XXIII Seminary, Weston, Massachusetts

"…Through scholarly research and documentation, the author presents the universal Mary, Mother of all nations, of all races, of all times. This book is informative about the breadth of Marian devotion among the laity and is valuable as a devotional to enrich one's spiritual life. Although most of the images and selections have not universal ecclesiastical approbation, the book can help to increase one's devotion to Mary."

—Sister Charlene Altemose, M.S.C.,
author of What You Should Know About Mary

"This beautiful and stunning tribute to Mary will become an instant classic treasured for generations by all those mere mortals like us—followers of her Son—who are also privileged to call her…'Mother.'…a volume of rare scholarship which is *both* a *history* book and a *prayer* book. I can't elevate it any higher than to suggest that only Mary could have inspired it."

—William O'Shaughnessy,
President and Editorial Director, Whitney Radio

"Anthony Chiffolo has done all of us a favor. *100 Names of Mary* presents a comprehensive look at Mary that will enhance our spiritual lives. The combination of Scripture, tradition and contemporary prayers provides a powerful portrait of Mary that will appeal to people from many different cultures and backgrounds. This book aids contemporary spiritual seekers to embrace Mary, as the universal guru, disciple, companion, mother, advocate, who continues to guide us on the path to holiness."

—*Bridget Mary Meehan,*
author of 20 books, including award-winner Praying with
Visionary Women *and* Praying with Women of the Bible

"Through Baptism the Father of Jesus becomes our Father, and the mother of Jesus becomes our mother. This is why we can call upon God as our loving Father, and this is why we can call on Mary as our mother to pray for us with a mother's love. Anthony F. Chiffolo's book is a wonderful way to get to know our Blessed Mother better."

—*Mitch Finley,*
author of Surprising Mary: Meditations and Prayers on
the Mother of Jesus *and* Your One-Stop Guide to Mary

"...a work to complement and enrich any Catholic's Marian library. The story of each title is briefly presented along with a beloved tradition and a sparkling new prayer. The reader will meet some old favorites like Fatima, Star of the Sea and the Assumption. In addition, Chiffolo introduces us to many Madonnas little known here in the U.S. Our Lady of Gyos, of Sinj, of Tinde, of Marija Bistrica, of Neocaesarea and of Trsat are only a few of the titles whose stories will delight any Catholic devoted to Mary."

—*Ann Ball,*
author of Modern Saints: Their Lives and Faces
and The Saints' Guide to Joy That Never Fades

"Add to the 100 names of Mary 'Guiding Light to Aspiring Teenagers.' In 1940 she answered my prayers for a successful cartoonist's career. This book is a treasury of revelation."

—*Bil Keane,*
creator of "The Family Circus"

"This wonderful book is absolutely needed and long overdue. It is graciously compiled with marvelous sensitivity. It brings together not just an expansive history of the wonders of Mary, but also a more complete continuity of the auras of beauty, superlative love and sustaining hope that extend and bloom from her presence and appearances through time."

—*Ingo Swann,*
author of The Great Apparitions of Mary: An Examination
of the Twenty-Two Supranormal Appearances

100 Names *of* Mary

Stories & Prayers

ANTHONY F. CHIFFOLO

ST. ANTHONY MESSENGER PRESS

Cincinnati, Ohio

Nihil Obstat: Hilarion Kistner, O.F.M.
                Rev. Robert A. Stricker

Imprimi Potest: Fred Link, O.F.M.
                Provincial

Imprimatur: +Most Rev. Carl K. Moeddel, V.G.
                Archdiocese of Cincinnati
                October 9, 2001

The *nihil obstat* and *imprimatur* are a declaration that a book is considered to be free from doctrinal or moral error. It is not implied that those who have granted the *nihil obstat* and *imprimatur* agree with the contents, opinions or statements expressed.

Library of Congress Cataloging-in-Publication Data

Chiffolo, Anthony F., 1959-
  100 names of Mary : stories and prayers / Anthony F. Chiffolo.
      p. cm.
Includes bibliographical references and index.
  ISBN 0-86716-441-7
  1. Mary, Blessed Virgin, Saint—Titles I. Title: One hundred names of
Mary. II. Title.
  BT670.T5 C45 2002
  232.91—dc21
                                    2001005136

Art: Front Cover, Page xvi: *Blessed Virgin and Christ Child.* Vatican mosaic at the Chapel of St. Gregory the Great, Athenaeum of Ohio/Mount St. Mary's Seminary, Cincinnati, Ohio. Photo by Janine Spang. Used with permission.

Page vi: *Assumption of Mary* by Heinz Hindorf. Stained glass window at Worms Cathedral, Worms, Germany. Copyright photo by The Crosiers/Gene Plaisted, O.S.C. Used with permission.

Page xii: *Immaculate Conception* by Steve Erspamer, S.M. Clip art printed from *Clip Art For Year B* by Steve Erspamer. Copyright ©1993, Archdiocese of Chicago: Liturgy Training Publications, 1800 North Hermitage Ave., Chicago, IL 60622, 1-800-933-1800. All rights reserved. Used with permission.

Page 26: *La Madonnina* by Roberto Ferruzzi. Painting, c. 1897.

Page 56: *Pieta* (after Delacroix) by Vincent van Gogh, 1889. Painting at Van Gogh Museum, Amsterdam, The Netherlands. Photo copyright: Art Resource, NY.

Page 98: *Our Lady of Guadalupe and Juan Diego of Mexico* by Robert Lentz. Copyright ©1986, Robert Lentz. Art courtesy of Trinity Stores, PO Box 44944, Eden Prairie, MN 55344, 1-800-699-4482. Used with permission.

Page 132: *Black Madonna,* a replica of Our Lady of Einsiedeln. Statue at Blue Cloud Abbey, Marvin, SD. Copyright photo by The Crosiers/Gene Plaisted, O.S.C. Used with permission.

Page 168: *Salus Populi Romani,* Madonna and Child attributed to Saint Luke. Painting at Basilica di S. Maria Maggiore, Rome Italy. Copyright photo: Alinari/Art Resource, NY.

Page 202: *Annunciation* by F. Schiavina. Sculpture at Church of the Annunciation, Nazareth, Galilee. Copyright photo by The Crosiers/Gene Plaisted, O.S.C. Used with permission.

Cover and interior design by Mary Alfieri

ISBN 0-86716-441-7

Copyright ©2002, Anthony F. Chiffolo
All rights reserved.

Published by St. Anthony Messenger Press
www.AmericanCatholic.org
Printed in the U.S.A.

$\mathcal{W}$hat shall I call you, full of grace?
  I shall call you Heaven: for you have
    caused the Sun of justice to rise.
  Paradise: for in you has bloomed
    the flower of immortality.
  Virgin: for you have remained inviolate.
  Chaste Mother: for you have carried in
    your arms a Son, the God of all.
  Pray to him to save our souls.

—*Fifth-century hymn*

To Rusty

Contents

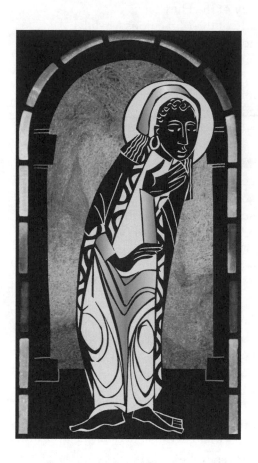

Acknowledgments

I thank Lisa Biedenbach and April Bolton of St. Anthony Messenger Press for believing in this project and shepherding it through the publication process.

My special thanks go out to Rayner W. Hesse Jr. for his assistance with proofreading, his practical suggestions, his invaluable theological insights, his sincere interest in my work and, most of all, his hearty support of all that I am.

Introduction

Some call her the Blessed Mother. Others, the Blessed Virgin Mary—BVM for short—or the Virgin, our Lady or, simply, Mary. The Gospels of Matthew, Mark and Luke name her Mary, while the Gospel of John refers to her only as the mother of Jesus. But over the centuries Christians have bestowed upon her innumerable titles of devotion—some lists include more than six thousand titles—from Ark of the New Covenant to Virgin of Tenderness, from Our Lady of All Nations to Our Lady of Zhyrovytsi. This proliferation of titles reflects the different ways people relate to Mary. Some communicate with her as with a very human mother; others approach her—mistakenly, the Roman Catholic Church maintains—as if she were a demigod; still others consider her a symbol of love, faith, hope or help. Fortunately, her various titles express her many qualities, so while one person may find her comfort in the Mother of Sorrows, another may find his center in the Queen of Peace. She also has many privileges, by which the faithful can express their devotion by addressing her as, for example, the Immaculate Conception or the *Panagia*. And then there are those titles that are linked to particular apparitions, among the most famous of which are Our Lady of Fátima and Our Lady of Lourdes, whose appeal to diverse people lies in the variety of messages, miracles and circumstances of the appearances.

But who was this woman? According to the Gospel of Matthew, she was the wife of Joseph of Bethlehem of Galilee and the mother of Jesus. Extracanonical sources and tradition add that her parents were Anne and Joachim of Nazareth. Little is known for certain of her life. Many of the Gospels' references to her are heavily overladen with symbolism and mythology, while others mainly situate her in the background of her son's ministry. The Scriptures do indicate that she was present at Jesus' crucifixion, that she was entrusted to the care of the beloved disciple, John, and that she was present with the disciples in the Upper Room at Pentecost.

The name *Mary*—probably Miriam or Miryam in Hebrew—comes from the Hebrew *mar* meaning "bitter, bitterly or bitterness." Secondary meanings include "great" and "heavy." Like many women of the Jewish faith, Mary was probably named after Miriam, the sister of Moses, an important Jewish prophet whose name means "fat, thick, strong" but can also mean "princess." Certainly, the Gospel writers highlighted the parallels between these two women. For example, Mary's Magnificat, delivered upon her visit to Elizabeth, strongly echoes the Song of Moses, which scriptural scholars now believe was originally ascribed to Miriam. Again, just as Miriam leaves Egypt to find the Promised Land in the company of Moses, the Deliverer, so Mary returns to the Promised Land with Jesus, the Messiah. And though they acted differently, both suffered on account of prophecy. When Miriam felt her prophetic voice was being marginalized, bitterness overtook her, caused her to rebel and brought a punishment from God. In contrast, Mary did not give voice to bitter prophecies but treasured all foretellings in the silence of her heart; though she did not rebel, her suffering on account of her son's death was nonetheless so extreme that the church names her Queen of Martyrs.

Indeed, some Christians ascribe to Mary's suffering a participation on her part in Christ's redemptive act, naming her Co-redemptrix. This is perhaps the most controversial of her titles currently, though through the centuries many of her names have caused debates, arguments, even excommunications. In the fifth century, for example, the Council of Ephesus was convened in order to decide whether Mary was the *Theotokos*, or God-Bearer; those who subsequently refused to honor the title approved by the council were excommunicated. Yet today some Christians prefer *Theotokos* to one of its alternative translations, *Mother of God*, a name that still causes heated debate because of its theological implications about the genesis of God. Even some of Mary's traditional titles, such as Immaculate Conception and Ever-Virgin, are not universally accepted and, consequently, have become stumbling blocks to Christian unity.

This is not to mention the amazing proliferation of Marian apparitions in the past one hundred years. Beginning in the nineteenth century with the appearance of our Lady in Paris, Mary is said to have appeared at Lourdes, Fátima, Akita, La Salette, Naju, El-Zeitoun, Knock, Amsterdam, Kibeho, Damascus, Medjugorje, Pontmain, Banneux, Beauraing, Dong Lu, Betania and a number of other locations until the present day. Mary has brought a unique message, charism, miracle or manifestation to each of these appearances and, thus, has often become known by a name unique to that apparition. For example, she is known as Our Lady of Light for her appearances at El-Zeitoun, Our Lady of All Nations for Amsterdam, Virgin of the Poor for Banneux and so forth. Otherwise, she is known simply as

Our Lady of Akita, Our Lady of Kibeho and so on.

The apparitions, of course, often raise more questions than they answer. Are they manifestations of the power of suggestion, mass hallucination or inexplicable natural events, or is the Divine really trying to send humankind a message via the Blessed Mother? And if so, why is she appearing in remote places to those who lack education or prestige or wealth instead of to heads of state or the assembled ambassadors to the United Nations, who might be able to effect some positive changes? And what about her messages? There are dire predictions of days of darkness, of the eschaton, of calamities and hardships because people have turned away from God. But plagues and earthquakes and wars have afflicted humans since history has been recorded: can a few appearances make any difference? And what kind of worship arises only from a desire to avoid sickness or pain anyway? Furthermore, what of Mary's apparitional claim to be Co-redemptrix? Is this an iconoclastic concept or a logical development of humankind's understanding of the Spirit's inclusivity?

Many people might believe that titles such as Co-redemptrix and Mother of God go too far, elevating the Blessed Mother to divine equality with Christ or with God—that is, replacing the Trinity with a quartet. On the surface, this may seem the case. Yet to understand how the church *honors* Mary—to comprehend that the people of God do *not* worship Mary as they worship God—it is essential to put aside emotional reactions and, digging beneath the surface, discover the origins and meanings of what the church believes about Mary.

This is the plan I have followed in writing this book. I have looked not only at Scripture, the writings of the early church, the pronouncements of the saints and papal statements, but also at recent biblical and theological scholarship. In so doing I have had to put aside my preconceived beliefs, to adopt a certain naiveté that would allow me to consider Mary's story anew. And as I reexamined what I had been taught about the Blessed Mother, I believe that I developed a deeper and more honest relationship with her. At the same time, I have, I feel, only just begun to recognize the magnificence of the redemption story.

My hope is that in challenging readers to reexplore their own beliefs about Mary, this book will also lead to a deeper appreciation of the glorious mystery of the Christian faith.

BLESSED VIRGIN AND CHRIST CHILD

Vatican mosaic at the Chapel of St. Gregory the Great
Athenaeum of Ohio/Mount St. Mary's Seminary
Cincinnati, Ohio

100 Names of *Mary*

Advocate
| INTERCESSOR |

HER STORY

*P*erhaps among all her titles, the Blessed Virgin Mary is best known as Advocate, or Intercessor—someone who pleads the cause of another or presents an entreaty in favor of another, often before a judicial court. In this sense the Blessed Mother is the advocate of all humankind, for she pleads the cause and presents the petitions of all people before God.

Mary's distinction as Advocate may have some basis in Old Testament images of the queen mother who intercedes on behalf of her subjects with her son, the king. Since Mary's son, Jesus the Christ, is King and Lord of All, she is Queen of the Universe (page 191), and she will petition him on behalf of her children. The New Testament also supports Mary's role as Advocate: the Gospels' (Luke 2:51 and John 2:1–11) depiction of Jesus' obedience to his mother leads to the belief that in heaven he will also grant her requests.

In the early days of Christian literature, Saint Irenaeus (second century) set the pattern by writing of Mary as Eve's advocate. Through the centuries many liturgies have developed this theme. For example, the preface for the Solemnity of the Immaculate Conception (page 23) reads, "You chose her from all women to be our advocate with you...." The Mass of the Blessed Virgin Mary, Queen of All Creation, includes this prayer: "You exalted her above all the choirs of angels...to intercede for all your children, our advocate of grace...." And the Mass of the Blessed Virgin Mary, Gate of Heaven, exclaims, "She is the Virgin at prayer, always interceding for sinners that they may turn to her son, who unseals the fountain of ever-flowing grace and opens the door of forgiveness." Indeed, there is hardly a prayer in the Roman liturgy that does not implore the Blessed Mother's intercession.

The earliest recorded prayer to Mary, the Sub tuum praesidium of the third or fourth century, reads, "We fly to thy patronage, O holy Mother of God. Despise not our petitions in our necessities, but deliver us from all danger, O ever glorious and blessed Virgin." This description of Mary as patron is another way of illustrating her advocacy. Just as knights would choose patrons to serve, many Christians put themselves under Mary's patronage by consecrating themselves to her honor. And just as patrons would intercede on behalf of their knights, so Mary advocates on behalf of her devotees.

Besides intercession and patronage, Mary's advocacy also includes protection, and Christians continue to appeal to her for assistance in times of danger. In the Memorial of Our Lady of Mount Carmel (page 135), for example, the church prays, "Father, may the prayers of the Virgin Mary protect us and help us to reach Christ her Son." The Mass of the Holy Name of Mary includes the following prayer: "Grant that we who call upon the holy name of Mary, our Mother, with confidence in her protection, may receive strength and comfort in our needs." These are but a few examples.

As Advocate, Mary is not the source of reconciliation, mercy or grace. She brings a human case before her son, pleading with him on behalf of each person in need. As Heavenly Mother, she will do all that she can—to the point of moving heaven and earth—to obtain all that her children require. Pope Paul VI wrote in *Credo of the People of God*, "We believe that the Holy Mother of God, the new Eve, Mother of the Church, continues in heaven to exercise her maternal role on behalf of the members of Christ."

So it is that people of God turn to the Blessed Mother as Advocate, placing themselves in her maternal care, that she might obtain from her son all that human hearts desire. She also obtains for her children the grace necessary to follow God's will. What's even more important, she pleads with her son to look with mercy and forgiveness upon all human transgressions. Intercessor, patron, protector—as Advocate, Mary leads all people back to right relationship with God.

✎ TRADITIONAL PRAYER

Steadfast Protectress of *Christ*-ians
Constant Advocate with *the Creator*,
Disdain not the cry of the sinful,
But of thy goodness,
Be ready to succor us,
Who do call with all confidence to thee.

Make haste to hear our petition!
Make haste to supplicate for us,
O Mother of *God*,
Who ever didst protect them that pay
    honor to thee!

—*Saints John Chrysostom and Basil*

Holy Mary, my advocate, I pray to you from the depths of my heart, for I have reached the absolute limit of my human resources. I am exhausted physically, depleted mentally, wrung out emotionally and dessicated spiritually. I have no one to turn to except you, my heavenly mother, nowhere to seek help except in your maternal heart. So, dearest Advocate, I bring to you my petition *[mention request]*. Please present it to your son, reminding him that I have turned to his mother in my hour of need, and implore him to look, therefore, upon me with his favor. O blessed Advocate, I thank you for your advocacy and pray that I may always be your loving child. Amen.

Ark of the New Covenant

HER STORY

From earliest times, Christians have seen in Mary and her pregnancy the reenactment of God's gift of the covenant to the chosen people. Indeed, through Mary's *fiat* God was able to enflesh a New Covenant. Numerous scriptural passages bear out this comparison.

Compare:

> Then the cloud covered the tent of meeting, and the glory of the LORD filled the tabernacle. (Exodus 40:34)

With:

> The Holy Spirit will come upon you, and the power of the Most High will overshadow you; therefore the child to be born will be holy; he will be called Son of God. (Luke 1:35)

As the book of Exodus describes, when the chosen people had built the ark of the covenant for the tablets of the Ten Commandments and had constructed the tabernacle to shelter it, God came to dwell there. The fathers of the church took this occurrence as a foreshadowing of the Incarnation, as announced to Mary by the angel Gabriel in the Gospel of Luke. God's glory, which filled the ark of the covenant, also came to dwell within the Blessed Mother.

Compare:

> How can the ark of the LORD come into my care? (2 Samuel 6:9)

With:

> And why has this happened to me, that the mother of my Lord comes to me? (Luke 1:43)

The words of King David and Elizabeth do not have exactly the same import, though both indicate a certain awe at the presence of holiness. What is remarkable is the prefigurement of Elizabeth's words in David's and the equation of "ark" and "mother."

Compare:

> So David and all the house of Israel brought up the ark of the LORD with shouting, and with the sound of the trumpet. As the ark of the LORD came into the city of David, Michal daughter of Saul looked out of the window, and saw King David leaping and dancing before the LORD.... (2 Samuel 6:15–16)

With:

> For as soon as I heard the sound of your greeting, the child in my womb leaped for joy. (Luke 1:44)

Both David and John leaped joyfully, indicating their delight in the presence of the Lord. And the Greek word used in Luke, *anafametzen,* meaning "shouts of joy," refers to liturgical celebrations, specifically those connected with the presence of the ark of the covenant. The Gospel's use of this word, then, is a powerful identification of Mary with the ark.

Compare:

> The ark of the LORD remained in the house of Obed-edom the Gittite three months; and the LORD blessed Obed-edom and all his household. (2 Samuel 6:11)

With:

> And Mary remained with her [Elizabeth] about three months and then returned to her home. (Luke 1:56)

Both the ark of the covenant and Mary remained in the hill country for three months, blessing their host's household with their holy presence.

To the chosen people, the ark of the covenant was the holiest object ever created, for it contained the tablets of the Law, Aaron's shepherd's staff and a sample of manna, the bread God provided in the desert. Further, it was the place and sign of God's presence among them, bringing blessings in peace and victory in battle.

At the same time, Christians believe Mary is the holiest of all humans, for she is the Immaculate Conception (page 23), the Full of Grace (page 48), the *Theotokos* (page 198). She carried within her the new Law as embodied in her son, who would be the Good Shepherd, the Bread of Life. He would be the New Covenant with the people of God. For this reason his mother is known as the Ark of the New Covenant, bearing witness to this new way as she continues to make the presence of Christ known to all.

∾ TRADITIONAL PRAYER

O Ark of the New Covenant, clad on all sides with purity in place of gold; the one in whom is found the golden vase with its true manna, that is the flesh in which lies the God-head.
—*Saint Athanasius* (attributed)

∾ NEW PRAYER

All-holy Ark of the New Covenant, when day is dawning and filled with potential, remind us of God's creative coming into the world.

All-holy Ark of the New Covenant, when day is present and filled with action, remind us of God's dynamic presence in the world.

All-holy Ark of the New Covenant, when day is closing and filled with completion, remind us of God's eternal embracing of the world.

O holy Mother, keep us mindful of God's immanence, that at every moment we might rejoice in God's great love. Amen.

Blessed Mother

HER STORY

Mary's recognition as the Blessed Mother comes from the nativity narrative in the Gospel of Luke. In announcing the Incarnation the angel Gabriel greeted Mary with these famous words: "Hail, favored one! The Lord is with you" *(NAS)*. Another translation reads, "Rejoice, highly favored one! God is with you! Blessed are you among women!" *(INT)*. God blessed Mary above all other women, preparing her for this very moment, upon which hung God's plan of salvation. And Mary's submission to God's will at this instant was certainly blessed, for without her cooperation Jesus would not have been conceived and God's plan of salvation would have been interrupted. The angel's words have become the opening to the Hail Mary, the world's most popular Marian prayer.

Mary soon went to visit Elizabeth, and the older woman immediately offered this benediction upon her pregnant cousin: "Blessed are you among women, and blessed is the fruit of your womb....And blessed is she who believed that there would be a fulfillment of what was spoken to her by the Lord." Elizabeth's words are the second part of the most popular prayer to Mary.

In her song of praise, delivered right after Elizabeth's greeting, Mary herself prophesied, "Surely, from now on all generations will call me blessed, for the Mighty One has done great things for me." The greatest of these things was her motherhood, conceived miraculously in Mary's womb by God's Spirit, preserved all through the journey to Bethlehem, recognized at the presentation at the Temple, protected during the flight to Egypt, obeyed at the wedding at Cana and honored by Jesus when from the cross he gave her into John's care and made her mother of all humankind. For these reasons all generations have held Mary in the highest esteem, honoring her with her most human title, that of Blessed Mother.

ᴄᴠ TRADITIONAL PRAYER

O Blessed Mother, whose love and protection have kept us faithful to your beloved son and his church, spread the mantle of your maternal care over us, fulfill our every need [mention request], and through your intercession with our Heavenly Father guide us to eternal joy in heaven, through Christ our Lord. Amen.

ᴄᴠ NEW PRAYER

O Blessed Mother, I have spent most of my life traveling in the wrong direction, trying to be someone God has not created me to be. And that journey has nearly destroyed me. Only in recent times have I been able to find the path God had intended for me all along. But I still lose my way because I am not always able to recognize myself, and I become afraid of losing myself again. O Blessed Mother, guide me along this new way, and stay with me when I feel that I don't know who I am anymore. Teach me what I need to know in order to be myself. Encourage me to persevere when the process of relearning how to live becomes overwhelming. Inspire me to dare to be the holy person God has created me to be, and raise up within me the courage to follow wherever God will lead. Amen.

Cause of Our Joy

HER STORY

From the moment of the Incarnation, the world was filled with a new joy. The angel Gabriel brought joyful news of her pregnancy to Mary, and the heavenly hosts proclaimed "good tidings of great joy" to the shepherds. The baby Jesus was the great joy for which Simeon and Anna had been waiting for years in the Temple. And after Jesus embraced his ministry, he brought great joy to those he cured of their sicknesses. To others he gave the joy of unconditional acceptance and welcome. Still others received from him the astonishingly joyful gift of faith in relationship with God. Finally, he presented to all the exceeding joy of resurrection life. Christians believe that Jesus the Christ is the source of all true joy and might even say that Jesus the Christ *is* Joy.

As his mother, Mary is Cause of Our Joy, for she brought Jesus to humankind. She delivered him into the world, shared him with the shepherds and wise men, presented him in the Temple. She raised him to be a child who needed to take care of God's business in God's house. She propelled him into his active ministry, urging him to replenish the wedding wine at Cana. And though it pierced her heart, she even endorsed his final sacrifice, for she understood who he was.

Mary continues to bring Christ to humankind. Over the centuries she has appeared many times as the Madonna holding the infant Jesus, and during her apparitions she has often spoken of her son, repeating his message to all who will listen.

She also brings people to Jesus, continually urging them to follow his way and accept his love. She even offers herself as Mediatrix (page 39) and Advocate (page 2) to help men and women approach Christ without fear and to enjoy a living and loving relationship with God. The keynote of her message is always joy—to bring Joy to the world and to bring the world to Joy.

❧ TRADITIONAL PRAYER

O Mary, who abandoned your soul to happiness by offering it to
    God, grant that in our gift to God, our joy may be complete.
O Virgin radiant with joy, grant that we may believe in the
    happiness which God in his love wills to offer us.
May joy flood again in hearts given over to sadness.
Teach us to detach ourselves from worldly pleasures and to

seek our happiness in God.
Help us to radiate the witness of Christian (and religious) joy.
Through your presence in our life, be for us the font of joy which
is ever new.
*"O Mary, who received from God the deepest joy, help us to live in true
joy, the joy of Christ."*

—*Jean Galot*

○ᴥ NEW PRAYER

Dearest Mother, Cause of Our Joy, I rejoice in the incredible blessedness of my life—in those relationships that bless my soul with love, in the natural beauty that fills my heart with peace, in the work that satisfies my days and the leisure activities that brighten my spare moments. I rejoice in love, the spirit of God that surrounds me and enlivens me and brings joy to my soul.

O Cause of Our Joy, surprise me with joy again and again. And when I forget my blessings and focus on my misfortunes, lead me back to joy. Help me refocus, that I may accept the priceless gift of joy that you present to me, the joy of your son and his resurrection life. Amen.

Cedar of Lebanon

HER STORY

*A*lthough the Promised Land to which God brought the tribes of Israel was "flowing with milk and honey," it was nevertheless a semiarid Mediterranean place, and large trees were unusual, if not unknown, there. But in the mountains of Lebanon, the land just to the north, the cedars grew tall and straight and were so highly prized that they came to symbolize whatever was precious. Thus in the Song of Solomon, the perfect bride was called forth from Lebanon: "Come with me from Lebanon, my bride....the scent of your garments is like the scent of Lebanon....Your channel is...a garden fountain, a well of living water, and flowing streams from Lebanon" (4:8–15).

The Old Testament includes many references to Lebanon and its cedars, which became a symbol of those who are righteous in the sight of God. The Psalms, for example, declare, "The righteous...grow like a cedar in Lebanon" (92:12) and "The trees of the LORD are watered abundantly, the cedars of Lebanon that he planted" (104:16).

But the cedars of Lebanon also represent those who have become proud: "For the LORD of hosts has a day against all that is proud and lofty, against all that is lifted up and high; against all the cedars of Lebanon, lofty and lifted up..." (Isaiah 2:12–13)—as if, having been raised up by the Lord, the haughty come to attribute all their righteousness to themselves. God will not permit the conceit to continue: "He will hack down the thickets of the forest with an ax, and Lebanon with its majestic trees will fall" (Isaiah 10:34).

Lebanon also figures in the messianic prophecies, which tell how God will raise up the lowly: "Shall not Lebanon in a very little while become a fruitful field, and the fruitful field be regarded as a forest?" (Isaiah 29:17). And the messiah will proceed from Lebanon: "The glory of Lebanon shall come to you..." (Isaiah 60:13); "He shall strike root like the forests of Lebanon....and his fragrance like that of Lebanon" (Hosea 14:5–6).

One group of early Christians, the Maronites, christianized this symbol. Descended from the Church of Antioch, Maronites were early monastics who fled to the Lebanese mountains in the fifth century during their persecution by the Monophysites (those who held that Christ did not take on human nature). Maronites were deeply devoted to Mary, honoring her as the Mother of the Light, and came to extol the strength of her purpose and her fidelity to God's will by referring to her as the Cedar of Lebanon. Just as the book of Sirach exalts the cedar—"I grew tall like a cedar in Lebanon" (24:13)—so the Maronites used the cedar to symbolize Mary's spiritual stature and excellence. Known for its longevity and resistance to decay, the cedar also came to symbolize Mary's sinlessness and eventual Assumption. Maronites also thought the fragrance and oil of the cedar could repel snakes, which symbolized evil, in the same way that Mary protected the church against heresy. In the Maronite tradition Mary was seen as the perfect bride of God, brought out from Lebanon to bear the Christ, the righteous one, who would be the redemption of God's people.

Maronites have carried their devotion to Mary with them as they have migrated to Africa, Australia and North and South America. Though their loyalty remains strong, they have adapted to current usages, and in many places now the Cedar of Lebanon is also called Our Lady of Lebanon. Even in Harissa, Lebanon, the Maronite shrine to Mary is known as the shrine to Our Lady of Lebanon. The faithful can find a replica of that shrine in North Jackson, Ohio, at the National Shrine of Our Lady of Lebanon. Despite modern adaptations of language, this title serves as a reminder of God's faithfulness to the people of God, the Messiah's inclusive love for all people and the Blessed Mother's essential role in redemption history.

⌘ TRADITIONAL PRAYER

Hail, O blessed spring of infinite joy,
Hail, O divine treasure of endless joy,
Hail, O shady tree of life-giving joy,
Hail, O Mother of God, unwedded bride,
Hail, O Virgin, unblemished after giving birth,
Hail, wondrous vision, far above any other marvel.

Who could describe your splendour?
Who could tell of your mystery?
Who could know how to proclaim your grandeur?
You have embellished human nature,
you have surpassed the angelic legions...,
you have surpassed all creatures...,
we acclaim you: Hail, full of grace!

—*Sophronius of Jerusalem*

⌘ NEW PRAYER

O Cedar of Lebanon, we praise you as the Immaculate Conception, we honor you as the All-Holy, we cherish you as the Full of Grace, we recognize you as the Righteous One whom God has raised up, and we celebrate you as the Bride of God. Thanks be to you for your obedience to the will of God, for from your *fiat* came forth our Messiah. Amen.

Comforter of the Afflicted
| CONSOLER OF THE AFFLICTED, OUR LADY OF CONSOLATION, OUR LADY OF LUXEMBOURG, OUR LADY OF CSÍKSOMLYÓ |

HER STORY

To become an effective person of consolation, must a man or a woman know affliction firsthand? Like her son, Mary was personally "acquainted with grief" (Isaiah 53:3 [KJV]). As Simeon prophesied to Mary, "A sword will pierce your own soul too" (Luke 2:35). And so it did—when the adolescent Jesus was lost in the Temple, when the rabbi Jesus refused to leave his disciples to speak with his mother ("Look, your mother and your brothers are standing outside, wanting to speak to you." But to the one who had told him this, Jesus replied, "Who is my mother, and who are my brothers?" [Matthew 12:47–48]), and when the crucified Jesus handed her over to John's care. When Jesus did so, he also entrusted the sorrowing John and, symbolically, all humankind to his mother's care, raising her up to be the consoler of all afflicted people.

Though stricken herself, Mary must have been a comfort to the guilt-wracked and desolate disciples just after Jesus' death. The reliance in providence that had enabled her to exclaim, *"Fiat!"* at Jesus' conception would have grown as she had observed the playing out of God's plan during Jesus' life and would have been strongest at the moment of Jesus' apparent loss. Even after the Resurrection, the early church must have called upon Mary for comfort during the periods of persecution and martyrdom. Indeed, the first recorded expression of devotion to Mary as Comforter of the Afflicted occurs in the writings of Saint Ignatius of Antioch, in the second century: "Mary, knowing what it is to suffer, is ever ready to administer consolation." And this she did abundantly, becoming known throughout Christendom as Comforter of the Afflicted.

Centuries later, in 1624, when the Thirty Years War was devastating the grand duchy of Luxembourg, a Father Brodquart inspired the citizens to build a small chapel for Mary, Comforter of the Afflicted. But in 1626 an outbreak of bubonic plague decimated the population, halting construction. Near death himself, Father Brodquart vowed to finish the chapel should he recover. He did, and the sanctuary, completed in 1628, was consecrated to Our Lady of Consolation. Immediately, it became a great center of pilgrimage as the people appealed to Mary for comfort and release from the afflictions of war, plague and famine. Many favors and several authenticated miracles were recorded.

In 1652 Pope Innocent X wished to foster devotion to Our Lady of Consolation, so he established a confraternity at the shrine. The number of pilgrims increased dramatically, necessitating the transfer of the devotion to the cathedral.

Because of the favors Our Lady of Consolation had granted, in 1666 the governor and the senators of the Conseil Provincial unanimously elected her as the patroness of the city of Luxembourg, and in

1678 she was elected patroness of the entire duchy of Luxembourg. From that time she has also been known as Our Lady of Luxembourg.

In the ensuing centuries, devotion to Mary as Comforter of the Afflicted has spread throughout the world. Sadly, the enormous popularity of this devotion indicates just how prevalent and deep-rooted human affliction is. But thankfully, it also indicates Mary's availability to people everywhere in times of hardship and grief. And through her miraculous interventions she has demonstrated time and again that she will not fail to comfort her afflicted children.

∾ TRADITIONAL PRAYER

Holy Mary, Mother of Jesus, Consoler of the Afflicted, I place myself this day under your special protection, and I invoke your motherly aid. I promise to be faithful to your divine son, and to honor you with my whole heart. Accept me, I implore you, as your child, and protect me now and forever. Ever guide my footsteps; comfort me in my pain and grief; teach me through life to do the will of God; and be with me in the hour of my death. Amen.

∾ NEW PRAYER

Dear Mother, Comforter of the Afflicted, we appeal for your comfort, not for ourselves, but on behalf of those who are truly sorely afflicted, those who suffer from war, sickness, famine, cold, homelessness, prejudice, unemployment and the innumerable evils that mark our disordered world. Send them the comfort of your spirit, that they may have hope in God's love. Then send us among them as comforters ourselves, to bring them peace, healing, food, warmth, shelter, acceptance, employment and goodness, that they and we may together experience the working out of God's providential plan. Amen.

🕊 Co-redemptrix

HER STORY

Co-redemptrix is perhaps the most controversial of all the Blessed Mother's titles. The controversy stems, in part, from an imperfect understanding of the title's meaning. Most people believe that a co-redemptrix is one who has an equal role in human redemption.

However, in this case the prefix *co-* does not mean "equal"; rather, it means "with," "together," "associated in action with another" or "having a usually lesser share in duty or responsibility." This is the manner in which Mary fulfills her role as Co-redemptrix.

Mary is seen to participate in Christ's redemption of creation in three ways:

1. She fully cooperated with God's plan of redemption by willingly becoming Mother of God (page 44).
2. She is known as Mother of Grace (page 48), distributing to humankind the graces of Christ's already accomplished redemption.
3. She joins her sinless suffering to that of Jesus, thereby actively sharing in Christ's redeeming action.

This last is the controversial point, and it is of relatively modern interpretation. The first pope to write about Mary's co-redemptive role was Leo XIII: "...we see that there stood by the Cross of Jesus his Mother, who in a miracle of charity...willingly offered Him up to divine justice, dying with Him in her heart, pierced by the sword of sorrow" (*Jucunda semper*, 1894). Pope Saint Pius X took up the theme: "Owing to the union of suffering and purpose existing between Christ and Mary, she merited to become most worthily the reparatrix of the lost world..." (*Ad diem illum*, 1904). Pope Benedict XV continued this discourse: "To each extent did she suffer and almost die with her suffering and dying Son; to each extent did she surrender her maternal rights over her Son for man's salvation, and immolated Him— insofar as she could—in order to appease the justice of God, that we may rightly say she redeemed the human race together with Christ" (apostolic letter, 1918).

Pope Pius XI wrote extensively on the concept of Mary as Co-redemptrix. For example, in *Miserentissimus redemptor* he explained, "She brought forth Jesus the Redeemer, fed Him, offered Him as a victim at the cross, by her hidden union with Christ, and an altogether singular grace from Him, was likewise the Reparatrix." Among other instances were these words he spoke to pilgrims in 1933: "We invoke her under the title of Co-redemptrix."

Pope John Paul II has used the term *Co-redemptrix*—which has sometimes been translated *co-operator*—more than any other pope. For example, he said, "Mary, though conceived and born without the taint of sin, participated in a marvelous way in the sufferings of her divine son, in order to be Co-redemptrix of humanity" (September 8,

1982). In his address at Guayaquil, Ecuador, he proclaimed, "Mary's role as Co-redemptrix did not cease with the glorification of her son" (January 31, 1985).

His apostolic letter *Salvifici doloris* offers a fuller explanation of his use of the term:

> In her, the many and intense sufferings were amassed in such an interconnected way that they were not only a proof of her unshakable faith, but also a contribution to the Redemption of all....It was on Calvary that Mary's suffering, beside the suffering of Jesus, reached an intensity which can hardly be imagined from a human point of view, but which was mysteriously and supernaturally fruitful for the Redemption of the world. Her ascent of Calvary and her standing at the foot of the cross together with the beloved disciple were a special sort of sharing in the redeeming death of her Son.

The idea these popes have presented is that as the mother of Christ, Mary had a special calling. Any good mother suffers with her children when they are sick or in need, sacrificing her time, her wealth, her health, her very life, if necessary, to assure the children's well-being. And doubtless, Mary countless times made this sacrifice for her son. But as Mother of the Church (page 57) and Mother of All People (page 43), Mary then had to sacrifice her own son for the good of all her children. By willingly offering up her son to death—by sacrificing him to the cross—Mary participated in a unique, though human, way in Christ's redemption of all people. By cooperating in the Redemption, she herself helped to redeem the world.

The church believes that all Christians are called to cooperate in the salvation of the world. Indeed, Christ's redemption would be pointless if it did not change lives. But Mary's role is unique among humankind, and for this reason she is called Co-redemptrix. John Paul II summarized her uniqueness:

> The collaboration of Christians in salvation takes place after the Calvary event, whose fruits they endeavor to spread by prayer and sacrifice. Mary, instead, co-operated during the event itself and in the role of mother; thus her cooperation embraces the whole of Christ's saving work. She alone was associated in this way with the redemptive sacrifice that merited the salvation of all mankind. In union with the Christ and in submission to Him, she collaborated in obtaining the grace of salvation for all humanity....Although God's call to cooperate in the work of salvation concerns every human being, the participation of the

Savior's Mother in humanity's Redemption is a unique and unrepeatable fact. (audience, April 9, 1997)

Mary's role as Co-redemptrix does not in any way lessen Christ's role as Redeemer, for the Scriptures clearly indicate Christ's preeminence. As Saint Paul wrote, God has brought us into the kingdom of God's "beloved Son, in whom we have redemption, the forgiveness of sins" (Colossians 1:13–14), and sinners are justified by grace "through the redemption that is in Christ Jesus" (Romans 3:24). And the early church's belief in Christ's redemptive power was certainly based upon ancient prophecies, which told the people that God proclaimed, "I am the LORD your Savior, and your Redeemer, the Mighty One of Jacob" (Isaiah 49:26). As the prophet Job asserted, "I know that my Redeemer lives, and that at the last he will stand upon the earth..." (19:25).

Mary does not usurp nor even equally share Christ's role as Redeemer, for she has her own role. As Co-redemptrix, she reflects her son's great love for humankind, sacrificing the human love she bears for him for the greater love he and she have for all people. Both mother and Co-redemptrix, Mary does all that is necessary for the redemption of her children.

❧ TRADITIONAL PRAYER

O Mother of love and mercy who, when thy sweetest Son was consummating the Redemption of the human race on the altar of the cross, did stand next to Him, suffering with Him as a Co-redemptrix..., preserve in us, we beseech thee, and increase day by day the precious fruit of his redemption and the compassion of his Mother.

—Pope Pius XI, *Prayer for the Solemn Closing of the Redemption Jubilee, April 28, 1935*

❧ NEW PRAYER

Dearest Mother Co-redemptrix, the traditional concept of the Redemption seems horrible to me—God sacrificing Jesus to an excruciating death on the cross because only the Son of God can completely liberate me from *my* sins. And your role in this scene? To willingly offer up your beloved son in sacrifice, for the fulfillment of God's plan. Such pain, such suffering, such sorrow make no sense to me. So I ask you to help me fathom this redemption. Demonstrate to me the necessity of this sacrifice. Explain to me this reparation. Teach me the meaning of this atonement. And show me the true purpose of your own cooperation. I want to believe, dear Mother, but I also want to understand. Please help me. Amen.

 Ever-Virgin
| AEIPARTHENOS |

HER STORY

*T*he doctrine of Mary's perpetual virginity is among the most debated of all Marian beliefs. It requires accepting, first, the idea that Mary was a virgin even though she conceived and bore a son, Jesus; and second, that Mary remained a virgin forever after Jesus' birth.

The first belief comes directly from Scripture. According to the Gospel of Matthew (1:18–25), before Mary and Joseph were married— that is, before they had intercourse—Mary "was found to be with child from the Holy Spirit." Upset at the news, Joseph decided to "dismiss her quietly," to end their betrothal. But an angel appeared to him to verify that Mary was still a virgin: "...the child conceived in her is from the Holy Spirit." The Gospel adds that the events confirmed the prophecy of Isaiah 7:14: "Look, the virgin shall conceive and bear a son," further explaining that Joseph married Mary but had no "marital [sexual] relations with her...."

The Gospel of Luke (1:26–38) confirms this story of the virgin birth. The angel Gabriel appeared to Mary while she was betrothed to Joseph and announced that she would conceive the "Son of the Most High." When Mary wondered, "How can this be, since I am a virgin?" Gabriel answered, "The Holy Spirit will come upon you, and the power of the Most High will overshadow you....For nothing will be impossible with God." And Mary submitted to God's plan.

An important extracanonical source supports the doctrine of the virgin birth. According to the Protoevangelium of James, written sometime around 120, Mary's parents, Anne and Joachim, married many years, were yet childless when an angel announced that they would have a daughter whom they would consecrate to God's service. Anne conceived and bore Mary, who when three was given to the Temple and avowed to perpetual virginity. When she came of age, however, she needed a guardian to protect her chastity, so Joseph, an elderly widower who already had children, was chosen by miraculous means as Mary's betrothed. The story then proceeds as already described in the Gospel accounts, except that the high priest, learning of Mary's pregnancy, put her and Joseph on trial, and the customary test proved them truthful in their account of Mary's virginal pregnancy.

Another extracanonical source, the Gospel of the Birth of Mary, tells a story very similar to that of the Protoevangelium.

This belief in the virgin birth is ancient, attested to by many of the church fathers and others who believed that it was necessary and divinely ordained, since only a virgin would be pure enough to be Mother of God. Saint Ignatius of Antioch (died c. 107), for example, wrote that the Lord was "truly born of a virgin." Saint Jerome (c. 342–420) exclaimed, "We believe that God was born of a virgin, because we read it." The Apostles' Creed (c. fourth century) affirmed, "He [Jesus Christ] was conceived by the power of the Holy Spirit and born of the Virgin Mary"; and the Council of Nicaea (325) codified the doctrine in its creed: "...by the power of the Holy Spirit he [Jesus Christ] became incarnate from the Virgin Mary...." The Lateran Council of 649 affirmed that Jesus was conceived "by the Holy Spirit without human [male] seed."

The second belief, that Mary remained a virgin forever after Jesus' birth, though much more controversial than the first, also has ancient origins. In asserting Mary's perpetual virginity, the church fathers looked to this passage from Ezekiel as a prophecy: "The LORD said to me: This gate shall remain shut; it shall not be opened, and no one shall enter by it; for the LORD, the God of Israel, has entered by it; therefore it shall remain shut" (44:2). The church fathers saw the gate as a symbol of Christ's passage through the door of Mary's womb. Saints Athanasius, Epiphanius, Jerome and Cyril of Alexandria, all of the fourth century, upheld this view. Saint Augustine (354–430) wrote that Mary "remained a virgin in conceiving her Son, a virgin in giving birth to him, a virgin in carrying him, a virgin in nursing him at her breast, always a virgin" (Sermon 186). The Second Council of Constantinople (553–554) affirmed the concept, twice referring to Mary as "ever-virgin."

Despite the debates over the centuries, the church has come to accept Mary's perpetual virginity as an article of faith, based on its long tradition, the agreement of the infancy narratives on this detail and the difficulty of explaining the idea's origins if not from some kernel of truth. As the *Catechism of the Catholic Church* summarizes:

> The deepening of faith in the virginal motherhood led the Church to confess Mary's real and perpetual virginity even in the

act of giving birth to the Son of God made man. In fact, Christ's birth "did not diminish his mother's virginal integrity but sanctified it" [*Lumen gentium*, 57]. And so the liturgy of the Church celebrates Mary as *Aeiparthenos*, the "Ever-virgin" [*Lumen gentium*, 52]. (499)

The *Aeiparthenos* gave herself completely to God by remaining ever-virgin, consecrating her entire being to embodying what God desired of her, trusting that her submission would be of much value in the plan of redemption history. Her faith has been justified, for she is still hailed as "blessed among all women."

❧ TRADITIONAL PRAYER

O most glorious Ever-Virgin Mary, Mother of Christ our God, accept our prayers and present them to thy Son and our God, that he may, for thy sake, enlighten and save our souls. Amen.

❧ NEW PRAYER

O Ever-Virgin, save me from my ennui, the dullness of orchestrating my every move and anticipating every possible result, of strategizing and maneuvering to achieve my own cherished goals, of protecting my preconceptions with my life because any surprise would upset all my plans. This way of being brings me little joy—yet I am unmoved. O Aeiparthenos, provoke me to recognize holy inspiration. Enlighten me to the limitless possibilities of my spirit. Open my soul to the infinite Divine! Help me to hear those inspired words of the angel, "With God all things are possible," that I may finally dare to abandon my routine, embrace uncertainty and seek the joyful destiny God has designed me for from the very moment of my creation. Amen.

℘. *Help of Christians*
| AUXILIUM CHRISTIANORUM |

HER STORY

"Spread devotion to Mary, Help of Christians, and you will see miracles." So advised Saint John Bosco, whose reverence to Mary as Help of Christians, or *Auxilium Christianorum*, led him to construct the

Church of Mary Help of Christians in Turin in 1863 and has helped make this title one of the Blessed Mother's most popular.

Bosco had two dreams that prompted his devotion. In the first, he faced a menacing crowd of cursing and fighting youths, whom he attempted unsuccessfully to subdue with his bare fists. A "majestic" man pulled him out of the fracas, then ordered Bosco back in to take charge "not with blows but with kindness."

Bosco objected: "Why do you ask impossible things of me? Who are you, anyway?"

The man replied, "Ask my Mother. I will give her as your teacher and guide, and she will make it all possible."

Suddenly, a woman stood beside Bosco and reassured, "In due time you will understand."

In the second dream, Bosco saw two pillars arising out of a storm-tossed sea to anchor Peter's bark (the church). The taller pillar, surmounted with the host, bore the inscription "The Salvation of Believers." The shorter pillar had a statue of Mary on top and was inscribed "Help of Christians."

Bosco was not the first to profess devotion to Mary as Help of Christians. In 1576 Bernardino Cirillo, archpriest of Loreto, published a litany, approved by Pope Clement VIII in 1601, that invoked Mary as Auxilium Christianorum. This invocation may have arisen out of the victory at the Battle of Lepanto, which many attributed to the intercession of the Blessed Mother. Because of her aid, Pope Pius V hailed her as Our Lady of Victory (page 175), Help of Christians.

Also, when Pope Pius VII was freed from captivity after the Battle of Waterloo, in thanks to God and Mary he instituted the feast of Our Lady, Help of Christians, to be celebrated on May 24.

In *The Glories of Mary*, Saint Alphonsus de' Liguori (1696–1787) recalled even earlier references: Saint John Damascene's (c. 676–eighth century) description of Mary as "the prepared and always ready help of Christians, by which they are all delivered from dangers" and Saint Cosmas of Jerusalem's (third century) depiction of Mary as "all-powerful to deliver us from sin and hell." Saint Alphonsus also related how Saint Bernard of Clairvaux (1090–1153) addressed Mary: "Thou art an invincible warrior in defense of thy servants, fighting against the devils who assail them." Historical writings are replete with references to Mary's helping her children in times of need, including the Sub tuum praesidium, the oldest prayer addressed to Mary. It was found on a papyrus dating from the end of the third century, a time of great danger for Christians, and praises

Mary for her assistance given in time of conflict.

Scripture also speaks of the feminine strength that will conquer evil and protect dependents. Genesis prophesies a woman whose seed will crush the serpent's head (3:15), and Revelation tells of a woman whose son will "rule all the nations with a rod of iron" (12:5). Mary is held to fulfill these prophecies.

As Help of Christians, Mary becomes for all Christians a model of the active, providing assistance to her children and moving heaven and earth to correct evil and bring about God's will.

❧ TRADITIONAL PRAYER

Most Holy and Immaculate Virgin, Help of Christians, we place ourselves under your motherly protection. Throughout the church's history you have helped Christians in times of trial, temptation and danger. Time and time again you have proven to be the Refuge of Sinners, the Hope of the Hopeless, the Consoler of the Afflicted and the Comforter of the Dying. We promise to be faithful disciples of Jesus Christ, your son, to proclaim his Good News of God's love for all people and to work for peace and justice in our world. With faith in your intercession, we pray for the church, for our family and friends, for the poor and abandoned and all the dying. Grant, O Mary, Help of Christians, the graces of which we stand in need [mention request]. May we serve Jesus with fidelity and love until death. Help us and our loved ones to attain the boundless joy of being forever with our Father in heaven. Amen.

❧ NEW PRAYER

O glorious Help of Christians, stand by my side when life asks what seems impossible, particularly [mention request]. Help me to persevere in this situation, reminding me that in the Spirit, all things are possible. Amen.

𝒫 Hodegetria
|"She Who Shows the Way"|

Her Story

The story of the *Hodegetria* is long and rich, for this icon has roots in Byzantium and Rus. In the Russian Orthodox tradition the three iconographic depictions of the Madonna and Child are the *Theotokos* (page 198), the Hodegetria and the Virgin of Tenderness (page 200). In the Byzantine tradition the major types of the Madonna and Child are the *Nikopoia*, the Hodegetria and the *Blacherniotissa*, which emphasizes Mary's role as intercessor.

Hodegetria means "she who shows the way," and this icon depicts the Blessed Mother holding the child Jesus in one arm, as if enthroning him, while pointing to him with her other hand. Her gesture and her gaze—looking out of the icon toward the viewer—call all people to recognize her son as the Way, the Truth and the Life. Thus, this icon is also known as the Signpost. Other commentators believe that this icon indicates that the Blessed Mother is herself the way to Christ, for she brought Jesus forth into the world and continues to manifest Christ to all peoples.

In the icon the child has his right arm raised in blessing. Though the size of a toddler, Jesus has the bodily proportions and visage of a young adult. This contradiction indicates that he is both son of Mary and Son of God, existing in time as human and in eternity as the Word, which is symbolized by the book he holds in his left hand. The Blessed Mother's posture and expression remind the viewer that her son is as human as we and yet much more than we are.

Simple yet symbolic, Mary Hodegetria indicates who Jesus is and the way Christians are to go. And in expressing these central mysteries of Christianity, she urges all viewers to meditate upon the meaning of faith.

ᴏᴠ Traditional Prayer

I beg you, O holy Virgin, that I may have Jesus from the Spirit from whom you conceived Jesus. May my soul receive Jesus through the Spirit, through whom your flesh conceived the same Jesus. Let it be granted to me to know Jesus from the Spirit, from whom it was given to you to know, to have and to bring forth Jesus. May I in my lowliness speak exalted things of Jesus in that Spirit, in whom you confess yourself to be the handmaid of the Lord, choosing that it be done unto you according to the angel's word. May I love Jesus in that Spirit in which you adore him as Lord, contemplate him as your Son. Amen.

—*Saint Ildefonsus of Toledo*

∾ NEW PRAYER

O holy Hodegetria, lately I find myself questioning my own faith, doubting what I've been taught and rejecting the doctrines of the church. Help me in my quest, that I may find Truth, the particular way that I must follow and the life that will bring me joy. Amen.

Immaculate Conception

HER STORY

*T*he dogma of the Immaculate Conception, that from the moment of her conception Mary was free from original sin, has a long and controversial history.

Scripturally, the Immaculate Conception is based first on the identification of the Blessed Mother as the New Eve (page 63). The letter to the Romans and the first letter to the Corinthians both describe Christ as the New Adam; just as Adam needed Eve as helpmate, so the New Adam would need a New Eve, a role fulfilled by Mary. Genesis 3:15, which speaks of a woman whose seed will crush the serpent, is held to prophesy the coming of the New Eve. And in the Gospel of John, Jesus' addressing his mother as "Woman" at the wedding at Cana and at the foot of the cross is believed to validate her role as the New Eve, that is, the new Mother of All People (page 43). Since Eve had been created immaculate, without sin, then, logically, Mary the New Eve would also have been immaculately conceived.

Second, the dogma of the Immaculate Conception draws on the scriptural recognition of Mary as "Full of Grace" (page 48). In the Gospel of Luke, Gabriel greets the young maiden: "Hail, Full of Grace!" (1:28)—literally, "completely graced" or "fully favored" one. Fully favoring Mary, God's grace kept her free from personal sin during her entire life, making her the only all-holy human. Many church fathers, such as Saints Justin, Irenaeus, Tertullian, Origen, Ambrose and Augustine, wrote on this theme, extolling Mary's purity.

None other than Saint Thomas Aquinas (1225–1274) methodically explained how Mary came to be the All-Holy (page 182). To paraphrase: God so prepares those chosen for a particular task that they are made capable of fulfilling it; since God chose Mary to be the mother of Jesus, there is no doubt that God made her worthy of that role. No one who had sinned would have been worthy to be Mother of God (page 44); therefore, God kept Mary free from all personal sin.

Aquinas did not go so far as to assert that Mary was, consequently, conceived immaculately, believing, along with Saints Bernard and Bonaventure and others, that every natural conception, including Mary's, transmitted original sin. Johannes Duns Scotus (c. 1265–1308) finally addressed this objection by maintaining the perfection of Christ's redemption: Mary obtained her son's greatest redemption when he preserved her from all sin, including original sin, from the very moment of her conception.

From the time of Duns Scotus, belief in the Immaculate Conception became officially sanctioned. The Council of Basle in 1439 affirmed the dogma, and in 1476 Pope Sixtus IV approved the feast of the Immaculate Conception, which for many centuries had already been observed on December 8. In 1708 Pope Clement XI made the feast an obligation. Finally, in 1854, Pope Pius IX issued the papal bull *Ineffabilis Deus*, which stated,

> We declare, pronounce and define that the doctrine which asserts that the Blessed Virgin Mary, from the first moment of her conception, by a singular grace and privilege of almighty God, and in view of the merits of Jesus Christ, Saviour of the human race, was preserved free from every stain of original sin is a doctrine revealed by God and, for this reason, must be firmly and constantly believed by all the faithful.

Remarkably, the declaration of the Immaculate Conception was the first papal teaching to be proclaimed infallibly, though the doctrine of papal infallibility was not to be officially approved until 1870.

In 1858, just a few years after Pius IX's pronouncement, the Blessed Virgin Mary appeared to Bernadette Soubirous at Lourdes and responded, "I am the Immaculate Conception" when asked for her name (page 122).

In present times the term *Immaculate Conception* has come to focus on the negative—that is, being without sin or being preserved from the stain of original sin. Because many people have found this negative focus harmful, the church has begun to state the dogma in positive terms, affirming that Mary was preserved for all time in a right relationship with God, that Mary was always a recipient of God's perfect grace, or—to adopt Duns Scotus's language—that Mary was graced with Christ's perfect redemption from the moment of her conception. These positive statements have the benefit of affirming both Mary's Immaculate Conception and Christ's primacy as Redeemer, thus directing the faithful through Mary to Christ.

❧ TRADITIONAL PRAYER

Holy Mary, Immaculate Mother of God, most pure and holy, in union with all the saints in heaven and the just on earth and with most heartfelt ardor, I consecrate my heart to you. I implore you to receive my homage of respect, love and confidence. I come to you, O Refuge of sinners, in my present distress, and implore you to exercise in my behalf the full measure of your influence in heaven.

Present my earnest petition to God and obtain for me [mention request]. Protect me, O holy and Immaculate Mother of God, watch over me, love me, now and forever. Amen.

❧ NEW PRAYER

I praise you, O Immaculate Conception, for the Lord has done great things through you.

I praise you, O New Eve, for the Lord has made of you a new beginning for humankind.

I praise you, O All-Holy, for the Lord has favored you with such holiness as made you fit to mother our Savior.

I praise you, O Full of Grace, for the Lord has so filled you with God's grace that its abundance overflows upon us in our need.

I praise you and thank you, O Immaculate Conception, for through you the Lord has done great things for us. Amen.

❧ Madonna della Strada
|"MADONNA OF THE STREETS"|

HER STORY

The image of the Madonna of the Streets is familiar to many people. Seeming very modern, she has become a favorite illustration for Christmas cards. But few people know that there are at least two Madonnas of the Streets and that together they have inspired Christians for centuries.

LA MADONNINA

Roberto Ferruzzi
c. 1897

The first Madonna of the Streets, known as *Santa Maria della Strada*, or Saint Mary of the Wayside, is an icon dating from the fourteenth century. It was originally placed in the Astalli family's small Church of Our Lady of the Wayside. In 1541 Pope Paul III gave this neighborhood chapel to Saint Ignatius of Loyola to use as the headquarters for the newly formed Society of Jesus. Though conveniently located in Rome, it was much too small for the expanding order. So a larger church was commissioned, to be called Il Gesù; it was finally consecrated in 1584, after Ignatius's death. Within Il Gesù was constructed an intimate chapel for the Santa Maria della Strada, which is still its main altarpiece.

The icon is located between an altar dedicated to Saint Ignatius and one dedicated to the Holy Name of Jesus. This location symbolizes the Blessed Mother's characteristically intercessory role. Il Gesù itself is dedicated to God, the Virgin and Jesus—again emphasizing Mary's important relationship with the Divine.

The icon depicts our Lady holding the child Jesus. Both are crowned with gold, with other decorations in gold and precious gems. She wears a golden sunburst on her right shoulder, and Jesus makes a gesture of blessing with his right hand. Although extremely ornate, the icon was considered a representation of poverty, symbolizing the humble origins of our Lord and the simple life of the Holy Family.

The second Madonna of the Streets is a contemporary depiction and is, to the modern eye, more evocative of our Lord's love of the poor. This is the image with which most people are familiar. It was actually titled *La Madonnina*, or Little Madonna, and was first exhibited in Venice in 1897. It is believed that the artist, Roberto Ferruzzi, used as models a peasant girl, Angelina Cian, age eleven, and her baby brother. The painting came to be known as the Madonna of the Streets because the image suggests hardship and poverty, and the little Madonna seems to be standing on a doorstep, pleading for food and shelter for herself and her sleeping, trusting baby. The painting offers observers a direct and personal challenge, and modern sensibilities, easily imagining Mary and Jesus in such a scene, feel compelled to reach out and offer help to those in need.

The concept of the Madonna of the Streets goes beyond the details of poverty or physical need. Certainly, there are many street people who lack the necessities of food, clothing, shelter, a job. But other people lack necessities, too: kind words, friendly gestures, loving acceptance. In a sense, all people are street people—all are on their way from the here and now to an unknown time and place. All need guideposts, and all need someone to reach out in charity to help them along. That is the Madonna della Strada's enduring message.

⌒ TRADITIONAL PRAYER

I greet you, Mother, morning and evening; I pray to you as I go upon my way; from you I hope for the inspiration and encouragement that will enable me to fulfill the sacred promises of my earthly vocation, give glory to God, and win eternal salvation. Amen.

—*Pope John XXIII*

⌒ NEW PRAYER

Cara Madonna, when I feel myself hungry or thirsty, remind me of those who are hungrier and thirstier. When I think I need a fancy new jacket or a pair of designer sneakers, remind me of those who have no coat or shoes. When I begin to make plans to buy a bigger house, remind me of those who have no house or apartment. When I despair of ever paying off my credit cards, remind me of those who have no job. And when I begin to drown in all my anxieties, lift me out of my funk and push me out into the streets among those whose needs are life threatening, and show me what I can do to help them. Then let them guide me to what's important. Amen.

ℬ *Mary of the Annunciation*

HER STORY

A number of the Blessed Mother's titles refer to her given name, Mary. Titles such as Mary of Nazareth, Mary of Bethlehem and Mary of Galilee commemorate those places where the Virgin experienced God's providence. Other titles, such as Mary of the Visitation and Mary of Calvary, mark milestone events in her life. Of these titles, Mary of the Annunciation is particularly inspiring to the people of God, for it memorializes a young girl's complete trust in the goodness of her creator.

The Gospel of Luke (1:26–38) provides the only account of the Annunciation in the Bible, relating that the angel Gabriel went to Nazareth to tell Mary, a maiden engaged to be married, that she was going to bear the long-awaited anointed one. Gabriel announced to this teenager, "And now, you will conceive in your womb and bear a son, and you will name him Jesus. He will be great, and will be called the Son of the Most High."

Because this announcement puzzled Mary, who was certain of her virginity, Gabriel explained how God would make the impossible pregnancy occur: "For nothing will be impossible with God."

Despite the angel's reassurances, Mary must have been terrified. Not even married, and pregnant! No one would believe this miracle, so she would be stoned or exiled. Was this to be her only reward for faithful service to God? Yet she found the courage within her young soul to submit to God's designs: "Here am I, the servant of the Lord; let it be with me according to your word."

Mary's cousin Elizabeth—or rather, Elizabeth's unborn child, John—confirmed the angel's message for Mary in what amounted to another annunciation: "And why has this happened to me, that the mother of my Lord comes to me? For as soon as I heard the sound of your greeting, the child in my womb leaped for joy" (Luke 1:43–44). Elizabeth also prophesied Mary's faith that through her God would bring to fulfillment what had been foretold of old.

While Mary responded to the angel's annunciation with submission, she greeted Elizabeth and John's annunciation with rejoicing: "My soul magnifies the Lord, and my spirit rejoices in God my Savior..." (Luke 1:46–47).

Mary's twofold response to the Annunciation—first her trusting submission to divine providence, then her joyful praise of the Lord's ways—has inspired the people of God for two millennia. She challenges the faithful to become the persons God created them to be and then to rejoice in the transformation, trusting that with God all things are possible.

❧ TRADITIONAL PRAYER

May all generations proclaim you blessed, O Mary.
You believed the Archangel Gabriel, and in you were fulfilled all
    the great things that he had announced to you.
My soul and my entire being praise you, O Mary.
You had faith in the incarnation of the Son of God in your virginal
    womb, and you became the Mother of God.
Then the happiest day in human history dawned. We received the
    Divine Master, the sole eternal Priest, the Host of reparation,
    the universal King....Amen.

Tune me the tune and word me the words! O Mary of the Annunciation, teach me that song of praise, that hymn of joy. Rhyme me the rhyme and beat me the beat! I will smile away sadness and laugh away melancholy. My God has created a wonderful life, a life of wonders, for my very own delight. O Mary, I will rejoice and be glad in it! Amen.

Mary of the Assumption
| Our Lady of the Assumption, Maria Assumpta |

Her Story

The most recent Marian dogma, that of Mary's Assumption, defines the belief that Mary was assumed body and soul into heavenly glory. Pope Pius XII infallibly defined this dogma on November 1, 1950, in his *Munificentissimus Deus:* "We pronounce, declare, and define it to be a divinely revealed dogma: that the Immaculate Mother of God, the ever Virgin Mary, having completed the course of her earthly life, was assumed body and soul into heavenly glory."

The pope, however, was not pronouncing in a vacuum, for the belief in Mary's Assumption, body and soul, dates at least from the fifth century, when the feast of the Assumption was celebrated in Syria. Prior to that, certain extracanonical works, such as *The Passing Away of Mary* and *The Obsequies of Mary,* spoke of her death amid miraculous circumstances and allege that she was either assumed into heaven or resurrected. The authority of these sources was rejected, but extraordinary legends persisted. One tradition asserted that Dionysius the Pseudo-Areopagite, the presumed disciple of Saint Paul, had witnessed the Assumption. According to another tradition, Juvenal, bishop of Jerusalem, told the Emperor Marcian and his wife, Pulcheria, that the apostles had witnessed Mary's death but that her tomb had been found empty. The Jerusalem church celebrated the feast of the Assumption in the sixth century. By the end of the eighth century, the Western church universally observed the feast (first known as the feast of the Dormition of Mary) on August 15; and from the tenth century on, there was little dispute over belief in the Assumption. However, there is still disagreement about whether the

Blessed Mother died and was resurrected or was taken up into heaven without dying, as the Scriptures suggest of Enoch and Ezekiel and perhaps Moses. And some traditions still refer to Mary's *koimesis* (falling asleep), or dormition.

Scriptural support for the dogma of Mary's Assumption is inferential. Referring to Mary as the "ark of Christ," commentators have interpreted Psalm 132's "Rise up, O LORD, and go to your resting place, you and the ark of your might" (8) as indicating Mary's Assumption to her son's heaven. Again, commentators have looked to Isaiah's "I will glorify where my feet rest" (60:13) as a prophecy of Mary's glorification through her Assumption. Finally, commentators have understood Revelation's "...and the woman fled into the wilderness, where she has a place prepared by God" (12:6) as another prediction of Mary's Assumption to be with God.

Other beliefs about Mary support the idea of the Assumption. The doctrine of Mary's Immaculate Conception (page 23) logically led to the belief that unlike the children of Eve, Mary the New Eve (page 63) would not have suffered physical death—or at least would not have suffered bodily corruption. Similarly, the conviction that Mary was the All-Holy (page 182) Mother of God (page 44) led the church to believe that Jesus would not allow his beloved mother to undergo the corruption of human death.

Since Pius XII's decree in 1950, the church has continued to interpret the Assumption. The *Catechism of the Catholic Church* has this to say: "The Assumption of the Blessed Virgin is a singular participation in her Son's Resurrection and an anticipation of the resurrection of other Christians" (966). Because of her special relationship with her son, Mary was granted the grace of resurrection life immediately upon the close of her life on this earth, in anticipation of the resurrection life that Christ has promised to all people.

Christians thus look to Mary of the Assumption with awe, for she is now united with Christ. And this union enables her to extend her maternal love over the entire universe, to all of God's children, to bring them as well into union with her son.

⌘ TRADITIONAL PRAYER

O Immaculate Virgin, you are Mother of God and Mother of all people.

We believe with all the fervor of our faith in your triumphal assumption, body and soul, into heaven, where you are acclaimed as Queen by all the choirs of angels and all the legions of saints. We unite with them to praise and bless the Lord who has exalted you above all other pure creatures, and we offer you the tribute of our devotion and love....

And from this earth, over which we tread as pilgrims, comforted by our faith in future resurrection, we look to you, our life, our sweetness and our hope. Draw us onward with the sweetness of your voice that one day, after our exile, you may show us Jesus, the blessed fruit of your womb.

O clement, O loving, O sweet Virgin Mary.

—*Pope Pius XII*

ᕦ NEW PRAYER

The world is too much with me, dearest Mother, and sometimes I long to fall asleep and awake in heaven. But I know that the course of my earthly life is not yet finished, so I beg you to help me find the strength to run my race until the end. O Maria Assumpta, grace me with your endurance, that I may persevere through the pain, the sadness and the terror that too often afflict me. Remind me that your motherly love will guide me to my harbor of safety. And along the way, teach me to accept joy, to rejoice in the goodness that exists in my life now and to exult in the hoped-for bliss of resurrection life. Amen.

ᕲ Mary of the Immaculate Heart
| OUR LADY OF THE IMMACULATE HEART |

HER STORY

*M*any modern images of the Blessed Mother feature her immaculate heart, either surrounded by thorns or surmounted by a cross or flames or pierced by swords. These illustrations often pertain to her apparitions, when she has either manifested or spoken of, and even requested reverence for, her immaculate heart. Consequently, devotions to the Immaculate Heart are widespread in modern times. But this affection is not a new craze, and references to the Blessed Mother's heart are as old as Scripture.

The Gospel of Luke tells how Mary reacted to the shepherds' angelic vision: "Mary treasured all these words and pondered them in her heart" (2:19). Then Luke relates what Simeon prophesied to Mary: "And a sword will pierce your own soul too" (2:35)—the soul being synonymous with the heart in the vernacular of the time. Again, Luke recounts that after the adolescent Jesus ran away and spent three days in the Temple before returning with his parents to Nazareth, "his mother treasured all these things in her heart" (2:51). Parents are often unable to express the joyful wonder associated with having children, and Mary was no exception, as the Gospel indicates.

Parents are also sometimes unable to utter the heartbreak they may experience on account of their children. Again, Mary was no exception, for she stood absolutely silent at the foot of the cross.

Yet Mary's parenthood was indeed exceptional because she knew in advance, from God, that her child was destined to break her heart. Only the grace granted to her as Full of Grace (page 48) enabled her both to understand and to endure this heartbreak. This grace was hers by virtue of her immaculate conception (page 23). As her soul has come to be understood as immaculate, so, synonymously, has her heart.

Private devotion to Mary of the Immaculate Heart occurred among the saints and mystics of the Middle Ages, including Saints Anselm, Bernard, Gertrude the Great and Brigid of Sweden. Saint Bernardine of Siena was the best-known devotee of that age, describing Mary's immaculate heart as burning with seven flames representing the seven acts of love expressed in Mary's seven "words" recorded in the Bible.

In the seventeenth century the writings of Saint John Eudes popularized devotion to the Immaculate Heart, for he linked reverence for Mary's immaculate heart with the honoring of Jesus' sacred heart. He organized the first celebration of a feast in honor of the Immaculate Heart in 1648 and established the Order of Our Lady of Charity, dedicated to Mary's heart, and the Congregation of Jesus and Mary (the Eudists), dedicated to both hearts. In 1670 he published *The Admirable Heart of the Mother of God*, seeking to foster a churchwide feast to honor Mary's immaculate heart, but the times were not ripe for this celebration.

It seems that Mary herself had to intercede to bring about this feast. In 1840 she appeared to Justine Bisqueyburu and presented the Green Scapular (page 150), which depicts the Immaculate Heart blazing, pierced with a sword, surmounted by a cross and encircled by the words "Immaculate Heart of Mary, pray for us now and at the hour of our death." Subsequently, in 1855 the Office and Mass of the Most Pure Heart of Mary was approved for local celebration.

In 1917 two of the secrets Mary revealed at Fátima (page 91) concerned her immaculate heart. The first: "I promise salvation to those who embrace devotion to my Immaculate Heart. Their souls will be loved by God as flowers placed by me to adorn his throne. These souls will suffer a great deal but I will never leave them. My Immaculate Heart will be their refuge, the way that will lead them to God." The second: "You have seen hell where poor sinners go. To save them, God wishes to establish in the world devotion to my Immaculate Heart. If what I say to you is done, many souls will be saved and there will be peace in the world."

The apparitions at Fátima, particularly Mary's request that Russia be consecrated to her immaculate heart, did much to spread the cult of the Immaculate Heart, and Mary reinforced the devotion when, in 1932, she exposed her immaculate heart during her apparitions at Beauraing (page 74).

Given the rapid spread of the devotion, Pope Pius XII consecrated the world to Mary's immaculate heart in 1942. In 1944 he instituted the feast of the Immaculate Heart of Mary, in 1945 extending it to the universal church.

Just as Mary's immaculate heart represents a single-minded and radical commitment to the way of her son, so devotion to Mary of the Immaculate Heart includes a complete submission to the Blessed Mother's maternal care. As Mary has promised, those who dare to so abandon themselves to her immaculate heart come to experience a greater union with Christ, who is present in a special way in her mother-heart.

❧ TRADITIONAL PRAYER

Immaculate Heart of Mary, full of love of God and all people, I consecrate myself entirely to you. I entrust to you the salvation of my soul. With your help may I hate sin, love God and my neighbor, and reach eternal life with those whom I love. Amen.

❧ NEW PRAYER

O Mary of the Immaculate Heart, I consecrate myself to you.
O Mary of the Immaculate Heart, I trust you with my soul.
O Mary of the Immaculate Heart, I abandon myself to your
    maternal care.
O Mary of the Immaculate Heart, I promise to follow where
    you lead.
O Mary of the Immaculate Heart, I dedicate myself to your
    service.

O Mary of the Immaculate Heart, I commit my life to your treasure,
the Sacred Heart of your son.
O Mary of the Immaculate Heart, I cherish your immaculate heart.
O Mary of the Immaculate Heart, I love you with my entire heart.
Amen.

🦋 Mary Reconciler of People and Nations
| Our Lady of Betania |

Her Story

*O*n the small farm of Betania, not far from Caracas, Venezuela, our Lady has been appearing to María Esperanza Medrano de Bianchini since 1976.

The story begins when Saint Thérèse of Lisieux appeared to the five-year-old María and gave her a rose. Then the Blessed Mother appeared to twelve-year-old María when she was very sick with acute bronchial pneumonia, recommending certain medications that saved the girl's life. During her adolescence she was healed from a paralyzing illness after an apparition of the Sacred Heart of Jesus. Her continuing visions led María to enter a Franciscan convent, but on October 3, 1954, Saint Thérèse indicated to María in a vision that her vocation was to be a spouse and mother. That same day, the Sacred Heart told her to travel to Rome. There she met and, in 1956, married Geo Bianchini Giani.

The Blessed Mother had already told María about a special place reserved in Venezuela for prayer and pilgrimage and had shown her the farm in a vision. María and Geo finally found and purchased the spot in 1974.

The first apparition at Finca Betania occurred on March 25, 1976. Though a number of people were present for a prayer meeting, María was the only one to see our Lady, who introduced herself as "Mary Reconciler of People and Nations." Thereafter, the apparitions continued on an irregular basis, and by 1990 our Lady had appeared thirty-one times. During the first few years few people saw Mary, though many witnessed strange phenomena, such as mist coming from the hill, a profusion of flowers, the sound of an invisible choir, the scent of roses and irregular movements of the sun.

However, on March 25, 1984, after a large group of people had attended Mass at noon, our Lady appeared to a group of children near a waterfall. They ran to bring the adults over, and Mary appeared again when all had assembled. This time all 108 people present could see her. She appeared seven times that afternoon.

The message that Our Lady of Betania brought is one of reconciliation and love:

> Behold, children, the love of a Mother, who cherishes you...and comes as a starting point to lead you toward a law of justice, love, peace and reconciliation!
>
> I call you, for the great moment of reconciliation has arrived....I extend my love to all my children, dwellers on earth, and be loyal to Jesus, so you may discover the wonderful secret of unity...which will help us find the key to God's kingdom!
>
> ...Forgive one another. Love one another. Serve one another....All of you are children of God. All are loved.

The bishop of the diocese opened an investigation in 1984. He interviewed witnesses and examined the more than five hundred cures attributed to Our Lady of Betania, among which was the cure of a baby's spina bifida, as documented at Westchester County Medical Center in Valhalla, New York. In 1987 he wrote, "...these apparitions are authentic and of a supernatural character."

The miracles of Betania have continued. María has herself received the stigmata, and she displays the gifts of healing, levitation, bilocation and prophecy. The Eucharist has materialized in her mouth, and she exudes the scent of roses. One of the most remarkable phenomena is the rose that spontaneously bursts forth from her chest: this miracle has occurred sixteen times.

During Mass at Betania on December 8, 1991, the consecrated host began to bleed. This was a further sign of the sacredness of the farm.

More than two thousand people claim to have witnessed Our Lady of Betania. María continues to receive visits from the Blessed Mother, whose messages, though often filled with dire predictions of wars and other calamities, continue to remind people of God's great love and to call all of humankind to reconciliation.

❧ TRADITIONAL PRAYER

O Holy Mary, my mother, into your blessed trust and custody, and into the care of your mercy I this day, every day, and in the hour of my death, commend my soul and my body. To you I commit all my anxieties and miseries, my life and the end of my life, that by your most holy intercession and by your merits all my actions may be directed and disposed according to your will and that of your Son. Amen.

—*Saint Aloysius Gonzaga*

ᘓ NEW PRAYER

Most Blessed Mother, I have become too accustomed to the cold war. I have held so fast and so long to past hurts and insults that the bad feelings existing between me and *[mention name]* have become a familiar, even comfortable, part of my life. Yet even though this discord tears me apart inside whenever I dare to think of it, I feel stuck in the silent battle-to-the-death. Please, dear Mother, instill in me the desire for reconciliation. Help me to put aside my pride, my hurt feelings, my grudges, so that we may begin to be reconciled. Though sometimes I cannot even bear to think about *[person's name]*, soften my heart so that I might pen *[person's name]* a letter or even send an E-mail message. Compose my tongue so that I might call *[person's name]* on the telephone and have an authentic conversation. And strengthen my limbs, my will and my soul so that I might someday be able to visit with *[person's name]* and, confronting our differences, come to a moment of reconciliation and peace. I ask this in your name, O Reconciler of People and Nations. Amen.

ᘓ *Mary the Dawn*
| OUR LADY GATE OF DAWN, DAWN OF THE NEW WORLD |

HER STORY

*I*nterpreting the writings of the Jewish prophets, the early Christians began to identify the "sun of righteousness" (Malachi 4:2) with the Christ who had lived among them. The New Testament writers reinforced this identification by recounting the words of the prophecy of Zechariah, the father of the great forerunner John the Baptizer: "By the tender mercy of our God, the dawn from on high will break upon us, to give light to those who sit in darkness and in the shadow of death, to guide our feet into the way of peace" (Luke 1:78–79). The meaning was clear: God sent the Christ to illumine the darkness of the human soul and light the pathway to God.

But the sun never appears unannounced; the dawn always precedes its rising. In the same way, God sent a precursor, someone to proclaim the coming of the Son. Some would call this prophet John the Baptizer: "He came as a witness to testify to the light, so that all might believe through him. He himself was not the light, but he came to testify to the light. The true light, which enlightens everyone, was coming into the world" (John 1:7-9). But a greater prophet was among the people, Mary, Queen of Prophets (page 190), and she spoke these words: "He has helped his servant Israel, in remembrance of his mercy, according to the promise he made to our ancestors" (Luke 1:54–55). Mary was the prophet of the sunrise, the Morning Star (page 41), the dawn that heralded the coming of the Lord into the world.

A Parisian manuscript of the twelfth century is the first recorded reference to Mary as the "*lux matutina*," or "light of the morning" or "dawn." The identification of Mary as the Dawn captured the imagination of Christians, for this title encapsulates the necessary participation of humanity in the story of redemption. As Pope John Paul II has written, "the Church has constantly been aware that Mary appeared on the horizon of salvation history before Christ" (*Redemptoris Mater,* 3). Before God could become incarnate, humanity had to submit to God's plan; Mary's *fiat* is the horizon, and it is both obedience and prophecy. It is in this sense that the pope explicitly calls Mary "the dawn": just as the dawn comes before the sunrise, "so Mary from the time of her Immaculate Conception preceded the coming of the Savior, the rising of the 'Sun of Justice' in the history of the human race" (*Redemptoris Mater,* 3).

Though her son has arisen in time and space, Mary still heralds the eternal Son-rise, the Resurrection that leads to the ongoing resurrection of each human soul through Christ. Furthermore, as the Dawn, she is also the sign that will lead the church into the age to come.

◌◌ TRADITIONAL PRAYER

Mary the Dawn, but Christ the perfect Day;
Mary the Gate, but Christ the heavenly Way;
Mary the Root, but Christ the mystic Vine;
Mary the Grape, but Christ the sacred Wine;
Mary the Wheat, but Christ the Bread;
Mary the Rose-tree, Christ the Rose blood-red;
Mary the Fount, but Christ the cleansing Flood;

Mary the Chalice, Christ the saving Blood;
Mary the Temple, Christ the temple's Lord;
Mary the Shrine, but Christ its God adored;
Mary the Beacon, Christ the haven's Rest;
Mary the Mirror, Christ the Vision blest. Amen.

∾ New Prayer

O blessed Dawn, when the moment arrives, will I be ready? Will my spirit dare to move forward along the path you are announcing to me, along the way God wants me to travel? Will I be able to commit myself to my destiny? Will I even be able to discern what God created me to be?

With your illuminating help, dear Mother, I will. Amen.

Mediatrix

Her Story

Mary's role as Mediatrix is complementary to her roles as Advocate (page 2) and Co-redemptrix (page 13). The tradition naming Mary as Mediatrix is ancient, and almost from the very beginning, the church has believed that God chose the Blessed Mother to be a mediator, placed "in the middle" between God and humankind in order to help effect a reconciliation.

Some Christians raise strenuous objections to naming Mary Mediatrix, asserting that Jesus Christ is the one and only mediator between God and humans. Indeed, the first letter of Paul to Timothy states clearly, "...there is also one mediator between God and humankind, Christ Jesus, himself human, who gave himself a ransom for all" (2:5–6). Roman Catholics, however, believe that Christ's perfect mediation does not prohibit others from mediating in a subordinate way. Rather, Christ's mediation seems to require the active participation of others. As the Second Vatican Council explained,

> No creature could ever be counted along with the Incarnate Word and Redeemer; but just as the priesthood of Christ is shared in various ways both by his ministers and the faithful, and as the one goodness of God is radiated in different ways among his creatures, so also the unique mediation of the Redeemer does not exclude but rather gives rise to a manifold

cooperation which is but a sharing in this one source. (*Lumen gentium*, 62)

As the church has taught for ages, the Mother of God highlights the perfect efficacy of Christ's mediation. In the words of the Second Vatican Council, "Mary's function as Mother of men in no way obscures or diminishes this unique mediation of Christ, but rather shows its power" (*Lumen gentium*, 60). And Pope John Paul II has stated, "Mary's mediation appears as the highest fruit of Christ's mediation and is essentially oriented to making our encounter with Him more intimate and profound" (audience, January 12, 2000).

The pope's encyclical *Redemptoris Mater* more fully explains the Blessed Mother's role as Mediatrix:

Mary places herself between her Son and mankind in the reality of its wants, needs and sufferings. *She puts herself "in the middle,"* that is to say, *she acts as a mediatrix not as an outsider, but in her position as mother.* She knows that, as such, she can point out to her Son the needs of mankind and in fact, she "has the right" to do so. (21)

As the pope has amplified, "[God] willed that this woman—the first to welcome his Son, should communicate Him to all humanity. Therefore, Mary is on the road that goes from the Father to humanity, as the mother who gives everyone her Savior Son. At the same time, she is on the road that men must take to go to the Father through Christ in the Spirit" (audience, January 12, 2000). Because Christ came to people through Mary, it is also possible—and, perhaps, sometimes necessary—for people to come to Christ through Mary. She can be called the doorway to Christ.

Through this doorway the graces of heaven are said to flow. In the words of Pope Benedict XIV, "Our Lady is like a celestial stream through which the flow of all graces and gifts reaches the soul of all wretched mortals." And Pope Saint Pius X has said that she is the "dispensatrix of *all* the gifts acquired by the death of the Redeemer." Not only is Mary Mediatrix, but she is Mediatrix of All Graces.

Indeed, because Mary's *fiat* empowered the Incarnation, she has great influence with her son. As Pope Pius XII has said, "...it is the will of God that we obtain *all favors* through Mary." For this reason, the faithful pray to Mary Mediatrix. She transmits all petitions to her son, convincing him to look favorably upon humankind's requests and always obtaining the grace of his mercy.

In her role as Mediatrix, Mary does not wish to draw attention to herself. Certainly, she would never condone any worship of herself. Rather, she points without fail to her son, always encouraging her children to focus on Christ and to follow God's will, always facilitating the communication that will bring all her children into loving relationship with the Divine.

∾ TRADITIONAL PRAYER

O Maiden and most holy Mother of the Word...from the depths of your compassion welcome the people who have recourse to you. Nourish, with the outflow of your loving kindness, the flock which the son born of you with his blood redeemed.

Offer your bosom to all who are created, you who nourished the creator of all. As a reward of service to you extol all who come to pay their homage. And we who are happy to serve you will always be protected by your mediation.

—*Visigothic Book of Prayer*

∾ NEW PRAYER

Mother Mary Mediatrix, we place before you our needs and our hopes and the secret desires of our hearts. And we ask you to bless us with the assurance that you will carry our petitions *[mention request]* to your son, obtaining for us from him the graces that we seek. Amen.

Morning Star
| STELLA MATUTINA |

HER STORY

*T*he morning star is the bright star that appears in the east just before the dawn. Known as a forerunner, the morning star predicts and announces the rising of the sun. In the same way, Christians perceive the Blessed Mother as the star announcing the rising of the Son. Like the morning star, Mary shines most brightly among all the other stars, or saints, in the heavens. Like the morning star, Mary heralds the imminent rising of the sun, the birth of the Son of God. Like the morning star, Mary directs the eyes of the watchful toward the emerging light, the Sun of Justice.

The title Morning Star, or *Stella Matutina*, first appeared in the

Paduan version of the Litanies of Loreto in the fourteenth century. The Paduan author probably combined two titles that had been in use since the twelfth century: *Stella Marina*, or *Stella Maris* (Star of the Sea, page 196), and *Lux Matutina* (Light of the Morning). Saint Anthony of Padua (1195–1231) himself held that "the morning star among the clouds" mentioned in the book of Sirach (50:6) referred to the Blessed Mother. Earlier, Saint Bernard of Clairvaux (1090–1153) had urged all of God's children to call on Mary "the star."

Pope John Paul II has continued this tradition, referring to Mary as "a true 'Morning Star'" who "precedes the rising of the sun." As he explains, "Mary from the time of her Immaculate Conception preceded the coming of the Savior, the rising of the 'Sun of Justice' in the history of the human race" (*Redemptoris Mater*, 3).

The people of God look first to Mary, the Morning Star, for guidance, for her light directs the faithful to look toward that brighter light, the Son of God, who is coming again into the world.

❧ TRADITIONAL PRAYER

We ask you then, our Lady, that as you are the morning star, you may by your splendor drive away the cloud of the devil's suggestions which covers the earth of our minds. Do you, who are the full moon, fill our emptiness and scatter the darkness of our sins, so that we may be able to come to the fullness of eternal life, to the light of unending glory. May he grant this, who brought you forth to be our light, who made you to be born on this day, that he might be born of you. To him be honor and glory forever and ever. Amen.

—*Saint Anthony of Padua, on the feast of Mary's Nativity*

❧ NEW PRAYER

I hail you, O Morning Star, with thanks for your hopeful illumination! For when sadness and depression had extinguished all light from my soul, you appeared in your full glory, promising that the darkness within would give way to a joyful brightness. Thanks be to you for your encouragement, for without it I would not have been able to reach the dawn.

As you did for me, dear Morning Star, shine brilliantly now for all those who are in despair, that they, too, may rejoice in the hope of the coming dawn. Amen.

ℬ Mother of All People

*T*he belief that Mary is Mother of All People has two sources. The first is the story of the crucifixion in the Gospel of John, which tells that just before his death Jesus put his mother into John's care: "When Jesus saw his mother and the disciple whom he loved standing beside her, he said to his mother, 'Woman, here is your son.' Then he said to the disciple, 'Here is your mother.' And from that hour the disciple took her into his own home" (19:26–27).

Jesus' use of the words *woman* and *mother* are taken to suggest the universality of Mary's motherhood. No longer, Jesus seemed to be saying, was Mary just his own mother; she was from that point the mother of all humankind, just as the young John became the prototype for all people whom Jesus still calls to follow his way.

The second source is the concept of the New Eve (page 63). Christians call Mary the New Eve because her obedience to God, which brought life and joy, succeeded Eve's disobedience, which resulted in death and sorrow. As the new Eve, Mary replaced the first Eve and became the new mother of all humanity.

As the spiritual mother of all persons, not only does Mary advocate and mediate for the well-being of all, she calls each one personally, leading each to a life of faith in her son according to her example. And her motherly love knows no bounds, overflowing so abundantly that she bathes all people, the good and the bad, with her lovingkindness, while always pointing the way back to God, the true source of life.

ᴄ⌇ TRADITIONAL PRAYER

O Mother of all people, you know their sufferings and their hopes. You feel in a motherly way the struggles between good and evil, between light and darkness, that shake the world. Accept our cry, addressed in the Holy Spirit directly to your heart. Embrace the people who are most awaiting this embrace, and at the same time the people whose trust you also particularly expect. Take under your motherly protection the whole human family, which we entrust to you with affectionate joy, O Mother. May the time of peace and freedom, the time of truth, justice and hope, approach for everyone. Amen.

—*Pope John Paul II*

Dearest Mother, how we long for your embrace, the sweet hugs and tender kisses of a loving mother who knows how to caress and soothe her children! And how we long for persons whose physical touch has the power to uplift our spirits! Yet we long—for despite the needs of our souls we have somehow erected fortresses around ourselves that keep other people at a distance. Open our eyes to the barriers we have created, that with your motherly help we may understand why we have raised them up. Encourage our determination to live in community, that we might begin to tear down and sweep away anything that separates us from loving relationship with others. And fill us with your courage, that we may finally open our arms to other people, daring to embrace them as we desire to be embraced. Amen.

Mother of God

HER STORY

Controversy over calling Mary the Mother of God has existed for centuries because the New Testament does not explicitly mention this title. The texts do speak of the "mother of Jesus" (John 2:1–3 and Acts 1:14), and they also affirm that Jesus is God (John 20:28: "Thomas answered him, 'My Lord and my God!'"; Luke 1:43: Elizabeth calls Mary "the mother of my Lord."). By deduction, Mary, as Jesus' mother, is seen as the Mother of God.

But the difficulty arises over the matter of calling a mortal woman the mother of the eternal God, and the title Mother of God might seem to imply that Mary is somehow a supergoddess, the creator of God. This inference betrays a misunderstanding of the Incarnation. When the Holy Spirit came upon Mary and the power of the Most High overshadowed her (Luke 1:35), the Son of God (Luke 1:35) was eternally begotten of God but was conceived in time by and took his human nature from Mary. Thus Mary brought forth the incarnate Son of God into the world. As Pope John Paul II has explained, "In proclaiming Mary 'Mother of God,' the Church thus intends to affirm that she is the 'Mother of the Incarnate Word, who is God'" (general audience, November 27, 1996).

The controversy became a source of division in the church during the fifth century, when Nestorius and his followers, unable to admit the unity of the human and the divine in Jesus, objected to calling Mary the Mother of God. To resolve the disagreement, the fathers of the church came together at Ephesus in 431. The result of that council was this declaration:

> We confess, then, our lord Jesus Christ, the only begotten Son of God perfect God and perfect man of a rational soul and a body, begotten before all ages from the Father in his godhead, the same in the last days, for us and for our salvation, born of Mary the virgin, according to his humanity, one and the same consubstantial with the Father in godhead and consubstantial with us in humanity, for a union of two natures took place. Therefore we confess one Christ, one Son, one Lord. According to this understanding of the unconfused union, we confess the holy virgin to be the Mother of God because God the Word took flesh and became man and from his very conception united to himself the temple he took from her.

The council actually used the word *Theotokos* (page 198), which can also mean "God-bearer" or "the one who gave birth to God." In the current age, some people prefer this title as less confusing than Mother of God.

On the other hand, the Second Vatican Council reaffirmed Mary's role as Mother of God: "The Virgin Mary, who at the message of the angel received the Word of God in her heart and in her body and gave Life to the world, is acknowledged and honored as being truly the Mother of God..." (*Lumen gentium*, 53).

Mary, Mother of Emmanuel—"God is with us" (Matthew 1:23)— brought God to the world. Through her ongoing intercession in human affairs, the Mother of God continues to bring God to all people, demonstrating as only she can that God is always "with us."

ॐ TRADITIONAL PRAYER

Hail, O Mary, Mother of God! You did enclose in your sacred womb the One Who cannot be encompassed. Hail, O Mary, Mother of God! With the shepherds we sing the praise of God, and with the angels the song of thanksgiving. "Glory to God in the highest and peace on earth to men of good will!" Hail, O Mary, Mother of God! Through you came to us the Conqueror and triumphant Vanquisher of hell.

—*Saint Cyril*

O Mother of God, despite the busy noise filling my life, a deep silence has enveloped my soul. It is the silence of the absence of God. I have pushed God away—with my mistakes and with my mistrust—and now God and I no longer parley. Yet I hope and believe that God is still with me, and I ask you, dear Mother of God, to carry the divine Godhead to me and to propel the divine in me toward the Godhead, that God and I might once again fill this silence with the joyful noise of relationship. Amen.

Mother of Good Counsel
| OUR LADY OF GOOD COUNSEL,
OUR LADY OF GENAZZANO, OUR LADY OF SHKODRA |

HER STORY

*M*other of Good Counsel is a title that describes one of Mary's motherly attributes, for she is to all people a mother who is able and willing to give good advice in times of difficulty. She is also always able to direct people toward God, providing the good counsel that removes doubt and confusion and makes the way to holiness and wholeness stand out clearly. At the same time, and more importantly, the title refers to Mary's motherhood of the Christ, who as the Way, the Truth and the Life is *the* Good Counsel leading people directly to God.

The title was well established early in Christian history, but a Renaissance legend served to spread devotion to Our Lady of Good Counsel. The Albanian people had venerated the Blessed Mother as *Zoja e Bekueme* (the Blessed Lady) for many centuries, but they were particularly devoted to an ancient icon of the *eleousa* type (page 200) that hung over the main altar in a church built beneath the fortress of Shkodra. This icon was famous for its sweetness and for the protection it afforded its devotees.

According to the legend, when Turks invaded Albania in the fifteenth century, two of the defenders sought refuge in Shkodra to beseech Zoja e Bekueme for deliverance. During their prayers they noticed that the icon was moving through the air. They followed it—all the way to Rome! There it disappeared. But the two men soon heard that a miraculous image had appeared suddenly in Genazzano, a small town thirty miles southeast of Rome. They went there immediately and upon seeing the miraculous painting recognized their Zoja e Bekueme.

Previously in Genazzano, a widow named Petruccia de Geneo had contributed money to renovate the fifth-century Church of Our Lady of Good Counsel, which had fallen into disrepair. Her funds fell far short of what was required, and the legend recounts how the Lord made up the difference. On April 25, 1467, the entire city was enjoying the yearly festival in honor of Saint Mark. At about four o'clock, a mysterious cloud descended upon the decrepit church. When the cloud evaporated, a fragile portrait of the Madonna and Child was found to be suspended in midair above an unfinished wall. The portrait was on paper-thin plaster, and the legend relates that a thread could be passed entirely around the painting without disturbing it.

The painting became an immediate sensation. From April 27 to August 14 of that year, no less than 171 miracles were attributed to the image, which became known as *Madonna del Buon Consiglio,* or the Madonna of Good Counsel. The number of pilgrims was so great that their donations completely funded the renovation of the church.

Though much of the church was destroyed in World War II, the painting was undamaged. Reportedly, it is still suspended in the air, as it has been for more than five hundred years. The church has been rebuilt and is now a vibrant center of pilgrimage. The church in Shkodra has also been restored and serves as a center of spiritual inspiration for Albanians.

Because of her great love, Our Lady of Good Counsel has a large following. Many churches and institutions throughout the world are named after her, and Pope Leo XIII authorized the insertion of *Mater Boni Consillii* (Mother of Good Counsel) into the Litany of Loreto in 1903. She continues to favor those who appeal to her, giving counsel about God and obtaining the light of truth for all those who ask in her name.

ᐯ TRADITIONAL PRAYER

Most glorious Virgin, chosen by the eternal Counsel to be the Mother of the eternal Word made flesh, thou who art the treasurer of divine graces and the advocate of sinners, I who am thy most unworthy servant have recourse to thee; be thou pleased to be my guide and counselor in this vale of tears. Obtain for me through the Most Precious Blood of thy divine Son, the forgiveness of my sins, the salvation of my soul and the means necessary to obtain it. In like manner obtain for Holy Church victory over her enemies and the spread of the kingdom of Jesus Christ upon the whole earth. Amen.

—*The Raccolta*

ᴄᴡ NEW PRAYER

Cara Madonna del Buon Consiglio, I come to you in this time of confusion as I face a decision about *[mention request]*. Shine the light of your good counsel upon my predicament, that I may choose wisely. O Zoja e Bekueme, be with me during my deliberations, that I may always seek to honor God and bring good and love to all who are involved. Amen.

Mother of Grace
| OUR LADY OF GRACE,
SANTA MARIA DELLE GRAZIE, NOTRE DAME DE GRÂCE |

HER STORY

The title Mother of Grace, or Our Lady of Grace, is one of Mary's most popular titles and has two possible origins. The earliest reference comes from France. In 1440 an icon of the Madonna and Child in the *eleousa* style (page 200) was moved from Rome to Cambrai, France, where people began to venerate *Notre Dame de Grâce* (Our Lady of Grace) as patron of the small town. The icon was, and still is, carried in procession through the town the day before the feast of the Assumption.

The second reference comes from Italy. When an image of the Madonna painted by Lodovico Sforza at the end of the fifteenth century was installed in the shrine of *Santa Maria delle Grazie* (Saint Mary of Grace) in the refectory of the monastery in Milan, the plague ceased to afflict the citizens of that city. The people of the region have venerated Our Lady of Grace ever since.

Theologically speaking, the title Mother of Grace refers to Mary's motherhood of Christ, the grace from whom all graces flow. The linking of Mary with grace is at least as old as the Gospel of Luke, which relates Gabriel's greeting to the young maiden: "Rejoice, highly favored one!" (1:28 *[INT]*). The Greek word translated as "highly favored one" is *kecharitomene,* which means literally "completely graced" or "fully favored." Saint Jerome translated the phrase into the

Latin *gratia plena*, "full of grace." In the Gospel *kecharitomene* is a noun, a renaming of Mary.

Mary's own fullness of grace is the result of her Immaculate Conception (page 23). As Our Lady of Grace, she serves as the mediator of grace to the faithful. She is often referred to as the Mediatrix of Grace.

ᴼᵛ TRADITIONAL PRAYER

It becomes you to be mindful of us, as you stand near him who granted you all graces, for you are the Mother of God and our Queen. Help us for the sake of the King, the Lord God and Master who was born of you. For this reason, you are called full of grace. Remember us, most holy Virgin, and bestow on us gifts from the riches of your graces, Virgin full of graces.

—*Saint Athanasius*

ᴼᵛ NEW PRAYER

Hail, *Kecharitomene!* Please look on us with the tenderness with which you first beheld your beloved son, and be for us the mother of grace in our hearts as you were mother of God's perfect grace. Lead us to moments of grace throughout our days, that we may remain conscious of the constant presence of the Divine in our lives. O Full of Grace! Help us so to live that we may reveal the working of God's grace to everyone we encounter. Amen.

Mother of Mercy
| OUR LADY OF MERCY, QUEEN OF MERCY |

HER STORY

Mary had a profound understanding of the mystery of God's mercy. Soon after learning of the Incarnation within her, she prophesied in the Magnificat God's fulfillment of the promise of mercy made to Israel: "His mercy is for those who fear him from generation to generation" (Luke 1:50) and "He has helped his servant Israel, in remembrance of his mercy, according to the promise he made to our ancestors..." (Luke 1:54–55). Certainly, Joseph would also have shared with her the message he received from the angel: "She will bear a son, and you are to name him Jesus, for he will save his people from their sins" (Matthew 1:21). Who but a merciful God would provide an instrument to release the chosen people from their bondage, who would, like his namesake, mercifully lead the people of God, despite their transgressions, to the Promised Land? With complete certainty, Mary knew within her immaculate heart (page 32) that the baby she was carrying was a manifestation of God's mercy toward humankind.

When her son began his ministry, she came to understand even more about the meaning of God's mercy. The Gospel of Matthew indicates that Jesus said to his disciples, "I desire mercy, not sacrifice" (9:13). When Jesus stood in the synagogue at Nazareth, he read, "The Spirit of the Lord is upon me, because he has anointed me....to proclaim the year of the Lord's favor" (Luke 4:18–19). The Jubilee Year was a time when all debts were forgiven—a year of unlimited mercy. Who but a merciful God would take notice of the outcasts of society and lovingly welcome them back into the fold? Jesus related the story of the Prodigal Son, for whom the father mercifully forgives all transgressions, rejoicing at his return (Luke 15:11–32). And Jesus exhorted his disciples to follow God's merciful example: "Blessed are the merciful, for they will receive mercy" (Matthew 5:7). Mary would have heard these pronouncements firsthand, would probably have discussed them with her son, too, and as God's Full of Grace (page 48), she would have intuitively understood her son's mission of mercy. Finally, as her son was entrusting her to John's merciful care, she would have experienced with Jesus the agonizing mercy that made his death necessary.

Saint Odo, Abbot of Cluny in the tenth century, is thought to have been the first to refer to the mother of the Divine Mercy as the Mother of Mercy. The title was accepted without question. It was incorporated in the famous eleventh-century prayer known as the Salve Regina. Numerous depictions of the Mother of Mercy have helped to spread devotion to Mary under this title. Our Lady of Ransom, for example, holds in her hands the chains that the Divine Mercy has removed from those imprisoned in sin; again, the enthroned madonna depicts Mary offering the merciful Redeemer to the world.

Pope John Paul II has written at length of Mary as the Mother of Mercy:

Mary, then, is the one who has the deepest knowledge of the mystery of God's mercy. She knows its price, she knows how great it is. In this sense, we call her the Mother of Mercy: our

Lady of Mercy, or Mother of Divine Mercy; in each one of these titles there is a deep theological meaning, for they express the special preparation of her soul, of her whole personality, so that she was able to perceive, through the complex events, first of Israel, then of every individual and of the whole of humanity, that mercy of which "from generation to generation" people become sharers according to the eternal design of the Most Holy Trinity. (*Dives in misericordia*, 98)

Mary's *fiat* brought the Divine Mercy to the world. For this cooperation in God's plan of mercy, Christians everywhere esteem and praise her.

ᴄᴠ Tʀᴀᴅɪᴛɪᴏɴᴀʟ Pʀᴀʏᴇʀ

Hail, holy Queen, Mother of Mercy, hail, our life, our sweetness and our hope. To you do we cry, poor banished children of Eve: to you do we sigh, mourning and weeping in this vale of tears. Turn, then, most gracious Advocate, your eyes of mercy toward us, and after this our exile, show unto us the blessed fruit of your womb, Jesus. O clement, O loving, O sweet Virgin Mary!
—*Salve Regina*

ᴄᴠ Nᴇᴡ Pʀᴀʏᴇʀ

O Mother of Mercy, behold our tears! We are filled with remorse for our transgressions, which are many. We have not been faithful to God. We have not been humane with others. We have not been kind to ourselves. For turning away from the way of your son, we are sorry. Guide us back to his way, and make our repentance known to him, imploring him to bestow on us the smile of his divine mercy, that we may one day come to share, with you, the promises of eternity. Amen.

ℬ. *Mother of Perpetual Help*
| Oᴜʀ Lᴀᴅʏ ᴏꜰ Pᴇʀᴘᴇᴛᴜᴀʟ Hᴇʟᴘ |

Hᴇʀ Sᴛᴏʀʏ

The Mother of Perpetual Help story begins in the fifteenth century, when, according to legend, a merchant stole a miraculous painting from a church on Crete and set sail across the Mediterranean.

Nearly shipwrecked in a wild storm, he made landfall and eventually brought the stolen painting to Rome.

There he became ill. Upon his deathbed he revealed the secret of the painting to a friend, begging that the icon be placed in a church for public veneration. The merchant died, the friend having promised to fulfill his wish. But the friend's wife so loved the image that she refused to part with it.

After the friend died the Blessed Mother herself intervened, appearing to the couple's six-year-old daughter. Referring to herself as the Mother of Perpetual Help, Mary asked the child to tell her mother and grandmother to have the icon venerated in a church between the churches of St. Mary Major and St. John Lateran. At the time the Church of St. Matthew the Apostle was found in that location, and with much reluctance, on March 27, 1499, the child's mother obeyed Mary's request.

Over the next three hundred years, the icon's beauty and wonder-working powers attracted the devotion of the people. When in 1798 Napoleon's troops nearly destroyed the Church of St. Matthew, the icon moved with its Augustinian caretakers to a nearby monastery. Then in 1819 the Augustinians took the painting with them to the Church of St. Mary in Posterula. As Our Lady of Grace (page 48) was already venerated there, the Mother of Perpetual Help was placed in a private chapel, forgotten by all except Brother Augustine Orsetti, who ensured that one of his altar boys, Michael Marchi, knew the icon's story.

In 1855 the priests of the Congregation of the Most Holy Redeemer, known as the Redemptorists, acquired the lands of the Villa Caserta, which included the spot where the Church of St. Matthew the Apostle had been located. There they constructed the Church of St. Alphonsus. Becoming interested in the history of their land, the Redemptorists turned up the story of the Mother of Perpetual Help icon. Michael Marchi, then a Redemptorist novice, remembered what Orsetti had said and directed his confreres to the image. Pope Pius IX granted the Redemptorists custody of the painting, telling them to make the Mother of Perpetual Help known throughout the world. Thus in 1866 the icon was retrieved, cleaned and installed in the very spot between St. Mary Major and St. John Lateran that the Mother of Perpetual Help had chosen as her sanctuary centuries before. Her feast was established on June 27.

With help from Mary herself the Redemptorists have indeed made her known throughout the world, and Our Mother of Perpetual

Help now has shrines in Boston, New York and St. Louis; Haiti, where she is the country's patron; Santiago, Chile; Curitiba, Belém and Manaus, Brazil; Tequisquiapán, Mexico; Belfast and Limerick, Ireland; Torun and Kraków, Poland; Singapore; and Manila, Philippines. The perpetual novena to Our Mother of Perpetual Help, which was first established in St. Louis in 1927, has helped spread the devotion and attracts hundreds of thousands of people in India, Sri Lanka, Singapore, Malaysia and Thailand.

The painting itself depicts the Madonna and Christ child, with Saints Michael and Gabriel in attendance. All are identified by Greek lettering. The two angels are holding the instruments of the Passion: the cross, the spear, the crown of thorns and the sponge. The child, having been shown this vision of his future, has in his fright rushed into Mary's lap. He is still staring at the cross with fear, and his sandal has fallen off his right foot, a detail that emphasizes how quickly he has run to his mother.

Though she has taken hold of his hand to comfort him, she is staring out of the image at the observer, her sorrowful eyes drawing all her children into her perpetual care and protection. The star on her forehead emphasizes her role as Mother of God (page 44) and Mother of All People (page 43). At the same time, with the hand with which she is holding her child's hand, she directs the observer to focus on Jesus, the Son of God. As always, Mary guides the faithful to her son, her mission being to bring all people to Christ, the source of all salvation.

❧ TRADITIONAL PRAYER

O Mother of Perpetual Help,
To thee we come, imploring help.
Behold us here from far and near,
to ask of thee, our help to be.
Perpetual Help, we beg of thee,
our souls from sin and sorrow free.
Direct our wandering feet aright,
and be thyself our own true light.
And when this life is over for me,
this last request I ask of thee:
obtain for me in heaven this grace,
to see my God there face to face. Amen.

—*The Redemptorists*

Dearest Mother of Perpetual Help, I fly to you in my fear, for I have had a vision of my hell—the isolation I am creating for myself now. And I ask your help in getting myself off this hellish path. Guide me to the way that will lead me to my heaven, the way of your son. Show me how to become, like him, a soul who knows how to relate to other souls. Help me to discover within myself that person who can be intimate with other people, that friend who can sincerely communicate with friends, that lover who can actually love my beloved. Teach me how to live a life of community instead of isolation, of relationship instead of aloneness, so that I may escape this hell I have seen and begin to experience the joy of my heaven on earth. Amen.

8. *Mother of Sorrows*

| MATER DOLOROSA,
MOTHER OF DOLOURS, OUR LADY OF SORROWS |

HER STORY

*M*ary's very name has roots in the Hebrew word *marah* meaning "bitterness" or "bitter sea," which first appears in the book of Exodus, when the Israelites came to a place called Marah where the water was bitter. The word *marah* appears again in the book of Ruth, when Naomi, whose name means "pleasant," told her kinswomen, "Call me no longer Naomi, call me Mara, for the Almighty has dealt bitterly with me" (1:20). In a sense, Naomi is herself a prototype of Mary, for just like Mary centuries later, Naomi lost her husband and her sons and was left on her own without male kinsmen. Indeed, her lament is the antithesis of Mary's Magnificat. But Mary's joy at her pregnancy too soon turns to unexpected woe.

This comparison of Mary to Naomi is notable because these women are, in a sense, related. Naomi was the mother-in-law of Ruth, who was King David's great-grandmother and, according to Matthew's Gospel, an ancestor of Mary's betrothed, Joseph.

Given her name's heritage—a joy turning to woe—it is no surprise that Mary's "My soul magnifies the Lord, and my spirit rejoices in God my Savior" (Luke 1:46–47) becomes, in the words of the *Stabat Mater*, "At the Cross her station keeping, / Stood the mournful Mother weeping." The actual title Mother of Sorrows arises from a title given to Jesus: just as he is seen as the Man of Sorrows (Isaiah 53:3), so his mother is held as the Mother of Sorrows.

Traditionally, the sorrows of our Lady number seven: Simeon's prophecy, the family's flight into Egypt, the family's loss of the boy Jesus in the Temple, Mary's meeting Jesus on the road to Calvary, Jesus' crucifixion, the removal of Jesus' body from the cross and Jesus' burial. Thus events fulfilled the prophecy of the first sorrow, for as Simeon foretold, "A sword will pierce your own soul too" (Luke 2:35). Such griefs as these would have destroyed any other person—indeed, Mary's suffering was so great that the church considers her the greatest of martyrs and calls her Queen of Martyrs (page 186). But Mary was able, with God's help, to overcome her crushing grief, and among the early Christians she emerged as a leading witness to the soaring joy of her son's resurrection life.

Devotion to the Mother of Sorrows has a long history but became popular during the Middle Ages, when the church elucidated a vast theology of suffering.

This theology gave rise to a thirteenth-century legend: Bearing a black garment in her arms, Mary appeared as the Mother of Sorrows to seven Florentine councillors, telling them to wear this mourning garb and to meditate on her sorrows. These men founded the Order of Servites in 1240, devoting themselves to the service of the Mother of Sorrows.

Devotion to the Mother of Sorrows became even more widespread in the fifteenth century with the popularizing of the *pietà* image. The juxtaposition of the Madonna embracing the child with the Mother holding the son's body proved edifying, encapsulating Christ's human existence.

Saint Alphonsus de' Liguori (1696–1787) did much to spread devotion to the Mother of Sorrows. According to his *The Glories of Mary*, Saint Elizabeth of Hungary (1207–1231) had a vision in which Saint John the Evangelist desired to see Mary again after her assumption. Christ granted this favor, promising four graces to those who are devoted to Mary's sorrows: true repentance; protection, particularly at the hour of death; mindfulness of his Passion, with its concomitant reward of everlasting life; and safekeeping in grace.

In modern times, theologies of suffering do not have much appeal. Still, many people say the Litany of the Seven Sorrows of the Blessed Virgin Mary, celebrate the feast of Our Lady of Sorrows on September 15, recite the Rosary of the Seven Sorrows, pray the Sequence in Honor of the Sorrowful Heart of Mary and the Novena to

PIETA (after Delacroix)

Vincent van Gogh
1889

the Mother of Sorrows and otherwise commemorate Mary's griefs. At the same time, they share with her their overpowering human sorrows, seeking empathy, comfort and compassion. Hearing the cries of all her children, the Mother of Sorrows does not fail to remind her son of the promises he made to those who call upon her sorrowful heart.

∾ TRADITIONAL PRAYER

O Mother of Sorrows, by the anguish and love with which you stood at the cross of Jesus, stand by me in my last agony. To your maternal heart I commend the last three hours of my life. Offer these hours in union with the agony of our dearest Lord in reparation for my sins. Offer to the Eternal Father the most precious blood of Jesus, mingled with your tears on Calvary, that Holy Communion with the most perfect love and contrition before my death that I may breathe forth my soul in the adorable presence of Jesus. Dearest Mother, when the moment of my death has at length come, present me as your child to Jesus. Ask Him to forgive me for I knew not what I did. Beg Him to receive me into His Eternal Kingdom to be united with Him forever. Amen.

—*Saint Paschal Baylon*

∾ NEW PRAYER

O Mater Dolorosa, my sorrows sometimes overpower and paralyze me. At such times, when I am unable to act for my own good—when I am unable even to think clearly—I fall in desperation upon your sorrowful heart. O Mother of Sorrows, pray for me now, at the hour of this death! Ease my fears, still my heart and calm my soul. Help me to place the overwhelming events of my life in your care. And open my senses to Jesus' abiding presence, that I may find peace in his promise to be with me always and never to abandon me to a lonely experience of suffering. Amen.

𝕭 Mother of the Church

HER STORY

*B*erengaud, bishop of Treves (twelfth century), was the first to use the title Mother of the Church (*Mater Ecclesiae*) in his writings, though the concept is ancient. From earliest times Mary was understood to have been Jesus' first disciple—she was the first person to praise God for the Incarnation (Luke 1:46–55)—and thus was held up as the first member of the church. Because Jesus appointed her to be mother of his followers just before his death (John 19:26–27), she is also considered the mother of all other members of the church.

The early church also looked to Mary as the model of persevering prayer. According to the Acts of the Apostles, after Jesus' ascension the disciples were in the Upper Room "constantly devoting themselves to prayer, together with certain women, including Mary the mother of Jesus" (1:14).

Finally, Mary was presumed present with the disciples when the Holy Spirit descended upon them at Pentecost, the so-called birthday of the church.

Renaissance writers, including Saint Antoninus of Florence (c. 1389–1459) and Saint Lawrence Justiniani (1381–1456), invited the faithful to venerate Mary as Mother of the Church, and modern popes, such as Leo XIII and John XXIII, called her by this name.

But it was not until November 21, 1964, during the celebration of the Mass concluding the Second Vatican Council's third session, that Pope Paul VI officially extolled Mary as Mother of the Church: "...we proclaim the Most Blessed Mary to be the Mother of the Church, that is to say, of all the people of God....And we wish that the Mother of God shall be still more honored and invoked by the entire Christian people under this most sweet title." As he explained, "She, who has given us the fountainhead of grace in Jesus, will not fail to succor the Church."

He also added these words on Mary's discipleship: "In her...the entire Church, in its incomparable variety of life and work, attains the most authentic form of the perfect imitation of Christ."

Looking to Mary as mother, the people of the church admire her perfect example of true discipleship and implore her aid as they seek to follow Christ. And just as she led the disciples during her own lifetime, she continues to inspire today's Christians to lives of holiness.

❧ TRADITIONAL PRAYER

O Virgin Mary, Mother of the Church, to you we recommend the entire Church....You who were given as mother to the best-loved Disciple by your divine Son at the moment of his saving death, remember the Christian people who entrust themselves to you. Remember all your children; support their prayers addressed to God; make strong their faith; make firm their hope; increase their love.

Remember those who are in tribulation, in need, in danger, above all those who are suffering persecution and who have been cast into prison for the Faith. For these, O Virgin, obtain fortitude, and hasten the longed-for day of their just liberation....O Temple of light, without shadow and without blemish, intercede with your only Son, the Mediator of our reconciliation with the Father, so that he may have mercy on our shortcomings and remove all dissension among us, granting to our souls the joy of loving. To your Immaculate Heart, O Mary, we finally recommend the entire human race...remove the scourges provoked by sin; give to the entire world peace in truth, in justice, in freedom, and in love. Make it possible for the whole church...to raise to the God of mercies, a majestic hymn of praise and of thanksgiving, a hymn of joy and exultation, because of the wonderful things the Lord has wrought through you, O clement, O loving, O sweet Virgin Mary.

—*Pope Paul VI, November 21, 1964*

Ꮒ NEW PRAYER

Dear Mother, it seems as if the church is falling apart. Discussions about birth control, women's ordination, homosexuality, divorce, financial stewardship and bias-free language turn into raging debates. Factions are formed, sides are taken and soon there is a giant chasm between two groups of people—who yet all remain devoted to the church, the church they wish to create. Infuse us with your wisdom, dearest Mother, so that we may put aside our emotions and consider the issues that divide us with a sincere desire to search for the truth. Unite us in this search, so that we all may be open to the Spirit's leading. Teach us again the ageless lesson that the church is the coming together of God's people, and help us to rejoice in the simple fact that we are all on the way. Amen.

Ꮒ *Mother of the Unborn*

HER STORY

When the Virgin Mary "was found to be with child by the Holy Spirit" (Matthew 1:18), Joseph planned to divorce her quietly so as not to cause her scandal. Fortunately, an angel forestalled Joseph's intentions and helped him comprehend both the sacredness of the life that was within Mary and his responsibilities toward her and her child.

Today, many people still do not recognize the sacredness of unborn life. As a result, unwanted pregnancies break many relationships or, in a great number of cases, lead to abortion. In these times Christians appeal to Mary as Mother of the Unborn because she knew firsthand the scandal and the terror of unplanned pregnancy, knew firsthand the subsequent rejection of loved ones, knew firsthand the need to place her life and the life of her unborn child utterly in the hands of divine providence.

Mary's distinction as Mother of the Unborn also stems from her appearances at Guadalupe (page 96). The portrait that miraculously appeared on Juan Diego's *tilma* depicts our Lady during her pregnancy. At the time the Aztecs still believed in human sacrifice, and Mary's apparition helped to end this practice. As a result, Our Lady of Guadalupe is today known as the patron of the pro-life movement.

Although the Blessed Mother may have a special love for the unborn, she is also the loving Mother of All People (page 43). Some members of the pro-life movement forget this, invoking Mary's name even as they engage in terrorist tactics that maim and kill. The church believes that Mary weeps over these injuries and deaths as much as she weeps over the souls wounded by abortion, that her loving heart is pierced anew when people of violence invoke her name.

As the church professes, Mary, Mother of All the Unborn—those yet to be born physically, and those yet to be born again of the Spirit—has but one desire as loving mother: to lead all her children safely to God.

∾ TRADITIONAL PRAYER

O Mary, Mother of the Unborn, protect the gift of human life that your divine son has allowed to be given. Give strength and joy to all parents as they await the birth of the precious child they have conceived. Give courage to those who are fearful, calm those who are anxious and guide all of us, with your motherly care, to treasure and protect the miraculous gift of human life. We ask this through your son, Jesus Christ our Lord. Amen.

∾ NEW PRAYER

O Mother of the Unborn, do I kill the pregnant joys of family members, or stifle the potential talents of my own [child/children], or murder the unborn ideas of my *[partner/spouse]*, or execute the incipient plans of my *[colleagues/friends]*, or slaughter the spirit of newness and enthusiasm and energy wherever I find it? If so, dear Mother, help me recognize the violence within my own soul, the hatred that murders all that is positive and good. Teach me to let go of anger, negativity and any need to be right or first or in control. Inspire me to become a person of support, a soul of peace, a heart of love. And send me your grace, that I might treasure the precious unborn. Amen.

Mystical Rose
| Rosa Mystica |

Her Story

*F*or all of recorded history the rose has been called the queen of flowers, so it is no surprise that the rose has come to be identified with the Blessed Mother.

There are three references in Scripture that support this link. In the first, from the book of Sirach, Wisdom explains that the Creator told her to take root in Jacob and Israel, with the result that "I grew tall like a palm tree in Engedi, and like rosebushes in Jericho..." (24:14). Commentators have interpreted this verse as a reference to the mysterious Incarnation of Christ in Mary's womb.

The second reference is from the book of Isaiah, who prophesies, "A shoot will spring from the stock of Jesse, a new shoot will grow from his roots. On him will rest the spirit of Yahweh..." (11:1–2 *[NJB]*). Commentators have explained these verses as predicting the Christ as the heavenly flower (rose) coming forth from the rosebush, his mother.

The third is from the Song of Solomon: "I am a rose of Sharon, a lily of the valleys" (2:1). The reference is to the exemplary bride and, symbolically, to Mary, the perfect bride of God who will bring forth from the Spirit the anointed one.

The early Christians embraced these metaphors. They saw the red rose as symbolic of Christ's blood, and thus it came to represent charity and martyrdom. And they saw the white rose as symbolic of purity, innocence and chastity and thus associated it with the Blessed Mother.

As gardeners know, the beautiful rose also has many painful thorns. Here is a symbolic union of opposites: in the blossoms, beauty, life, hope, resurrection; in the thorns, pain, martyrdom, blood, death. Mary embodies this union, having suffered the martyrdom of seeing her own flesh and blood die on the cross, yet also having experienced the hope of the Resurrection.

Christians believe that God gave the Mystical Rose, alone among humankind, a special insight into these mysteries—of the Incarnation, the Resurrection and her own role in the Redemption. The church thus appeals to Mary for the grace of her mystical wisdom.

○ᴗ Traditional Prayer

O Mary, mystic rose, whose lovable heart, burning with the living fire of love, adopted us as thy children at the foot of the Cross, becoming thus our most tender Mother, make me experience the sweetness of thy motherly heart and the power of thine intercession with Jesus, in all the dangers that beset me during life, and especially at the dread hour of my death; in such wise may my heart be ever united to thine, and love Jesus both now and through endless ages. Amen.

—*The Raccolta*

○ᴗ New Prayer

O Mystical Rose, my existence often seems a complete mystery to me. Where am I going? and Why am I here? are questions for which I have found no satisfactory answers. I pray you, grace me with your mystical wisdom, that I may begin to find the answers I seek. But more than that, keep me from questioning life to death. Inspire me to accept the answers that are right in front of me, in the poetry and symbols and metaphors that surround me, in the people I encounter, in the beauty of creation, in the God-events that surprise me daily. Teach me to enjoy life's mystery, to embrace its uncertainty, to caress its holy secrets, placing myself completely in God's hands and trusting the Holy Spirit to make of my most mysterious life something beautiful. Amen.

𝕭 The New Eve

*T*he identification of the Blessed Mother as the New Eve dates from the earliest Christian traditions, and this mariological concept is the basis for much of what the church has come to believe about Mary.

The scriptural evidence for this comparison is manifold. Genesis 3:15 speaks of another woman whose seed will crush the serpent, and this passage is held to prophesy Mary's motherhood of Christ. In the Gospel of John, Jesus addresses his mother as "Woman" at the wedding at Cana and at the foot of the cross, indicating her representation of all women and her role as the new mother of humankind. And the epistle to the Romans and the first letter to the Corinthians speak of Christ as the New Adam, with the implication that just as God created Eve to be with Adam, so God created Mary, the New Eve, as a necessary complement to the New Adam in the redemption story.

This and other scriptural evidence led the early church fathers to say, "Death through Eve, life through Mary." Even though these women were not the ultimate causes of humankind's death or redemption, respectively, death and life entered human experience as a result of their decisions. Saint Irenaeus of Lyons was perhaps the first to directly compare Mary and Eve, but at the heart of the comparison was a belief in Mary's virginity, which parallels the original virginity of Eve. In 189 he wrote in *Against Heresies*, "The knot of Eve's disobedience was loosed by the obedience of Mary. What the virgin Eve had bound in unbelief, the Virgin Mary loosed through faith." Further, he asserted, "As by a virgin that human race had been given over to death, by a virgin it is saved."

Tertullian in 210 continued the analogy in *On the Flesh of Christ*:

> It was while Eve was still a virgin that the word of the devil crept in to erect an edifice of death. Likewise through a Virgin the Word of God was introduced to set up a structure of life. Thus what had been laid waste in ruin by this sex was by the same sex re-established in salvation. Eve had believed the serpent; Mary believed Gabriel. That which the one destroyed by believing, the other, by believing, set straight.

As the early church maintained, just as the fall began with Eve, the work of redemption began with the New Eve, Mary. Eve's entire being disobeyed God, and thus humankind stepped off the path leading to eternal life; but Mary's entire being was obedient, and her submission to God's will—her willingness to be the mother of eternal life—reversed the disorder of the fall and put humankind back on its rightful path.

Several doctrines grow out of this identification of Mary as the New Eve. The first is the dogma of the Immaculate Conception. If Eve were created immaculate, without sin, then so, too, Mary the New Eve. Another is the profession of Mary the New Eve as the Mother of All People (page 43). The third is the dogma of the Assumption: while Adam and Eve both died as a consequence of their disobedience, Mary the New Eve participated in the resurrection of the New Adam and was physically "raised up" to God in heaven.

The Blessed Mother's role as the New Eve is ongoing. She continues to mother all people, always pointing to the New Adam and always leading all nations to God. And thus she manifests the greatest love of all, God's loving provision for the ongoing redemption of creation.

ᘏ Traditional Prayer

Radiant
mother of sacred healing!
you poured salve on the sobbing
wounds that Eve sculpted
to torment our souls.
For your salve is your son and you
wrecked death forever,
sculpturing life.

Pray for us to your child,
Mary, star of the sea.

O life-giving source and gladdening
sign and sweetness of all
delights that flow unfailing!

Pray for us to your child,
Mary, star of the sea.

Glorify the Father,
the Spirit and the Son.

Pray for us to your child,
Mary, star of the sea.

—*Saint Hildegard of Bingen*

O Blessed Mother, despite our best intentions, we have—in little ways or big—stepped off the path leading to God. Lead us back to the Way, that we may rediscover our true purpose. Lead us back to the Truth, that we may lead lives of honesty and integrity. Lead us back to the Life, that we may become life-giving and life-affirming people. O New Eve, inspire us to become ourselves new Eves and Adams birthing the love of God into the world. Amen.

 Nikopoia
|"BRINGER OF THE VICTORY"|

HER STORY

*I*n the Byzantine tradition the major types of the Madonna and Child are the *Hodegetria* (page 22); the *Blacherniotissa*, which emphasizes Mary's role as intercessor; and the *Nikopoia*, Bringer of the Victory.

This iconic representation is extremely regal, usually depicting the Blessed Mother enthroned. She is facing forward, with her feet on a royal footrest, dressed in an imperial costume of royal purple. She has seated the child on her lap, supporting him with her left hand on his left leg and her right hand on his right shoulder. To iconographers this pose symbolizes the majesty of the child. Oftentimes, two angels, holding the orb and the scepter, which are also symbols of royalty, frame the Madonna and Child.

By presenting Mary and Jesus in isolation on a throne, the icon calls to mind the adoration of the magi who brought royal gifts of gold, frankincense and myrrh to the child and bowed down before him and his mother to worship him (Matthew 2:11).

Heraclius might have attached the nickname "Bringer of the Victory" to this icon, having named the Madonna and Child as depicted herein as his protectors when he sailed from Carthage to victory over Constantinople in 610 and became Eastern Roman emperor.

The icon symbolizes Christ's victory over the world itself and is our Lady's reminder to all people to share in and enjoy that victory.

TRADITIONAL PRAYER

You are most blessed, O virgin Mother of God, for through him who was incarnate of you, Hades is despoiled, Adam is recalled, the curse is destroyed, Eve is set free, Death is slain, and we are brought to life. And so we shout aloud our hymn of praise: Blessed is Christ our God, Glory to you who deigned to accomplish this!

↬ NEW PRAYER

O holy Nikopoia, I thank you for reminding me of your son's great victory, and I ask you to remind me again and again. Encourage me when I feel embattled or defeated, that I might remember the words of your son, who told his people to "be of good cheer" because he had overcome all. Help me to see the details of my day-to-day enervations from an eternal point of view, to cast aside my despair of the minute, to embrace the joy of the moment that God has conceived for me. Teach me to rejoice in my very life. I ask this in the name of your son triumphant. Amen.

ℬ Our Lady of Akita

HER STORY

As at Naju (page 137) and the Philippines (page 159), Mary has brought her message to the remote mountain village of Akita, Japan, by means of a bleeding, weeping statue.

The story began on June 12, 1973, when Sister Agnes Katsuko Sasagawa entered the chapel of her convent for eucharistic adoration. Suddenly, a blinding light blazed forth from the tabernacle. Agnes, a convert who had just joined the Handmaids of the Eucharist, fell prostrate, powerless to rise for more than an hour. An identical experience the next day convinced Agnes that the Lord was manifesting his true presence in the Eucharist to her.

The vision was repeated on June 28, whereupon Agnes felt an excruciating pain in her left palm. The following day, after an angel recited the rosary with her, she noticed a cross-shaped wound in her left hand. On July 5 it began to bleed.

On July 6 Agnes saw the chapel's statue of the Blessed Virgin suddenly come to life in the midst of a brilliant light. Though Agnes was completely deaf, she heard a beautiful voice requesting the prayer of the Handmaids of the Eucharist. During the recitation, the angel added the words *truly present* to the phrase "Jesus present in the Eucharist."

Agnes and the novice mistress examined the statue later, finding in its right palm a crosslike wound with blood flowing from the center. The statue bled again on July 12, 13, 26 and 27, the angel explaining to Agnes that Mary was shedding her blood to ask for conversion and peace and in reparation for human sins. When the statue's bleeding ceased, the wound in Agnes's palm healed without a scar.

On August 3 Agnes heard the heavenly voice speak of the need for "a cohort of victim souls," and on September 29 Agnes and a companion remarked a sweetly fragrant fluid flowing like perspiration from the statue. On October 7 the angel told Agnes that the flow of fluid would continue until October 15—and it did stop as predicted.

On October 13, 1973, the anniversary of Fátima's sun miracle (page 91), the statue described the "terrible punishment" to come and implored Agnes, "Pray very much the prayers of the rosary. I alone am able to save you from the calamities which approach. Those who place their confidence in me will be saved."

On October 13, 1974, Agnes's hearing was restored, as the angel had predicted. The cure lasted until the following March.

On January 4, 1975, the statue of the Blessed Virgin began to weep. Hundreds of people subsequently observed the weeping, which occurred 101 times before ceasing on September 15, 1981. The angel explained to Agnes the special meaning of that number—the first "1" representing Eve, the second representing the Virgin, and "0" representing God.

The University of Gifu analyzed the tears, perspiration and blood from the statue, determining that the blood was of human group B and the tears and perspiration belonged to group AB. A subsequent analysis of the tears placed them in group O. In 1976 an inquisitor accused Agnes of causing the statue's emanations by means of "ectoplasmic powers," but her blood was group B and was thought incapable of accounting for the statue's tears.

On March 25, 1982, the angel predicted a complete cure of Agnes's deafness. This occurred on May 30. Previously, in 1981, a woman with terminal brain cancer had received immediate healing while praying before the statue.

On April 22, 1984, Bishop John Ito declared the events at Akita to be of supernatural origin, authorizing the veneration of Our Lady of Akita. The Vatican approved the events and messages as reliable and worthy of belief in 1988.

Some Roman Catholics interpret the events at Akita as the culmination of Mary's apparitional messages. Nevertheless, reports of new appearances by our Lady continue to make headlines. The truth is that no one knows when or if Mary might appear again. What is known is that her message at Akita, like her messages to people the world over, has brought countless souls to faith in her son, Jesus.

∾ TRADITIONAL PRAYER

Most Sacred Heart of Jesus, truly present in the holy Eucharist, I consecrate my body and soul to be entirely one with your heart, being sacrificed at every instant on all the altars of the world and giving praise to the Father, pleading for the coming of his kingdom. Please receive this humble offering of myself. Use me as you will for the glory of the Father and the salvation of souls. Most holy Mother of God, never let me be separated from your divine son. Please defend and protect me as your special child. Amen.

∾ NEW PRAYER

Dear Mother, Our Lady of Akita, I do not wish to cause you pain, but please be with me as I weep over my failures, and console me in my remorse. Most of all, lead me back to wholeness, that in embracing my mistakes I may understand how and why and where I went wrong and may make my way to the path that God intends me to travel. O bleeding, tearful Mother! Invoke the Divine Mercy on my behalf. And pray for me, that with your assistance I may accept God's forgiveness and love and learn to be truly the person God created me to be. Amen.

ℬ Our Lady of All Nations

HER STORY

On March 25, 1945, the feast of the Annunciation, near the close of World War II, Isje Johanna Peerdeman, called Ida, was talking in her living room with her sisters and her spiritual director, Joseph Frehe, O.P. Suddenly, Ida saw a light coming from an adjoining room and felt drawn to it. Then the room seemed to disappear, and she saw a lady coming toward her out of empty space. Ida thought her to be the Blessed Mother. The woman told Ida to slowly repeat what she said, and Father Frehe had Ida's sisters transcribe the words. Thus began a long series of visits and supernatural experiences that would continue for decades.

When the first vision occurred, Ida was forty years old. Although Ida's spiritual director and one or two of her sisters were present during many of the apparitions, only Ida saw or heard the lady. Information about the apparitions was not made public for many years.

The lady did not identify herself definitively until 1951, when on February 11 she said, "I am the Lady—Mary—Mother of All Nations. You may say, 'The Lady of All Nations' or 'Mother of All Nations.' I wish to be known as this. Let all the children of men, of all the countries in the world, be one!"

Most of our Lady's messages were extraordinarily prophetic, predicting such events as the division of Korea into North and South, the landing on the moon, the construction of the Berlin Wall, even the development of chemical and biological weapons. In some cases the prophecies predated the events by more than twenty years. Mary even anticipated the Second Vatican Council, explaining, "I, however, will deliver the message of the Son: The doctrine is correct, but the laws can and must be changed" (February 11, 1951). She also asked the faithful to introduce Our Lady of All Nations and her message of grace, peace and redemption to the whole world.

Perhaps most remarkably, Mary began to prepare the hearts and minds of humankind for a new Marian dogma, telling Ida on May 31, 1951, "It is the wish of the Father and the Son to send Me into the world in these times as the Co-redemptrix, Mediatrix, and Advocate." Again, on July 2, 1951, our Lady said,

> The following is the explanation of the new dogma: As Co-redemptrix, Mediatrix and Advocate, I am standing on the globe in front of the Cross of the Redeemer. By the will of the Father, the Redeemer came on earth. To accomplish this, the Father used the Lady. Thus, from the Lady the Redeemer received only—and I am stressing the word "only"—flesh and blood, that is to say, the body. From my Lord and Master the Redeemer received His divinity. In this way the Lady became Co-redemptrix.

As our Lady was also quick to point out, on April 4, 1954, "I am not bringing a new doctrine. I am now bringing old ideas." Indeed, the fathers and mothers of the church believed that as Christ was the New Adam, so Mary was the New Eve (page 63).

While our Lady continued to visit Ida until 1959, on May 31, 1958, Ida began experiencing eucharistic visions and locutions, which included communications from all three persons of the Trinity. The messages were overwhelmingly hopeful, pointing not only to Christ's redemption of humankind but also to the victory of our Lady over Satan. Ida experienced 56 apparitions and 151 mystical experiences associated with the Eucharist, most during the Mass, the last occurring on March 25, 1984.

Because of her experiences, Ida suffered ridicule and persecution, but the ecclesiastical approval of the apparitions, granted on May 31, 1996, by Bishop Henrik Bomers and Auxiliary Bishop Josef Punt, of the Haarlem-Amsterdam Diocese, was a great solace to her. Shortly thereafter, Ida died, on June 17, 1996.

Following is the prayer to Jesus that Our Lady of All Nations bequeathed to humankind through her apparitions in Amsterdam.

ॐ TRADITIONAL PRAYER

Lord Jesus Christ, Son of the Father, send now your Spirit over the earth. Let the Holy Spirit live in the hearts of all nations, that they may be preserved from degeneration, disasters and war. May the Lady of All Nations, who once was Mary, be our Advocate. Amen.

ॐ NEW PRAYER

Dearest Mother, Our Lady of All Nations, I am overwhelmed with joy! I rejoice to recognize and honor you as Co-redemptrix, Mediatrix and Advocate. I am moved to dedicate my life to your spirit of *fiat*. And I feel myself bursting with my love for you and with your love for me. O holy Mother, be my co-redeemer, bringing good out of all that I attempt, even when I fail. Be my mediator, reconciling me to God's will and integrating my spirit with the Holy Spirit. And be my advocate, leading me to your son, that I may embrace the Way, the Truth and the Life. Most of all, be to me always a dearest and most loving mother. Amen.

ॐ Our Lady of Aparecida
| NOSSA SENHORA DE CONCEIÇÃO APARECIDA |

HER STORY

*D*evotion to Our Lady of Aparecida dates from 1717, when the villagers of Guaratingueta, near São Paulo, Brazil, were preparing for the visit of the governor. Because it was a day of abstinence, three men—Domingos Garcia, João Alves, and Felipe Ramos—

went fishing to provide food for the reception.

Spending many hours on the Paraiba River, they caught nothing at all and became quite discouraged but continued casting their net. One time, Alves noticed that it had twisted around the body of a small statue. Made from obarro, a black material, the statue was of a woman, but the head was missing. The men kept the statue, proceeding down the river. Later, when the net pulled in the head belonging to the statue, the men recognized it as an image of the Blessed Virgin Mary.

Having yet to catch any fish, Garcia, Alves and Ramos threw their net again, and it suddenly filled to overflowing with fish, so many that their boat could not carry the full load without sinking. The villagers attributed the men's good fortune to the intercession of the Blessed Mother and named the statue *Nossa Senhora de Conceição Aparecida* (Our Appeared Lady of the Conception).

The villagers subsequently venerated the statue, and many miracles were attributed to our Lady's intercession. In fact, the people believe that the grace she showered on the land led to the abolition of slavery in Brazil.

A large church was built to enshrine the statue in 1888, and the first organized pilgrimage took place in 1900. Our Lady of Aparecida was proclaimed Queen of Brazil in 1929 and, in 1931, Queen and Patroness of Brazil.

Nowadays, from August 31 to September 7, many thousands of people embark on the Pilgrimage of Those Without, walking the hundred miles from São Paulo to Aparecida. The pilgrimage culminates at the Cathedral of Aparecida in the *Grito dos Excluídos* (Cry of the Excluded Ones), a national protest on behalf of "those without"— without employment, homes, education, healthcare, land or food. The object is to focus attention on the problems devastating Brazil's poor, to call upon the government to change its policies and to appeal to Our Lady of Aparecida, as patroness of the people of Brazil, to appear once again to aid those who suffer from exclusion and deprivation.

❧ TRADITIONAL PRAYER

Lady Aparecida, a son of yours who belongs to you unreservedly—*totus tuus*—called by the mysterious plan of Providence to be the Vicar of your Son on earth, wishes to address you at this moment. He recalls with emotion, because of the brown color of this image of yours, another image of yours, the Black Virgin of Jasna Góra.

Mother of God and our Mother, protect the Church, the Pope, the bishops, the priests and all the faithful people; welcome under your protecting mantle men and women religious, families, children, young people and their educations.

Health of the sick and Consoler of the afflicted, comfort those who are suffering in body and soul; be the light of those who are seeking Christ, the Redeemer of all; show all people that you are the Mother of our confidence.

Queen of Peace and Mirror of Justice, obtain peace for the world, ensure that Brazil and all countries may have lasting peace, that we will always live together as brothers and sisters and as children of God.

Our Lady Aparecida, bless all your sons and daughters who pray and sing to you here and elsewhere. Amen.

—*Pope John Paul II*

∾ NEW PRAYER

Appear to us again, Nossa Senhora de Conceição Aparecida. Shower your abundance upon those of us who have little, that we might have all that we need. And shower your grace upon those of us who have much, that we might have the generosity of spirit to become agents of your abundance to all our sisters and brothers. Amen.

Our Lady of Banneux
| VIRGIN OF THE POOR |

HER STORY

*O*n the cold evening of January 15, 1933, in the small Belgian village of Banneux, eleven-year-old Mariette Beco was awaiting her brother's return for dinner. As she peered out the window, she caught sight of a luminous figure. A beautiful young woman, about five feet tall, dressed in a white flowing gown and veil, with a bright blue sash and a golden rose on her right foot, was standing near the family's vegetable garden, holding a rosary and smiling at Mariette.

Becoming excited, Mariette called to her mother. Able to discern only a shadowy figure, Mrs. Beco was frightened that her daughter had seen a witch. As the young girl began praying the rosary, the glowing woman gestured to her to approach. But her mother had locked the door to keep Mariette in. When she returned to the window, the woman had vanished.

Convinced that she had seen the Blessed Virgin, Mariette exhibited a profound change in her behavior, returning to school, studying her catechism, attending Mass and saying her prayers.

Three nights later, Mariette was waiting outside for the woman, kneeling on the frozen ground and praying the rosary. She suddenly perceived the woman floating toward her. Mr. Beco, having found Mariette on her knees, quickly summoned a neighbor as witness. As the girl continued to pray, the woman came closer, then beckoned Mariette to follow her to a nearby spring. There she spoke for the first time: "Thrust your hands into the water." When Mariette obeyed, the woman asserted, "This spring is mine." Then she retreated into the sky.

The following evening, when the woman appeared for the third time, Mariette asked her name. "I am the Virgin of the Poor," she replied. Leading Mariette to the spring, she explained that it was "reserved for all nations, for the sick." Then she vanished as before.

During the fourth apparition, on January 20, the Virgin requested that a chapel be built near the spring. "I have come to relieve suffering," the Virgin disclosed on February 11, the fifth apparition. She entrusted a secret to Mariette during the sixth visit. In subsequent appearances the Virgin told Mariette, "Believe in me, and I will believe in you" and exhorted her to "pray hard." During the final visit, the eighth, the Virgin said, "I am the mother of the Savior, Mother of God." And again she advised Mariette to "pray hard."

Mariette was subsequently subjected to a battery of examinations by doctors and psychiatrists, who never found any trace of hysteria or deceit. After investigating the many miraculous healings attributed to the waters of the spring that the Virgin had claimed, the bishop authorized the cult of Our Lady of Banneux, Virgin of the Poor, in 1942. His approval was renewed and confirmed in 1947 and 1949.

The cures continue today as the Virgin draws thousands of pilgrims to Banneux, where she relieves their sufferings, exhorts them to "pray hard" and reaffirms their faith.

∾ TRADITIONAL PRAYER

Blessed Virgin of the Poor, lead us to Jesus, source of grace.
Blessed Virgin of the Poor, save all nations.
Blessed Virgin of the Poor, relieve the sick.
Blessed Virgin of the Poor, alleviate suffering.
Blessed Virgin of the Poor, pray for each one of us.
Blessed Virgin of the Poor, we believe in you.

Blessed Virgin of the Poor, believe in us.
Blessed Virgin of the Poor, we will pray hard.
Blessed Virgin of the Poor, bless us.
Mother of the Savior, Mother of God, we thank you. Amen.

❧ NEW PRAYER

Dearest Lady of Banneux, we thank you for believing us worthy of your gift of healing and for placing that gift in the hands of an innocent child, a child who believed in you as you believed in her.

Help us to believe, not only in the gifts that you shower upon us but also in the grace and forgiveness and joy that your son, our redeemer, bestows upon us moment by moment. Give us the hearts of children, accepting and thankful hearts, that we may put aside our skepticism and trust completely in God's love, believing that this is the only gift that is not too good to be true.

O Virgin of the Poor, teach us to trust others with our own most precious gifts. Teach us that though we may consider ourselves poor and in need and our gifts of little value, what we each have, if we put it together with what our neighbors have, is so much more than is needed. Teach us that this is the way of God's providence. Amen.

𝕽. *Our Lady of Beauraing*
| VIRGIN WITH THE HEART OF GOLD |

HER STORY

*O*ur Lady first appeared in Belgium on the night of November 29, 1932, in the obscure town of Beauraing, about sixty miles southeast of Brussels, to five children: Fernande Voisin, fifteen; Gilberte Voisin, thirteen; Albert Voisin, eleven; Andrée Degeimbre, fourteen; and Gilberte Degeimbre, nine.

That evening, Fernande and Albert, along with the Degeimbre children, had gone to the school of the Sisters of Christian Doctrine to bring home their sister, Gilberte. After ringing the convent's bell, Albert looked across the courtyard and was astonished to see a figure walking along the facing viaduct. He shouted, and all the others looked and saw her, too. Frightened, they rushed home, where no one believed their story.

They returned to the courtyard the next night and again saw the woman. On the third night the figure appeared in the garden near a grotto of Our Lady of Lourdes. The children believed she was the Blessed Mother, for she was dressed entirely in white, with a white veil, and she was standing upon a cloud. One child, overcome with emotion, had to be taken home, but three children returned to the garden, where the woman appeared on the lowest branch of a hawthorn tree. This was the spot where she manifested herself during her remaining thirty apparitions.

The woman spoke to the children for the first time on December 2, nodding her assent when Albert asked if she were the Immaculate Virgin and asking that they should always be good.

Beginning on December 4, the children noticed that the Virgin carried a rosary. During subsequent visits she asked for a chapel to be built and exposed her immaculate heart, which burned with a radiant gold. She also told the children, "Pray, pray very much."

On December 8, in the presence of ten thousand or more spectators, the children entered into a state of ecstasy, remaining impervious to pinches, pinpricks, bright lights, even the touch of flames. After they emerged from the ecstasy, their skin showed no signs of these tests.

On January 1, 1933, the Virgin said that her last visit would be on January 3.

In the presence of an estimated thirty thousand people, the Virgin kept her promise, appearing to all but Fernande, whose sobs of disappointment accompanied the joyous shouts of the other four. During this apparition the Virgin spoke to each of the children privately. Her messages were brief: "I am the Mother of God and the Queen of Heaven. Pray always." "I will convert sinners." And she imparted to each a secret. Then she disappeared.

Heartbroken, Fernande refused to leave with the others. Suddenly, the crowd heard a loud crash, and a great ball of fire appeared on the hawthorn. Fernande was overjoyed to see the Virgin, whose final words were, "Sacrifice yourself for me. Adieu."

The apparitions inspired both extreme skepticism and sensational devotion. In the first year more than two million people visited the convent garden, reporting many cures and favors due to Our Lady of Beauraing's intercession. After another seer, Tilman Come, witnessed several apparitions of the Virgin with the golden heart and was healed of a spinal disease, the bishop of Namur opened an investigation. The Vatican approved the cult of Our Lady of Beauraing in 1943. On July 2, 1949, citing the miraculous cures of Marie Van Laer and

Marie-Madeleine Acar-Group, the bishop affirmed that "the Queen of Heaven appeared to the children of Beauraing during the winter of 1932–33 especially to show us in her maternal Heart the anxious appeal for prayer and the promise of her powerful mediation for the conversion of sinners." Since then millions have visited the church constructed near the site of the apparitions, imploring the intercession of the Virgin with the Heart of Gold—praying just as our Lady urged.

ᐁ TRADITIONAL PRAYER

Our Lady of Beauraing, Immaculate Virgin, ever victorious in all your battles for the kingdom of God, we beseech you, convert sinners, as you have promised. Exercise on their behalf the power of your immaculate heart! Bring back to the love of God all souls who, deprived of sanctifying grace, stand in danger of eternal perdition. O heavenly Mother, cast your eyes of mercy on your poor children, and be our help in all tribulations! Be the health of the sick and comforter of the afflicted. Queen of Heaven, crowned with eternal glory, our love and our gratitude proclaim you also queen of our hearts and sovereign of the world. We shall work for the extension of your kingdom in ourselves by sacrifice and imitation of your virtues, and around us by frequent prayers and good works. May you reign over the whole world and spread everywhere the kingdom of your son, our Lord Jesus Christ. Amen.

ᐁ NEW PRAYER

Dearest Lady with the Heart of Gold, it seems hypocritical of me to pray "for the conversion of sinners" when I so often fall short of the mark myself. Please pray to your son for me, that he may look upon my life with forgiveness and grace me with his boundless mercy. And ask him to teach me to treat others who disappoint me just as I implore him to treat me, just as I would like them to treat me, with forgiveness, mercy and love. Amen.

ℬ Our Lady of China

HER STORY

*T*he presence of Roman Catholicism in China essentially dates from 1582, when Matteo Ricci, an Italian Jesuit, set up a small residence in Zhaoqing and became director of Jesuit activities in China. Immersing himself in Chinese culture, Ricci eventually mastered both Mandarin Chinese and Confucian thought and developed a system of theology that accommodated Catholicism and Confucianism. Accepted in Peking, he won many converts to the Roman Catholic faith.

Over the next century the Chinese emperors allowed Catholic priests to work in China, but these missionaries were increasingly hostile to Chinese culture and refused to support Ricci's Confucian Catholicism. In 1704 the Holy Office banned all Confucian ceremonies in the Christian communities, confirming the prohibitions in 1739. In the meantime, in 1721, as a result of the Vatican's intransigence, the emperor prohibited all Europeans from proselytizing in China.

While the emperors continued to enforce the bans over the centuries, the flame of Catholicism was never extinguished in China, for Ricci's work continued to inspire numbers of Chinese people to become Confucian Catholics. Tong Lu, a poor village in northern China that had sprung up around an old Vincentian mission, became a center for Chinese Christians.

In April 1900 during the Boxer Rebellion, ten thousand rioters attacked Tong Lu as part of a countrywide effort to extirpate all Western influences. To create panic, the attackers began shooting into the air, but they suddenly fled. According to legend, a woman in white had appeared in the sky above the village and a strange, fiery horseman had then dispersed the rioters. Father Wu, the Chinese Catholic pastor of the village, was said to have invoked the Blessed Mother's intercession during the attack.

When the villagers rebuilt their church, Father Wu placed a painting of Mary above the altar. She was depicted wearing the royal robes of a Chinese empress, with the Christ child in her hands. The bishops of China named this image Our Lady of China in 1924.

Pope Pius XI consecrated the church at Tong Lu as the Shrine of Our Lady of China in 1932, and in 1938 the Vatican lifted its ban on Confucian ceremonies in Catholic communities.

Attempting to eliminate all Western practices from China, the

Communists destroyed the Marian shrine at Tong Lu in 1951. Fortunately, the painting of Mary had been hidden and is now believed to be in the possession of Chinese priests who carry out their pastoral duties secretly, relying on the continued protection and grace of Our Lady of China.

Despite persecutions, Tong Lu has remained a center of worship for Chinese Catholics. On the vigil and feast of Our Lady of China, May 23 and 24, 1995, thousands of Catholics surmounted roadblocks and endured physical abuses to pray at the shrine. Their reward was a spectacular miracle of the sun followed by the apparition of Our Lady of China and the child Jesus, the Holy Family, the heavenly Father and the Holy Spirit—all witnessed by more than thirty thousand pilgrims and certified by the bishop.

Since then the government has forbidden the annual May pilgrimage, and Communist forces have attacked underground Catholics and arrested and tortured Catholic clergy. Some have been "disappeared."

Nevertheless, underground Chinese Catholics continue to call upon Our Lady of China for protection and freedom. She sustains the faith of these persecuted souls, giving them hope that one day Christians will again be free to worship God in China.

❧ TRADITIONAL PRAYER

O blessed Lady, with Jesus always before you, you watch over all your children. You resist war and persecution, and so we come before you with confidence to implore your motherly intercession. We beseech you to help end all division, violence and persecution. We look for your protection in our trials. Remove all that separates us from one another, and lead us into unity with Jesus. Hear our prayer, O blessed Lady, and draw us closer to one another. Amen.

❧ NEW PRAYER

Dear Lady of China, we implore you to send your legions of angels to protect those souls who suffer indignities and violence because of their faith in your son. Defend people everywhere—especially the people of China—from religious persecution, and sustain in them the hope of religious freedom. They are true witnesses, persevering in the practice of their faith despite expulsion, arrest, torture, even death. Be with them during their anguish, comforting them as only you, our heavenly mother, can. And reveal to us their sorrow, that we might do all in our power to lift the yoke of persecution and oppression from their souls. Amen.

𝒳 Our Lady of Csíksomlyó
| COMFORTER OF THE AFFLICTED |

HER STORY

*N*ow part of Romania, Transylvania, a borderland between Europe and Asia, has been crossed and conquered by innumerable invaders over the centuries. Fortunately, the people of this region have had recourse to Our Lady of Csíksomlyó, Comforter of the Afflicted (page 11), who has graced them with her miraculous protection.

Csíksomlyó is a small place north of Bucharest. Here is found a miraculous wooden statue of our Lady, presently honored in a shrine so spectacularly bright and colorful that it rivals any religious sanctuary the world over. More than six feet tall, the statue depicts our Lady standing in the sun, holding the Christ child in her left arm and a scepter in her right. As might be expected, she and her son exhibit Slavic features.

The origins of the statue are unknown. According to one legend, local artisans may have carved it in the fourteenth century. Another tradition ascribes it to the great German sculptor Veit Stoss of the sixteenth century. Another possibility is that the Franciscan monks brought it with them when they were driven north by the Turks. In any case, the Franciscans who settled in Csíksomlyó bonded with the inhabitants and became caretakers of the shrine. Given the recurring misfortunes of this land at the crossroads of so many routes of war, the townsfolk came often to implore the intercession of Our Lady of Csíksomlyó.

Since the sixteenth century many miracles attributed to her have been recorded. She is said to have protected her people from the attacks of foreign armies and from the despoilment of local warlords. She is said to have survived undamaged a Tartar officer's attempt to pierce her with his lance and to have remained untouched each of the six times the surrounding church was burned to the ground. On September 20, 1798, she was officially declared a wonder-working image and given a golden crown.

When the Communists took power in Romania after World War II, they sealed Our Lady of Csíksomlyó in her shrine and exiled her Franciscan guardians. The people never forgot her, however, and attribute their eventual triumph over Communism to her intercession. Now that her shrine has been opened again to the public, people continue to pray to her for comfort in their afflictions and deliverance from their burdens.

◌ TRADITIONAL PRAYER

Mother, I commend and entrust to you all that goes to make up earthly progress, asking that it should not be one-sided but that it should create conditions for the full spiritual advancement of individuals, families, communities and nations.

I commend to you the poor, the suffering, the sick and the handicapped, the aging and the dying. I ask you to reconcile those in sin, to heal those in pain and to uplift those who have lost their hope and joy. Show to those who struggle in doubt the light of Christ your son. Amen.

◌ NEW PRAYER

O Lady of Csíksomlyó, I ask for your comfort this day, not simply for my own afflictions, which are slight and transient, but more significantly for the tribulations of those innocents caught in the crossfires of war. Protect them from all harm. I pray especially for the people of [mention place], whose trials are particularly heavy at this time. Deliver them from their burdens, that they may soon know the joys of peace. Amen.

ℬ Our Lady of Czestochowa
| THE BLACK MADONNA |

HER STORY

Ranking fourth among the world's Christian pilgrimage sites, behind only Rome, Lourdes and Jerusalem, the shrine of Our Lady of Czestochowa is Poland's national shrine. More than five million pilgrims come here annually to view the sacred icon of our Lady, which, according to legend, Saint Luke the Evangelist painted on a table built by Jesus himself.

Saint Helena supposedly discovered the image in Jerusalem in 326 and took the icon back with her to Constantinople, where her son, the Roman emperor Constantine, had it enshrined. The painting quickly became a favorite among the people for its miracles and is credited with saving Constantinople from the attacking Saracens.

Whether the icon originally depicted the Madonna and Child as dark skinned is unknown. Perhaps fires burned the icon or smoke from centuries of votive candles turned it black, from which the popular title the Black Madonna arose.

Various legends tell of the painting's next move. According to one, it was a gift to Emperor Charlemagne, who later presented it to Prince Leo of Ruthenia. Another legend relates that a Greek princess received the icon as a wedding gift from the Byzantine emperor and brought it with her to Belz when she married a Ruthenian nobleman.

When the Tartars invaded Ruthenia in the fourteenth century, our Lady's intercession is said to have caused a mysterious cloud to envelope the chapel containing her image, protecting it from looting and confusing the invaders, who soon retreated.

Afterward, an angel appeared in a dream to Prince (Saint) Ladislaus of Opola and urged him to take the icon to Jasna Góra (Mount of Light), near an obscure village named Czestochowa. He founded a monastery of Pauline monks to care for the portrait. In 1386 the friars built a shrine, which because of the countless miraculous events occurring there soon became the most famous in Poland. King Jagiello thereafter built a great cathedral around the shrine.

When Swedish troops invaded Poland in 1655, a handful of soldiers and monks, determined to defend the shrine to the death, begged the icon for deliverance. They held off the invading army for forty days, and their small victory so encouraged the Polish people that they drove the Swedes out. In gratitude, King John Casimir declared Our Lady of Czestochowa the Queen of the Crown of Poland and placed the country under her protection.

The Soviet Army invaded the newly independent Poland in 1919 and by September 14, 1920, had arrived at the banks of the Vistula, ready to attack Warsaw. In desperation the people prayed to Our Lady of Czestochowa. The next day—the feast day of Our Lady of Sorrows—Mary is said to have appeared in the clouds above Warsaw, and the Soviet Army was routed in a series of battles that came to be known as the Miracle at the Vistula.

Though Pope Clement XI had recognized the miraculous nature of the icon in 1717, Pope Pius XI affirmed Mary's title as Queen of

Poland in 1925, designating May 3 as her feast.

During World War II, Hitler prohibited pilgrimages to the shrine, but people secretly made the journey to implore our Lady's aid. After Poland was liberated, pilgrims visited to express their gratitude. The shrine was the site of Poland's rededication to the Immaculate Heart of Mary on September 8, 1946, as well as a gathering in 1947 to implore Mary's intercession against the new danger of Communism. Certainly, the prayers of Our Lady of Czestochowa helped end Communist rule in Poland.

Now that Central and Eastern Europe are opening to tourists, the shrine of Our Lady of Czestochowa welcomes even more pilgrims, for her story has come to inspire freedom-loving people throughout the world.

℃ TRADITIONAL PRAYER

Holy Mother of Czestochowa, you are full of grace, goodness and mercy. I consecrate to you all my thoughts, words and actions—my soul and body. I ask for your blessings and especially prayers for my salvation. Today, I consecrate myself to you, good Mother, totally—with my body and soul amid joy and suffering—to obtain for others and myself your blessings on this earth and eternal life in heaven. Amen.

℃ NEW PRAYER

Dear Lady of Czestochowa, our Black Madonna, teach me the lesson of human family. Remind me that whether we are black or white or red or yellow makes no difference, that we are all human. When I might be tempted to judge people in terms of race or ethnicity, send your image to me so that I remember that we are all your children, that we all come from God. And when I might hear racial or ethnic insults, strengthen your spirit of love within me, that I might speak up for the dignity of all people and not be a silent accomplice to prejudice. Remove the fear of difference from my heart, that I might look at and treat all people as loving and lovable brothers and sisters. Amen.

𝒷 Our Lady of Divine Providence

| QUEEN OF THE HOME |

HER STORY

*T*he title Our Lady of Divine Providence has its roots in the story of the wedding at Cana (John 2:1–11). During the celebration, Mary told Jesus that the host had run out of wine to serve to the guests. He told her to leave him alone, but she did not retreat. Taking matters into her own hands, she urged the servants to follow Jesus' instructions. Thus did the Blessed Mother corner divine providence into supplying the needs of the moment.

Mary is the mother of divine providence because she is the mother of Christ, the mother of the one who satisfies all human needs. When Jesus promised his disciples that God would supply all their needs (Luke 12:22–31 and Matthew 6:25–33), he was assuring them that he himself was both the agent and the fulfillment of divine providence.

According to one tradition, Saint Philip Benizi (1233–1285), superior of the Servants of Mary, was the first to spread devotion to Our Lady of Divine Providence. He invoked Mary's aid when his friars had nothing to eat, and a miraculous delivery of two baskets of food preserved the community.

But our Lady did not become well known until the Counter-Reformation Era. In 1611 the Barnabites were experiencing such grave financial difficulties that they had to stop construction on the Church of San Carlo ai Catinari in Rome. Blaise Palma, pastor, made a pilgrimage to Loreto to appeal for Mary's assistance. When he returned, the Barnabites received the money to complete the structure.

Experiencing money troubles again, the Barnabites had to abandon one of their Roman residences. In the move, a miraculous image of the Blessed Mother was shattered. In recompense they received in 1664 a painting of the Madonna by Scipion Pulzone, known as Gaetano, a student of Raphael. The gorgeous image depicts the Blessed Virgin Mary holding her toddler son, Jesus. What is most remarkable about the depiction is that the child has wrapped his fingers around his mother's hand. This pose symbolizes the sacred source of Mary's power, as if the child is telling her, "Mother dear, I place in thy hands the authority to act in my name. From my infinite treasure-house do thou *provide* good things to all who implore thy aid." The Barnabites referred to the painting as *Mater Divinae Providentiae*, or Mother of Divine Providence, and placed it in the chapel where they would gather for the daily recitation of the Divine Office.

Not long afterward, Januarius Maffetti, a member of the Barnabite community, was moved to make the painting known to the public. Soon all of Rome came to venerate our Lady. In 1774 Pope Benedict XIV established the Confraternity of Our Lady of Providence, which over the years has spread to Spain, France, Belgium, Switzerland, Turkey, China, South America, Mexico, Crete and Malta. She is also well known in Puerto Rico, thanks to Bishop Gil Esteve Tomás, whose appeal to our Lady is said to have rescued the cathedral and the finances of his diocese from ruin.

In the United States Our Lady of Divine Providence is also known as Queen of the Home, thanks to the devotion of the Right Reverend Monsignor A. J. Rawlinson, an early-twentieth-century chaplain of the Sisters of Providence of Saint Mary-of-the-Woods, who made copies of Gaetano's painting available to thousands of Americans.

Though Gaetano's painting is not so well known now as previously, Our Lady of Divine Providence continues to watch over her children, ensuring through her foresight and persistent entreaties that her son will not forget the people of God in their moments of need.

ॐ TRADITIONAL PRAYER

> Our Lady of Providence, mother of grace and mercy, pray for us.
> Our Lady of Providence, help of the sick, pray for us.
> Our Lady of Providence, hope of the oppressed, pray for us.
> Our Lady of Providence, star of the sea, pray for us.
> Our Lady of Providence, tower of David, pray for us.
> Our Lady of Providence, queen of the home, pray for us.
> Our Lady of Providence, model of disciples, pray for us.
> Our Lady of Providence, mother of the Church, pray for us....
>
> Pray for us, Our Lady of Providence, that we may be made worthy of the promises of Christ.

—from the Litany of Our Lady of Providence

ॐ NEW PRAYER

When I enumerate my troubles, O Lady of Divine Providence, they seem but paltry things. Food, clothing, shelter, health, employment, safety are not my worries, as they are for so many millions throughout the world.

So, dearest Mother, please hear the entreaties of those millions as they cry for assistance. Take their cries right to the throne of divine providence. And implore your son to send his Spirit out into the world, to move those of us with few needs to open our hearts to the great needs among us.

O dear Lady, inspire us to become agents of divine providence ourselves. Dare us to take that first step. Only then can we learn the truth of divine providence, that our own little bit will be enough if we have enough little bits to put together. Amen.

ℬ Our Lady of Einsiedeln

HER STORY

The story of Our Lady of Einsiedeln begins in 853 with the monk Saint Meinrad, who built a hermitage in the wilderness just southeast of Zürich, Switzerland. He was known throughout the region for his kindness, generosity and sanctity, but on the night of January 21, 861, he was murdered by two thieves, who hoped to find jewels or gold in the holy man's cell.

Meinrad had had a small chapel near his hermitage, in which he had venerated a statue of the Madonna and Child. To commemorate the holy man's dedication to the Blessed Mother, Benedictine monks built a Lady Chapel in Einsiedeln on the supposed site of Meinrad's hermitage and installed the statue inside. According to legend, on September 14, 948, Bishop Conrad of Constance, who was to consecrate the chapel, had a vision in which Christ himself performed the Mass of Consecration, in honor of his mother. In confirmation, the next day, as the bishop arrived for the service, he heard a voice saying, "Stop, brother. The church has been consecrated by God." Pope Leo VIII confirmed the miraculous consecration in a bull issued in 964.

The statue in the Lady Chapel has come to be known as Our Lady of Einsiedeln. It is a black Madonna statue (see page 132), in that the figures of our Lady and the Christ child are dark colored. She is depicted standing, just under four feet tall, holding Jesus in her left arm.

Fire has damaged the church and monastery at Einsiedeln a number of times, but it is said that the Lady Chapel and the statue have always escaped harm. However, there is some evidence that the statue currently in the chapel was carved in 1466, after the third major fire.

Tens of thousands of pilgrims once made their way to Einsiedeln each week, and many miracles have been attributed to our Lady's intercession over the centuries. Though her popularity has waned in favor of more recent shrines, Our Lady of Einsiedeln still attracts two hundred thousand pilgrims yearly, bestowing spiritual graces upon all those who seek her aid.

❧ TRADITIONAL PRAYER

Hail, Mary, queen of mercy, olive-branch of forgiveness, through whom we receive the medicine that heals our sickness, the balsam of pardon; Virgin Mother of the divine offspring, through your Son, your only Child who stooped to become the brother of humankind, you are the true Mother of us all. For the sake of his love, take me, unworthy as I am, into your motherly care. Sustain, preserve, and enlighten my conversion. Be for me for all eternity my cherished mother, tenderly caring for me throughout my earthly life, and enfolding me in your arms at the hour of my death. Amen.
—Saint Gertrude the Great

❧ NEW PRAYER

Dearest Lady of Einsiedeln, I implore your protection from the many thieves of this world. There are thieves of money or property, who deprive me of all that I have earned. There are thieves of time, who fill up my days with pointless busyness or waste my nights with inefficiencies. There are thieves of credit, who refuse to acknowledge my insights and contributions. There are thieves of dignity, who insult and reject me and leave me feeling less than human. There are thieves of trust, who take advantage of my faith in them. And there are even thieves of love, who take my affection for them and reply with hate or disdain or indifference. Though they may not assault me physically, all these thieves injure my spirit. Please, dear Mother, protect me from their depredations. As well, remind me that not all people are thieves, that I may continue to place my trust in the basic goodness of humankind made in God's image. Amen.

25 Our Lady of El-Zeitoun
| OUR LADY OF LIGHT |

HER STORY

El-Zeitoun, or Zeitun, was a quiet suburb of Cairo, Egypt, when the Blessed Mother began appearing atop St. Mary's Coptic Church there. In ancient times El-Zeitoun was known as Mataria, the place where the Holy Family, according to tradition, either lived or rested during its journey into Egypt to escape from King Herod's jealous rage. A shrine had been built here to commemorate their sojourn. Another legend recounts that in 1918 Mary appeared to Khalil Pasha Ibrahim, requesting that a church be built on this site and promising to bring a special blessing to the place fifty years later. St. Mary's was constructed, and the apparitions of Our Lady of Light began in 1968—as Mary had promised.

It was Tuesday, April 2, 1968, the feast of Our Lady of Light. A group of Muslim workers had arrived for its shift at the bus garage, which was across the street from the church. At 8:30 P.M. they noticed movement near the church's middle dome. Suddenly, a "white lady" appeared, kneeling beside the cross atop the dome. Believing a young woman was about to kill herself, Farouk Mohammed Atwa pointed toward her with his bandaged finger and implored her not to jump. When the figure rose to her feet, a woman below exclaimed, "Virgin Mary, Virgin Mary." Witnesses then saw a white dove hover around the glowing figure, which disappeared after a few moments. The next morning, when Atwa reported to the hospital for a scheduled operation on his finger, the doctors found it completely healed.

Word of the cure and the appearance spread quickly, fueled by reports of additional apparitions. Initially, the Virgin appeared two or three times each week. Immense crowds composed of Muslims, Christians, Jews and nonbelievers—sometimes as many as 250,000 people on a single night—congregated in the street to wait for the Lady of Light.

Bright lights in the night sky and soaring white doves, which otherwise do not fly after dark, accompanied the apparitions. Sometimes the doves or the lights would take the shape of a cross. Our Lady was observable to everyone in the crowd. She even allowed herself to be visible in photographs and on television—so that many millions more might see her. Although she never spoke nor gave any verbal messages, she appeared many times in the posture of prayer—

as if inviting all the world to join together in silent, prayerful contemplation of the Divine. She would often bow to or bless the crowd. She also appeared with one of various symbols: a cross, an olive branch, a rosary or a crown.

People of all faiths and backgrounds experienced miracles—cures of cancer, restorations of sight—that they attributed to her intercession. She was even said to have protected a child from being crushed by a train.

The stories prompted the Coptic hierarchy to investigate. Suspecting an elaborate hoax, the local police cooperated, searching a fifteen-mile radius around the site to uncover any device that might be projecting the images. No device was found. After a brief study His Holiness Kyrillos VI, Coptic Pope of Alexandria and Patriarch of the See of St. Mark in Africa and the Near East, issued a statement in 1969 authenticating the apparitions of the Virgin. Then Pope Paul VI asked Cardinal Stephanos I to make a further study. The apparitions finally received the Vatican's approval.

After the first few months the frequency of the apparitions dwindled to once or twice per week. The final apparition occurred on May 29, 1971. Yet miraculous cures have continued.

Why El-Zeitoun? Perhaps because the Arabic word *el-zeitoun* means "olives," a symbol of peace. Peace has been an important component of all Mary's messages to her children. And one of the great miracles of El-Zeitoun is that Our Lady of Light has been able to bring Christians, Muslims, Jews and people of other faiths or of no faith together to share moments of prayer and to be at peace with one another.

ᘯ TRADITIONAL PRAYER

O Mary, immensity of heaven, foundation of the earth, depth of the seas, light of the sun, beauty of the moon, splendour of the stars in the heavens...Your womb bore God, before whose majesty man stands in awe. Your lap held the glowing coal. Your knees supported the lion, whose majesty is fearful. Your hands touched the One who is untouchable and the fire of the divinity which is in him. Your fingers resemble the glowing tongs with which the prophet received the coals of the heavenly oblation. You are the basket for this bread of ardent flame and the chalice for this wine. O Mary, who nurtured in your womb the fruit of oblation...we pray to you with perseverance to guard us from the adversity which ensnares us and as the measure of water cannot be parted from the wine, so let us not be separated from you and your Son, the Lamb of salvation.

—Ethiopic *Anaphora in Honour of Mary*

ᴄᴠ NEW PRAYER

Most blessed Mother, be with me as I approach the Lord this day, that I may learn to quiet the clamor within my soul, that I may leave behind my worries and questions, that I may empty myself of all longing and need so that I may become attuned to holy silence and hear what God has to say to me within my heart. As well, help me approach all people in this way, that I may hear truly what each one has to say, without inserting myself into their messages, and so come to closer communion with each one. Amen.

📚 *Our Lady of Ephesus*

HER STORY

According to the narrative of the crucifixion in the Gospel of John, when Jesus died, the apostle John took Mary into his care: "When Jesus saw his mother and the disciple whom he loved standing beside her, he said to his mother, 'Woman, here is your son.' Then he said to the disciple, 'Here is your mother.' And from that hour the disciple took her into his own home" (19:26–27). Tradition has always affirmed that John and Mary moved to Ephesus, on the western coast of present-day Turkey, to avoid the persecution of Christians taking place in Jerusalem and that Mary ended her days in this obscure place.

The presence in Ephesus of the Church of the Virgin, the first basilica in the world dedicated to Mary, supports the belief that she once resided there because during the early days of Christianity, places of worship were dedicated only to persons who had lived or died in the area.

The tradition was so firmly established that the church fathers decided to hold a council at Ephesus in 431. Within the walls of the Church of the Virgin, also known as the Double Church, the council formally proclaimed Mary as *Theotokos* (page 198).

The basilica was destroyed in the seventh or early eighth century; a smaller brick church that replaced the basilica fell into disrepair in the thirteenth century. Though the site is in ruins today, it is still sacred in the memory of the church.

But Ephesus is also the location of another archaeological treasure, the house believed to have been Mary's last home. The information leading to the discovery of the house came from a remarkable source.

Anne Catherine Emmerich (1774–1824) was a German Augustinian nun favored with numerous visions of the life of the Blessed Mother. Inspired by Emmerich's writings, a priest, Father Jung, led a group of explorers to Mary's house in 1891. After excavating the area, they were amazed at the apparent accuracy of Emmerich's descriptions. In 1896 Father Jung presented his findings to the archbishop of Smyrna, who published a formal declaration of the discovery.

The Vatican has subsequently allowed religious ceremonies to be celebrated at the site. Pope Saint Pius X granted plenary indulgences for pilgrimages to the shrine and bestowed his apostolic blessing upon all those involved in the restoration of the house. In 1951 Pope Pius XII declared Mary's home an official sanctuary for pilgrims and confirmed the plenary indulgences. Pope John XXIII reaffirmed the plenary indulgences in 1961. Pope John Paul II has verified the significance of the house as a place of worship.

Although no documents or other artifacts proving Mary was ever in Ephesus have turned up, tradition and the Council of Ephesus have so intimately connected the Blessed Mother with this place that she is now known as Our Lady of Ephesus. Millions of pilgrims come annually to this out-of-the way city to venerate her under this title, experiencing, perhaps, something of what her life was like and praising the wondrous ways of God.

❧ TRADITIONAL PRAYER

Most holy and immaculate Virgin Mary, who followed the beloved disciple into Asia and who was proclaimed Mother of God at Ephesus, protect the Church of Smyrna, sole survivor of the Seven Churches of the Apocalypse, heir to all their traditions and mother of all the churches.

Bestow, we beseech you, your maternal and benevolent protection on the entire church, both in the West and in the East, the cradle of our faith.

Our Lady of Ephesus, queen assumed into heaven, you who are mother to all humankind, guard and protect us from all perils, both spiritual and physical. Intercede with your divine son for us who, following the example of our fathers, place in you all our trust and all our love. Amen.

O Lady of Ephesus, I, too, am a wanderer, making my way back to heaven, my true home. But I also have a home here. Please bless this home, that it may be a loving place for me and my loved ones, a safe refuge for those in need and a welcoming space for all the people of God. Teach me to fill my home with joy and laughter, with happy experiences and positive feelings, with beauty and tranquility and peace. And sanctify all who visit my home, that they may enter in the spirit of kindness and go out again refreshed in the spirit of love. Amen.

ᔓ *Our Lady of Fátima*

HER STORY

*O*ur Lady's apparitions at Fátima, Portugal, during the summer of 1917 are perhaps the most famous of all her appearances.

Fátima is in the very center of Portugal, a country known as the Land of Mary. Its every diocese is dedicated to the Blessed Mother under one of her titles, and Leiria, the diocese of Fátima, is dedicated to the Queen of Heaven. Indeed, the name Fátima is taken to mean "lady" in Arabic.

In 1916 while tending sheep in the hills, Lúcia dos Santos, age nine, and her cousins Francisco (eight) and Jacinta (six) Marto encountered the Guardian Angel of Portugal, who taught them this prayer: "My God, I believe, I adore, I hope and I love you. I ask pardon of you for those who do not believe, do not adore, do not hope, and do not love you." During subsequent visits the angel told them to pray, accept suffering and offer sacrifices, and brought them the Eucharist: to Lúcia, the host; to the others, the chalice. The children kept these events secret.

On May 13, 1917, Lúcia, Francisco and Jacinta were tending sheep in the Cova da Iria, a natural amphitheater. After lunch they said the rosary. When a flash of lightning interrupted their prayer, they prepared to hurry home, but a brighter flash caught their attention. They beheld a globe of light hovering above a holm oak tree and, within that light, a beautiful lady clothed in a white robe with a rosary on her right hand. When questioned, the lady said she came from heaven. She then asked the children to return to the same spot on the thirteenth of the next five months, and she promised to reveal her identity in October. Departing, she told them to say the rosary daily for world peace.

Despite Lúcia's warnings, Jacinta could not keep the vision to herself. The story spread quickly, and the children were chastised for telling lies.

On June 13 the lady announced that Francisco and Jacinta would be taken to heaven soon but that Lúcia would remain to establish devotion to the Immaculate Heart (page 32). Then she told the children to add this prayer after each decade of the rosary: "O my Jesus, forgive us our sins. Save us from the fires of hell, and lead all souls to heaven, especially those who are in most need of your mercy."

The next days brought the children ridicule, accusations and punishments. Lúcia, beginning to doubt, was given an internal assurance that the visions were not from the devil.

On July 13 about five thousand people gathered at the Cova, and many reported seeing a flash of lightning and a white light above the tree and hearing a buzzing sound. When Lúcia requested a sign for all to see, the lady promised a miracle during her October visit. Then she spread out her hands; light descended from her palms toward the center of the earth, giving the children a harrowing vision of the souls in hell. She predicted another war during the reign of Pius XI and then asked for the consecration of Russia to her immaculate heart and the Communion of reparation on first Saturdays. And she gave the children three secrets.

The county administrator abducted the children on August 13, threatening them with boiling in oil if they did not recant. But the children were resigned to die for the truth. He released them three days later, and on August 19, to make up for the missed visit, the lady appeared to the children in a different place.

Thirty thousand people gathered at the Cova on September 13 and witnessed a shower of white petals. The lady agreed that a chapel could be built on the site.

Anticipation of the October 13 appearance was overwhelming as seventy thousand pilgrims gathered. A torrential rain had completely drenched the people and turned the ground to mud by the time the children arrived to greet the lady.

When she appeared, she announced herself as the Lady of the Rosary. Then she opened her palms, and rays of light shot up toward the sun. Lúcia cried, "See the sun," and the people in the crowd were able to look at the sun without damaging their eyes and saw it whirl and pulse and change colors. Then it plunged toward the earth. When it returned to its place in the sky, the people found themselves and the ground completely dry.

During this miracle of the sun, the children had visions of our Lady and Saint Joseph with the child Jesus blessing the world, of Jesus in a red robe blessing the crowd and of Mary as Our Lady of Sorrows (page 54) and Our Lady of Mount Carmel (page 135).

Francisco and Jacinta both fell victim to the postwar influenza epidemic, Francisco dying on April 4, 1918, and Jacinta on February 20, 1920. Jacinta's body was found to be incorrupt when it was exhumed in 1935 and 1950.

Lúcia joined the Sisters of Saint Dorothy in 1926. She continued to receive visions of our Lady with the child Jesus, and in 1927 Jesus gave Lúcia permission to reveal the first two secrets—the vision of hell and the messages about Russia. In 1929 our Lady told Lúcia to ask the pope to consecrate Russia to the Immaculate Heart. Lúcia joined the Carmelites in 1948 and took the name Sister Santa Maria Lúcia of the Immaculate Heart. She is still living.

The church began investigating the appearances at Fátima in 1922, and on October 13, 1930, Bishop José Correia da Silva of Leiria declared the apparitions worthy of belief. A church was built at the Cova and is now one of the world's major pilgrimage destinations. An unexpected spring discovered nearby has been the source of many miraculous cures.

In June 1944 Lúcia finally transcribed the third secret and conveyed it to the bishop in a sealed envelope. He turned it over, unread, to the Vatican in 1957. Pope John Paul II finally released the secret to the world on June 26, 2000, interpreting it as a prediction of the assassination attempt that nearly killed him in 1981.

In early 1989 Lúcia announced that God had accepted John Paul II's March 25, 1984, consecration of Russia and the world to the Immaculate Heart and that the results would become known by the end of the year. It was in 1989 that the Berlin Wall fell, and the Soviet Union itself dissolved soon thereafter.

Though many people believe that Our Lady of Fátima's call to prayer and reparation changed the course of modern history, her messages are also timeless, warning humankind of the dangers of disregarding God's will while also offering the hope of love and peace through her caring and loving heart.

Beloved Mother, most holy Virgin, Our Lady of Fátima, we acknowledge with sadness the suffering of your immaculate heart, surrounded as it is with the thorns ungrateful people have placed around your heart. Moved by our love of you as our Mother, we place ourselves at your feet and humbly want to make reparations to you by means of our prayers and sacrifices for the grievances you have suffered.

Speak on our behalf, fairest Lady, and obtain for us pardon of our sins and grace to make amends for them. Hasten the conversion of all peoples so that they may learn to love the Lord. Turn your eyes of mercy toward us, so that we may love God with all our hearts while on earth and enjoy his presence forever in heaven. Amen.

∾ NEW PRAYER

Most holy Lady of Fátima, it seems to me that there are too many secrets in the world—secrets among governments, secrets within families, secrets between lovers, even secrets hidden in the recesses of my own heart—secrets that breed mistrust, foster insecurities and develop into hostilities. Help me to face up to my own secrets, that I may be honest with myself and come to know truth. Help me also to be open and truthful with others and with God in all that I do and say, that my relationships may be founded on truth. And help me to set an example of complete and guileless honesty, that others may see the joy of truth. I ask this in the name of your son, who named himself Truth. Amen.

🦋 Our Lady of Gietrzwald

HER STORY

About 120 miles north of Warsaw lies Gietrzwald, one of Poland's best-kept religious secrets. In this village is found the sanctuary of Our Lady of Gietrzwald, which houses both a miraculous icon of the Madonna and a statue of the Immaculate Conception commissioned in honor of the Blessed Mother's apparitions there.

The icon of Our Lady of Gietrzwald dates from the fourteenth century. Over the course of their turbulent history, the people of Poland have consistently appealed to Our Lady of Gietrzwald for assistance and have filled the church with precious gifts in thanksgiving for the healings received from her. The painting received a singular honor in 1967 when the primate of Poland bestowed a golden papal crown upon our Lady.

But it was the Blessed Virgin Mary's appearance at Gietrzwald that really made the village a pilgrimage destination. On June 27, 1877, thirteen-year-old Justina Szafrynska, who was preparing for her first holy Communion, and her mother knelt down to pray when they heard the angelus bell. Suddenly, Justina saw a dazzling light in a tree nearby. She became enraptured and in her state of ecstasy told her mother that she could see the Blessed Mother sitting on a brilliant chair surrounded by angels. The apparition lasted only a few moments, during which the lady asked Justina to return the next day.

She did, bringing along her friend twelve-year-old Barbara Samulowska. They began reciting the rosary when the lady appeared, both children seeing angels place a child on the lady's lap. The lady appeared again on June 30, telling the girls to pray the rosary every day.

The next time, when Justina asked the lady to identify herself, the apparition replied, "I am the Blessed Virgin Mary."

The apparitions continued daily for the next two months, and the growing crowds of onlookers told the girls to ask our Lady specific questions about people they knew. Our Lady's answer was always the same: "You must pray the rosary." She also requested that a shrine be built to enclose a statue of the Immaculate Conception. Once she instructed the girls to wash in a nearby spring, which she blessed for healings.

Church authorities quickly began an investigation, interrogating the girls separately after each apparition and testing them medically and psychologically during their ecstasies. The reports were positive, but it was not until 1977, on the hundredth anniversary of the events, that the local bishop declared the apparitions authentic.

Now that Communism has fallen in Poland, the fame of Our Lady of Gietrzwald is finally spreading, and she calls out to all the world, inviting pilgrims to come to her sanctuary and pray the rosary for healings both physical and spiritual.

❧ Traditional Prayer

Mother of our Lord, healer of human souls and bodies, Lady of Gietrzwald, you who blessed this place with your presence, please turn your loving eyes toward me and ask your son Jesus Christ for the favors I am in need of *[mention request]*. Compassionate and merciful Virgin Mother, I am forever yours. Amen.

❧ New Prayer

Most holy Lady of Gietrzwald, we come to you in our pain and sorrow. Please comfort us as you comforted your son, Jesus. Take us in your arms, wipe away our tears and reassure us that all will be well. Hear our needs *[mention request]* and bring them to the attention of your son, imploring him to grant our hearts' desires. Amen.

❧ *Our Lady of Guadalupe*

Her Story

When Mary appeared to Juan Diego in Tepeyac, Mexico, in 1531, she most probably spoke to him in his own language, Nahuatl, and called herself *coatlaxopeuh*, or "the one who crushes the serpent." This Nahuatl word *coatlaxopeuh*, which is pronounced "quatlasupe," sounds remarkably like the Spanish word *Guadalupe*—thus the language-crossing homophone.

Blessed Juan Diego, born in 1474 with the Aztec name Cuauhtlatoatzín, meaning "the one who talks like an eagle," worked in the fields and manufactured mats for a living. He and his wife owned their land and house but had no children. They were baptized by Spanish missionaries sometime around 1524, he taking the Christian name Juan Diego and she, María Lucía. When María Lucía died in 1529, Juan Diego moved in with his uncle Juan Bernardino in Tolpetlac, which was closer to the church in Mexico City. Every Saturday and Sunday he walked many miles to attend Mass and religious-instruction classes.

During his early-morning trek on December 9, 1531—the Spanish feast of the Immaculate Conception—Juan Diego heard a woman's voice calling him as he passed the hill at Tepeyac, a place of special significance in the Aztec religion. Climbing to the top, he saw a young woman wearing a robe of salmon and bluish green. Encircled with rays as bright as the sun, she said, "I am the Holy Mary ever-Virgin. I greatly desire that a church be built to me here, so that I may give all my love, compassion and help. For I am a compassionate mother to you and to all of my devoted children who will call upon me with confidence. It is here I wish to hear your pleadings and to cure your ills and your sorrow."

She instructed him to bring her request to the bishop of Mexico City, but he refused to hear Juan Diego. So our Lady appeared again the next day, repeating her message. This time, the bishop urged the visionary to ask the apparition for a sign that she was truly who she claimed. Juan Diego delivered the bishop's request during the third visitation, and the lady promised the proof for the following day.

But the next morning Uncle Juan Bernardino was gravely sick, and Juan Diego thought to summon a priest from the city to dispense last rites. Approaching Tepeyac Hill, he hurried to avoid the lady, but she intercepted him, promising that his uncle would be cured. Then she sent Juan Diego on a curious errand: to gather some flowers for her from the top of the hill. Since it was the freezing month of December, Juan Diego was astonished to find the hilltop blooming with roses. He picked a large number of blooms and placed them in his *tilma*, or "cloak," woven of fibers. Then he descended to the lady, who tied up his tilma and told him he was to show the flowers only to the bishop.

When Juan Diego was finally able to see the bishop, he opened his tilma. A stream of roses fell to the floor. But what most awed the bishop was the beautiful image of the Blessed Virgin that had been imprinted on the tilma: a depiction of the Immaculate Conception.

Our Lady not only cured but also appeared to Juan Bernardino, telling him that the image she had given Juan Diego would be used to stamp out the Aztec religion of "the stone serpent." The bishop ordered the construction of the church as our Lady had requested and enshrined the image from Juan Diego's tilma there. It can still be viewed at Our Lady of Guadalupe Basilica in Mexico City.

Over the years scientists have examined that life-size image in minute detail, concluding that no known artistic or scientific process can explain its creation. The tilma has yet to deteriorate, and the colors have not faded. Remarkably, in 1921, during the persecution of Roman Catholics, the image survived a dynamite explosion without a scratch.

The feast of Our Lady of Guadalupe continues to be celebrated on December 12, the anniversary of her gift of her image. In 1990 Pope

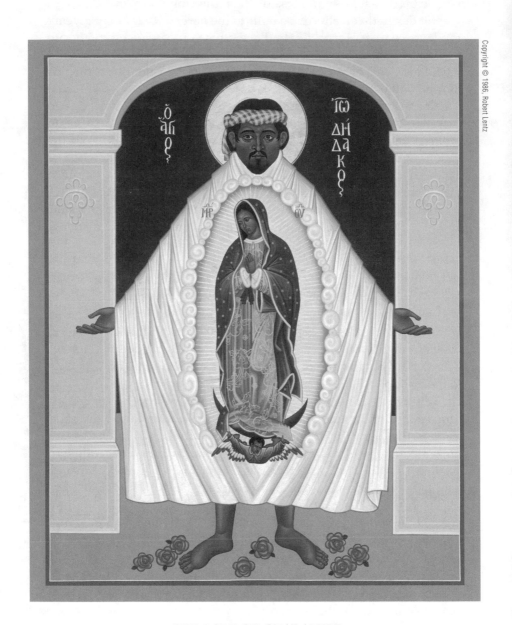

OUR LADY OF GUADALUPE
AND JUAN DIEGO OF MEXICO

Robert Lentz
1986

John Paul II beatified Juan Diego at the basilica in Mexico City.

The image seems to depict Mary during her pregnancy. Because the Aztecs had practiced human sacrifice, it is believed that our Lady's purpose was to end this custom. As a result, Our Lady of Guadalupe has become the patroness of the pro-life movement, and many people invoke her intercession on behalf of the unborn and pray to her in reparation for abortion.

❧ TRADITIONAL PRAYER

Remember, O most gracious Virgin of Guadalupe, that in your apparitions on Mount Tepeyac you promised to show pity and compassion to all who, loving and trusting you, seek your help and protection.

Accordingly, listen now to our supplications and grant us consolation and relief. We are full of hope that, relying on your help, nothing can trouble or affect us. As you have remained with us through your admirable image, so now obtain for us the graces we need. Amen.

❧ NEW PRAYER

Holy Mother, Our Lady of Coatlaxopeuh, I do not remember my mother's pregnancy, and I can only imagine what she may have felt: joy at the miracle that was taking place within her; worry about my health; discomfort because of the changes her own body was experiencing; anticipation to hold her firstborn in her arms; pain at my birth. Yet too soon afterward, she experienced the inevitable moving apart as her child grew and became an adult. Now we are virtual strangers. I do not know who she has become, and she cannot find in me the babe she once held in her arms. And in this distance lies a painful longing to know once again the unconditional maternal embrace. So dearest Mother, you who brought the Christ child into creation, help me to appreciate the woman who bore me into the world. Help me to reclaim what we experienced together, so that we might come to know each other again and experience the joyful love that God intended between mother and child. This I ask in the name of your son, Jesus. Amen.

🦋 Our Lady of Gyor

*T*he story of Our Lady of Gyor actually begins in Ireland. For many years the Cathedral of Clonfert, Ireland, had a painting showing the Blessed Mother gazing lovingly at the peacefully sleeping infant Jesus. Kneeling in a posture of prayer, she is wearing a crown, as is the babe. The Roman Catholics of Clonfert had a great devotion to this image.

When Oliver Cromwell's forces invaded Ireland in 1649, his army arrested many of the clergy, including Bishop Walter Lynch of Clonfert. The bishop escaped from prison in 1652, smuggling himself and the Madonna of Clonfert painting out of the country.

He ended up in Hungary, where the bishop of Gyor appointed him as his vicar general. Gyor is located in northwestern Hungary, midway between Vienna and Budapest. Bishop Lynch learned Hungarian and worked in Gyor for ten years. When the situation in Ireland improved, he thought to return to his homeland, but he became deathly ill. On his deathbed he bequeathed the Irish Madonna painting, as it had become known, to the local bishop.

The people of the diocese were overjoyed to hear that the Madonna would remain in their cathedral. Many pilgrims came to offer their petitions to her, the faithful attributing all their answered prayers to her intercession.

Meanwhile, in 1697 Parliament ordered the expulsion of all priests from Ireland and the British Isles. Roman Catholic churches were ransacked, confiscated or destroyed. Parliament's intention, to erase all traces of the Roman Catholic faith, caused great suffering among Irish Catholics.

Back in Hungary, thousands of people were attending Mass in the Cathedral of Gyor on March 17, 1697—Saint Patrick's Day—when the Irish Madonna began to weep bloodstained tears. When church officials removed the painting from its frame to examine it, they found no explanation for the phenomenon. The weeping continued for three hours. Hundreds of people, including the governor of the city, its mayor, all its council members, the bishop, priests, Calvinist and Lutheran ministers, as well as a rabbi, signed testimonies attesting to the miracle.

The Irish Madonna remains a cherished treasure because she has transcended national boundaries. Not only has she united the people of Ireland and Hungary in reciprocal sympathy for one another's suffering, she also annually attracts more than a million pilgrims. They bring to the weeping Madonna their petitions for her loving intercession, and they all leave comforted in the knowledge that Our Lady of Gyor, as she is now known, understands their pain and will do all that she can to bring them relief.

∾ TRADITIONAL PRAYER

Our Lady of Gyor, Virgin Mother, full of grace, I place myself before your holy picture with great reverence! My eyes are full of tears whenever I think of the sufferings of the church and your followers. For them you shed tears in this place for three hours.

O Mary, through your loving and tear-filled eyes, may you see me as a devoted child of yours. Increase in me a spirit of repentance, and enliven in me a greater faith and love of your son. Please unite all my tears with your tears and offer them as a sacrifice in order to gain mercy for me from your holy son, Jesus Christ. Amen.

∾ NEW PRAYER

O sorrowful Lady, weep not for me, for my sorrows are passing, my pains inconsequential, my needs but slight. Weep, rather, for the children of the world who cry themselves to sleep each night, and for the hardness of our hearts that keeps us from caring for these little ones.

Show us your tears, O Lady of Gyor, that they may dissolve our crust of indifference. Rain down on us your tears, O Lady of Gyor, that they may water and cultivate the spirit of love God has implanted in our hearts. Wash us all over with your tears, O Lady of Gyor, that we may be moved to become personally involved with children in need. Help us to ease their hunger, to clothe their nakedness, to shelter them from the cold, to provide them with education, to protect them from violence and abuse and to love them—to love them more than anything. Amen.

Our Lady of Hope of Pontmain

*I*n 1871 our Lady appeared to four French children in Pontmain to remind the world of the miraculous power of prayer.

France was at this time battered in the Franco-Prussian War. Napoleon III had lost the Battle of Sedan the previous September and been taken prisoner. Strasbourg and Metz had fallen; Paris was under siege. Many people believed that the events predicted by Our Lady of the Miraculous Medal (page 155) were coming to pass.

The villagers of Pontmain expected the Prussians to invade their district, located about 180 miles west of Paris, at any moment, so the morning of January 17, many people had joined Abbé Michel Guérin at Mass, imploring God's mercy through the Blessed Mother.

That bitterly cold evening, César Barbadette and two of his sons, Eugene, twelve, and Joseph, ten, were breaking fodder in the barn. At about 5:15 P.M. Eugene went to the open door and suddenly saw a beautiful woman in the sky. She was wearing a dress of deep blue covered with gold stars. On her feet were blue shoes with gold bows, and on her head, a black veil and a gold crown.

When César and Joseph came to the door, Joseph immediately described the lady exactly as Eugene saw her. But César, seeing nothing, told his sons that they were simply imagining things. His wife, Victoire, also chastised her sons but had them say five Our Fathers and five Hail Marys just in case.

After supper Eugene and Joseph found the lady just as before. Victoire sent for Sister Vitaline, one of the nuns who ran the village school, who could not see the lady either but did notice three stars arranged in a new way. Abbé Guérin noticed the same stars.

Conjecturing that Mary was revealing herself only to children, Sister Vitaline and a colleague, Sister Marie Edouard, brought some children from the school to the barnyard. Françoise Richer, eleven, and Jeanne-Marie Lebossé, nine, indicated that they could see our Lady.

When Sister Marie began the rosary, the children noted that a small red cross appeared over Mary's heart; sad now, she was suddenly surrounded by a blue oval frame and four candles. A white scroll appeared beneath Mary's feet when Sister Marie began the Magnificat. Words of gold appeared: "But pray, my children."

Sister Marie's recitation of the Litany of Loreto elicited more words: "God will soon answer your prayers," then, "My Son allows himself to be moved"—revealing the identity of the heavenly visitor.

A red crucifix with the words "Jesus Christ" appeared in Mary's hands when the crowd in the barn began singing "Mother of Hope." As the villagers sang "Parce nobis, Domine," the four candles were lit, the crucifix faded, two crosses appeared above our Lady's shoulders and she smiled. The star that had lit the candles came to rest over her head.

As Abbé Guérin called the people to say their night prayers together, a white veil rose from beneath our Lady's feet, slowly hiding her from the children. By 9:00 P.M. she had completely disappeared.

Earlier, the commander of the Prussian Army, General Schmidt, had announced plans to invade the district the next day, but all of France claims that sometime during the apparition he received an unexpected order forbidding him to advance. Instead, the Prussian Army withdrew. An armistice was signed eleven days later. Some of the Prussian soldiers spoke of "an invisible Madonna barring the way."

All of the soldiers from Pontmain returned home unharmed, and a number of miraculous cures were reported. Bishop Wicart of Laval made an investigation and on February 2, 1872, authorized devotion to Our Lady of Hope of Pontmain.

Both Eugene and Joseph Barbadette became priests, and Jeanne-Marie Lebossé became a sister of the Holy Family. While they were still alive, French Cardinal Dubois petitioned the Holy See for a Mass and Office proper to Our Lady of Pontmain, which Pope Pius XI authorized.

Our Lady of Pontmain gave hope to the people of France during a time of despair, but she also brings hope to all people at all times, that those who pray with perseverance to Mary can trust in her son's loving response.

∾ TRADITIONAL PRAYER

Mary, servant of the Lord, sweet Lady, humble Queen, we greet you. Mother of Jesus, our Savior and our brother, we love you. We are your children. Teach us to pray; come prepare in us a dwelling place pleasing to God, our Creator, Master of the universe, who makes the stars dance and fly on your beautiful dress. Mother, tender and pure, attentive to our needs as to the desires of the Holy Spirit, keep us in your love. Amen.

New Prayer

Dear Lady of Hope, lately I've so come to doubt the efficacy of prayer that I don't often pray, and praying now seems unnatural. Even saying this prayer seems formidably awkward: I've fallen out of practice and feel that I don't know how to begin or what to say. O Mother of Hope, I really want to know how to pray! I implore you, please teach me. Pray with me, that I may begin to pray again. Instill in me your spirit of prayer, that I may dare to speak with you in prayer as easily as I speak with my closest friends. Most of all, dear Mother, show me that prayer works. Give me that hope, and thus inspire me to a living renewal of prayer. Amen.

Our Lady of Kalwaria Zebrzydowska

Her Story

The story of Our Lady of Kalwaria Zebrzydowska dates from 1600, when a squire named Mikolaj Zebrzydowski built in Kalwaria, which is about twenty miles southwest of Kraków, a small sanctuary for a representation of the crucifixion. By 1617 the Franciscan friars who took care of the shrine had developed special services known as the Co-suffering of Our Lady, in which pilgrims would process, singing and praying, from a chapel representing the tomb of Christ to the Loreto House chapel.

Zebrzydowski had a great devotion to the Blessed Mother and had an image of the Madonna brought from Loreto to be installed in a special shrine inside the main church. The icon earned a reputation for granting special graces, and in 1887 the cardinal of Kraków bestowed a bejeweled golden crown upon the wonder-working image.

The icon of Our Lady of Kalwaria Zebrzydowska is a Byzantine depiction of the Virgin of Tenderness type (page 200). Mary is embracing the infant Jesus, who clings to her neck. With her left hand she indicates the Christ. The ornamentation is very ornate, the robes and crowns highly decorated.

Over the years forty chapels have been built throughout the hillside to represent the Via Dolorosa, and beginning in the seventeenth century a Passion play has been performed annually during Holy Week. The shrine of our Lady, the chapels and the Passion play attract more than one million pilgrims each year. Among the most famous of those has been Pope John Paul II, a native of a nearby village. He has a particular devotion to Our Lady of Kalwaria Zebrzydowska, who has inspired him to encourage reverence of the Blessed Mother of God.

❧ TRADITIONAL PRAYER

O beautiful and splendid Star, Our Lady of Calvary, in you we take refuge, O holy Mary. We have heard a lovely voice; the holy Virgin is calling us, "Come to me, my children, come, this is just the right time." The song of birds exalt her name; it's a voice of nightingales. This is why we should be here, bowing down with hearty prayer. Our Lady of Calvary, pray for us, O holy Mary, that we may be truly worthy to take part in future glory. Amen.

❧ NEW PRAYER

Most blessed Madonna, Our Lady of Kalwaria Zebrzydowska, remind us daily of all that your son endured for love of us. Keep before our mind's eye the events of his Passion, that we may remember how unconditionally God loves each one of us. And help us to imitate your son's utter truthfulness and to embody his perfect integrity, that we ourselves may become bearers of Christ to a world in need. We ask this in the name of your son, our Lord. Amen.

Our Lady of Kazan
| KAZANSKAYA |

HER STORY

*A*ccording to legend, the icon of Our Lady of Kazan dates from the time of the apostles. Various traditions mention the icon as early as the eleventh century, but art experts and historians generally agree that the icon could not have been painted before the thirteenth century and believe that it came from Constantinople.

When the Tartars besieged the city of Kazan, the capital of Tatarstan located about six hundred miles east of Moscow, in 1209, the icon disappeared, lost in the ruins of the monastery where it had been enshrined. In 1579, as the story goes, the Blessed Mother appeared to a nine-year-old girl named Matrona, telling her where the icon was buried. Matrona received three visits from Mary before finally going to the bishop. Excavations proved unsuccessful until Matrona herself finally took up the shovel. She found the icon wrapped in a red cloth on July 8, which the bishop established as the feast in honor of the Mother of God of Kazan.

Subsequently, the icon became known for its power to cure, and the people invoked Our Lady of Kazan, or *Kazanskaya*, as the Protectress of Russia, particularly during the Swedish, Polish and French invasions. A special church dedicated to our Lady was built in Kazan in 1679, but the icon—or a copy—eventually ended up in St. Petersburg, perhaps moved in 1713 by Czar Peter the Great to legitimate his new capital.

What happened to the icon during the twentieth century is unclear. Some sources say that it was stolen in 1904. Other sources assert that it disappeared during the 1917 Revolution, when the Bolsheviks destroyed the basilica where the icon was enshrined. Still others rumor that it was smuggled out of the country, to England or the United States. Mysteriously, sometime in the 1950s or 1960s John Haffert, the founder of the Blue Army of Our Lady of Fátima, purchased the icon and, in 1970, enshrined it at Fátima, Portugal. A few years later he brought it to the Vatican. There are current reports that the icon of Our Lady of Kazan in the Vatican has been authenticated and that Pope John Paul II will personally return it to Russia in the near future.

The icon depicts the Madonna and Child. Mary bows her head toward her son, who faces toward the viewer, his right arm raised in a gesture of welcome. The icon may be said to be a variation of the *Hodegetria* (page 22), in which the mother shows the way to the son and the son invites all people to follow his way. Over the centuries, even during the Communist regime's antagonism toward religion and even from abroad, Our Lady of Kazan has always directed people toward the faith in Christ that brings true freedom.

ᵔ TRADITIONAL PRAYER

Sweet Mother of Jesus! Be my mother always. Make me holy, obedient, humble and a true lover of Jesus, your son. May my life be an image of the life of Jesus, and may you guide me along the paths of life to the eternal happiness of heaven, and there be united with you who are united to God above all creatures. Dearest Madonna, give me the courage to do the will of God and enter into heaven as a true child of God. Amen.

ꙮ New Prayer

O Kazanskaya, the gravest danger we face is that we are lost— unable to find our way back to God. Illuminate the path for us, that we may come to join your son, who rests safely in your arms. Amen.

ꙮ Our Lady of Kevelaer

Her Story

*T*he story of Our Lady of Kevelaer begins in 1641, when Hendrick Busman, a peddler, was passing through the village of Kevelaer, which had been destroyed by fire during the Thirty Years War. When he stopped to pray by a wayside crucifix, he heard a voice saying, "At this place you shall build me a chapel." But he paid no mind. A week later he stopped again at the crucifix and heard the same words. When the message was repeated on a third occasion, he finally agreed to take on the task. But he had no funds, so the chapel remained only a challenging idea.

One night not long after, a bright light awoke Busman's wife, revealing to her a shrine with a small image of the Blessed Mother that she recognized as that of Luxembourg's Comforter of the Afflicted (page 11). The peddler's wife also saw in her vision two soldiers carrying the image.

The woman eventually found the soldiers and returned home with the image. Immediately, the cottage was mobbed by pilgrims who desired to pray to our Lady for healing. So Busman asked the local Capuchins to enshrine the image while he began the chapel he was instructed to build. The image was installed in the new sanctuary on June 1, 1641.

Astonishingly, healings began to occur almost every day at the shrine. Diocesan authorities began an investigation, concluding that many of the cures were miraculous.

A more impressive shrine was constructed in 1654. Aside from a hiatus during the French Revolution, it has displayed the miraculous image continuously to the present day. The shrine, which is located about sixty-five miles northwest of Cologne, is still one of the most popular pilgrimage destinations in all of Germany, and Our Lady of Kevelaer continues to provide comfort and protection for those who seek her aid.

ᴄᴡ Traditional Prayer

Mary, Mother of Jesus, I pray that I may receive a heart like yours, so beautiful, so pure, and without blemish—a heart filled with love and humility. Then I can love your son as you love him, and I can serve him by my works of charity and mercy. Mary, I pray that I may become a messenger of the love and peace of God. Amen.

ᴄᴡ New Prayer

Dearest Lady of Kevelaer, we ask you to comfort those who are afflicted with loneliness, especially *[mention name]*. Remind them that though their beloved may have died or their children may have grown up, though they may have separated from family or relocated to a new place, they are never completely alone. You are always with them, as near to them as a watchful mother is to her beloved children. And your son is present with them, too, as he promised, sharing with them the pain of their loneliness and loving them all the more because of their affliction. Help them to accept his love, to let it fill them up and displace their sorrow, to allow it to bring them out of their aloneness so that they can find new community and renewed joy in other people. Amen.

ᵴ Our Lady of Kibeho

Her Story

Among the Blessed Mother's most recent—and most terrifyingly prophetic—apparitions are those that occurred in Kibeho, Rwanda, not long before the massacres in that country.

On November 28, 1981, Alphonsine Mumureke, a sixteen-year-old student at the local Roman Catholic school, beheld a luminous lady in white who identified herself thus: "I am the Mother of the Word." The lady reassured Alphonsine that she had heard her prayers and had come because her companions had insufficient faith. At that the girl recognized the lady as the Blessed Mother.

When her schoolmates mocked Alphonsine for her story, she asked our Lady to appear to others. On January 12, 1982, our Lady manifested herself to Anathalie Mukamazimpaka, urging, "We must dedicate ourselves to prayer. We must develop in us the virtues of charity, availability and humility."

The ecstasies of the girls excited the villagers, and the local bishop's confidante, Marie-Claire Mukangango, twenty-two years old, tried to discredit the seers. Much to her surprise, on March 22, 1982, she received a vision of our Lady, who said, "I have come to prepare the way for my son for your good, and you do not want to understand. The time remaining is short and you are absent-minded. You are distracted by the goods of this world, which are passing. I have seen many of my children getting lost and I have come to show them the true way."

Appearances to other seers followed. On May 25, 1982, Stephanie Mukamurenzi, fourteen, received messages about repentance, conversion and mortification. On June 2 Agnes Kamagaju, twenty-two, saw our Lady; Jesus also appeared to her, calling all people to pray and exhorting young people to chastity. On July 2 Jesus appeared to Segatashya, fifteen, who was not yet a Christian, asking for prayers and repentance because the end of the world was near: "You will know my Second Coming is at hand when you see the outbreak of religious, ethnic or racial wars." Jesus also told him, "I am neither white nor black; I am simply Lord." On September 15 our Lady appeared to a Muslim woman, Vestine Salina, twenty-four, asking her to shepherd people to God.

Since our Lady announced her appearances in advance, a platform was built in the village courtyard so that the large crowds of people could observe the seers' ecstasies. Sometimes the visions lasted for hours. Observers would prick the seers with knives, burn them with candles or shine bright lights in their eyes, but the visionaries remained oblivious to these tests.

Various unnatural phenomena accompanied some apparitions. The sun danced and became blue and red, the sky changed color and the stars turned into luminous crosses. Our Lady also sent heavy rains to the drought-stricken region.

Then on August 15, 1982, came the terrifying prophecy. Five of the seers had a vision of rivers of blood. They saw bodies abandoned without burial, burning trees, decapitated heads. The vision was so disturbing that even the observers became frightened. This vision of terror was repeated several times. Finally, our Lady warned most of the seers to leave Rwanda, to escape the coming massacre.

The apparitions continued for Alphonsine until November 28, 1989, though they had stopped for the others by the end of 1983. The bishop had permitted public devotions at the site of the apparitions on August 15, 1988.

The massacres began in 1991. The majority Hutus murdered untold numbers of the ruling Tutsis; estimates of the number of dead run into the millions. The rotting of the unburied bodies polluted rivers and lakes and caused even more deaths from fever. Marie-Claire and perhaps Segatashya and the bishop were murdered. Alphonsine escaped, though not her family, and others of the seers are believed to have found safety in refugee camps.

During her last apparition our Lady left Alphonsine with this message: "I love you, I love you, I love you very much. Never forget the love I have for you in coming among you. These messages will do good not only now but also in the future." Despite the horrors of the Rwandan civil war, this is the message—the word of love—that our Lady wishes the people of God to learn from her apparitions at Kibeho.

Ꮸ TRADITIONAL PRAYER

We turn to you, O blessed Virgin Mary, Mother of Jesus and our Mother too. How could we, with trembling hearts, concern ourselves with the greatest problem of all, that of life and death, now over-shadowing all mankind, without trusting ourselves to your interces-sion to preserve us from all dangers?

This is your hour, O Mary. Our blessed Jesus entrusted us to you in the final hour of his bloody sacrifice. We are sure that you will intervene.

And now indeed we beseech you for peace, O most sweet Mother and Queen of the world. The world does not need victorious wars or defeated peoples, but renewed and strengthened health of mind, and peace which brings prosperity and tranquillity; this is what it needs and what it is crying out for: the beginning of salvation and lasting peace. Amen.

—*Pope John XXIII*

Ꮸ NEW PRAYER

Dear Lady of Kibeho, too often have I experienced the hatred of difference and exhibited it myself because of my own prejudices. Pray for me, that I may not hate in return those who hate me because of who I am. Pray for me, that I may forgive those who harm me because I am not who they want me to be. Pray for me, that I may allow the word of love to transform all prejudice within my own soul, replacing it with acceptance and love. Pray for me, that I may have the humility to seek the forgiveness of those I have harmed. And pray for me, finally, that I may find within me the courage to speak and act to protect all people who are terrorized by any hatred of difference. Amen.

25. Our Lady of Knock
| Our Lady of Silence |

HER STORY

Knock (Cnoc Mhuire) was just an unknown place in County Mayo, in the west of Ireland, in 1879 when a group of villagers there witnessed a heavenly tableau that is perhaps unique in the history of Marian apparitions.

The apparition occurred the evening of August 21. The day had been stormy and wet, and Mary McLoughlin, the village priest's housekeeper, noticed a number of "strange figures" when she passed by the chapel at about 7:00 P.M. on her way to visit a friend, Mary Beirne. McLoughlin did not stop, thinking that perhaps the priest, Archdeacon Cavanagh, had purchased some statues.

After visiting for half an hour, both women walked to the archdeacon's house. On their way Beirne noticed the figures near the chapel were actually people: the Blessed Virgin, Saint Joseph and a bishop she took to be Saint John the Evangelist. Beirne left McLoughlin standing watch and went off to fetch her mother, her sister Margaret, her brother Dominick, her niece Catherine and others—in all, eighteen witnesses, ranging in age from six to seventy years old. Someone told the archdeacon, but he declined to come out.

The witnesses generally described the tableau as follows: The Blessed Virgin appeared in the center and slightly above the others, wearing white, with a yellow crown on her head, and she was gazing upward, with her hands upraised. Saint Joseph was to her right, his head inclined toward his wife. His hair and whiskers appeared gray. Saint John, on the Virgin's left, appeared with his hand upraised as if to give an episcopal blessing.

Besides the three personages the witnesses saw a lamb resting on an altar. Some of them also saw a crucifix behind the lamb.

When she arrived on the scene, Bridget Trench went up to kiss the Virgin's feet. However, she felt nothing but the wall, but she did note that it and the grass beneath the figures were dry, despite the rain's blowing right against them.

The figures remained for about two hours, and witnesses generally agreed that the Blessed Virgin, Saint Joseph and Saint John did not move the entire time. All said that the three heavenly visitors spoke not a word.

The archbishop opened an investigation almost immediately. Fifteen witnesses were interviewed, and although the 1879 investigation found them trustworthy, the bishop did not publish the report.

Shortly after the apparition, people began reporting miraculous healings. Archdeacon Cavanagh kept careful records of these cures, which numbered 394 and included the notations that John O'Brien, born blind, had regained his sight after making a pilgrimage to Knock and that Mrs. Doble, lame for seventeen years, had recovered use of her foot. In addition, Archbishop Murphy of Hobart, Tasmania, recovered his sight at the age of eighty, and Archbishops Clune of Perth, Australia, and Lynch of Toronto, Canada, both received cures of their illnesses.

In 1936 the local bishop appointed another commission, which wrote a positive report. As a remarkable endorsement of the apparition's authenticity, Pope John Paul II made a pilgrimage to Knock in 1979, the centenary year of our Lady's appearance there.

Because of the unusual nature of the apparition, several natural explanations have been advanced: that the witnesses cooperated in fabricating the story to bring notoriety to their village; that a magic lantern projected the images; that luminous paint had been applied to the chapel wall; that the witnesses had experienced mass suggestion or hallucination. The investigations explored and dismissed all these possibilities. The only explanation given credence was the simple one: that, in fact, our Lady had appeared, along with Saints Joseph and John.

More than a century later the questions and inconsistencies are no less bothersome. But the miraculous cures continue, and even now, 1.5 million people every year make a pilgrimage to Knock to experience the place where Our Lady exhibited her silent adoration of God.

Our Lady of Knock, Queen of Ireland, you gave hope to your people in a time of distress and comforted them in sorrow. You have inspired countless pilgrims to pray with confidence to your divine son, remembering his promise: "Ask and you shall receive, seek and you shall find." Help me to remember that we are all pilgrims on the road to heaven. Fill me with love and concern for my brothers and sisters in Christ, especially those who live with me. Comfort me when I am sick or lonely or depressed. Teach me how to take part ever more reverently in the holy Mass. Pray for me now, and at the hour of my death. Amen.

Ｏ NEW PRAYER

Most blessed Lady of Knock, it is easy for me to recite the simple prayers I learned in my childhood or even to repeat the more complex formulas I've absorbed as an adult. But your example tells me that silence can also be prayer, that silent attention to God is worship. So dearest Lady of Silence, remind me again of the importance of silence. And help me, I pray, to silence the noise within my soul, that I may someday be fully attentive to the Divine and may finally be able to worship God with all my soul. Amen.

Our Lady of La Salette

HER STORY

"If my people will not submit I shall be forced to let go the hand of my Son. It is so strong, so heavy, that I can no longer withhold it." With these words Our Lady of La Salette greeted two young visionaries at a remote mountain spot outside the village of La Salette, France.

The two seers were from the town of Corps. Maximin Giraud, eleven years old, had been hired out by his father to watch cattle. Mélanie Mathieu-Calvet, fourteen or fifteen, also tended cows. Both children's families were poor, Mélanie's desperately so.

On the day of the apparition, September 19, 1846, Maximin and Mélanie were tending their charges on adjacent land. After lunch they napped. At about three o'clock Mélanie awoke and, fearing the cattle had strayed, awakened Maximin. Together they found the herds, then were startled by an extremely bright light near a dry spring. As they approached, they perceived a lady within the sphere of light. She was sitting with her head in her hands, weeping.

The lady wore white shoes, a white robe and cape, a white cap and a crown with roses. On a small chain around her neck hung a cross. She was dazzlingly bright.

The children were afraid, but the lady arose and said, "Come near, my children, be not afraid. I am here to tell you great news....For how long a time do I suffer for you! If I would not have my son abandon you, I am compelled to pray to him without ceasing. And as to you, you take no heed of it." The lady then chastised humankind for their sins, explaining that the rotting of the previous potato harvest had been an unheeded warning.

The lady had been speaking in French but switched to the children's patois. She predicted the potatoes, the wheat, the walnuts and the grapes would all go bad. As well, an epidemic would kill many children.

The lady then gave both Mélanie and Maximin private messages and charged them not to reveal these secrets to anyone except the pope.

Speaking to both children again, the lady exhorted them to say their prayers carefully morning and evening: "When you cannot do better say at least one 'Our Father' and a 'Hail Mary.' But when you have time and when you can do better, say more."

Then she disappeared into the sky, saying twice, "Well, my children, you will make this known to all my people."

Back in the village, Maximin told what they had experienced. The parish priest, Father Mélin, repeated their story during his homily, and a few people climbed the hill and found that the dry spring was flowing. Someone gave some of the water to a critically ill woman, who drank it, made a novena to Mary and was completely cured on the ninth day.

As the cures multiplied, the bishop of Grenoble opened an investigation. Cross-examined by ecclesiastics, lawyers and doctors, Maximin and Mélanie never changed their stories. Furthermore, the lady's prophesies were coming true almost immediately: The potatoes rotted that winter. In 1847 the grain and walnuts went bad. In 1849 a cholera epidemic killed many children. Approximately one million people throughout Europe would die of these calamities. Furthermore, phylloxera destroyed practically every vineyard in France in 1860.

The bishop asked the children to record the secrets the lady had imparted, promising that only the pope would read the letters. The messages moved Pius IX to say, "Here are the secrets of La Salette: unless you do penance you shall all perish." On September 19, 1851, the bishop authenticated the apparition and approved construction of a church at the site.

Mélanie and Maximin did not enjoy happy lives. Mélanie, drawn to the religious life but unable to find a suitable community, tried unsuccessfully to found her own. She died in 1904.

Maximin, failing seminary training, moved about France as a merchant and served in Rome as a papal Zouave. He wrote "My Profession of Faith in the Apparition of La Salette" to counter claims that he had recanted. It was said that Saint Jean Vianney doubted Maximin's truthfulness, but Vianney eventually declared, "I have asked for signs in order to believe in La Salette, and I have obtained them." On his deathbed in 1875 Maximin signed a statement reaffirming the truth of the apparition.

The secrets of La Salette have since become public. They accurately predicted the rise of Napoleon III, the exile of Pius IX and a series of devastating wars. They also asserted the necessity of repentance. Finally, Our Lady of La Salette issued a call to action relevant to all times: "I call on my children the true faithful, those who have given themselves to me so that I may lead them to my divine Son, those whom I carry in my arms, so to speak, those who have lived in my spirit....It is time they came out and filled the world with light. Go and reveal yourselves to be my cherished children. I am at your side and within you...."

❧ TRADITIONAL PRAYER

Remember, Our Lady of La Salette, true Mother of Sorrows, the tears you shed for us on Calvary. Remember also the care you have taken to keep us faithful to Christ, your son. Having done so much for your children, you will not now abandon us. Comforted by this consoling thought, we come to you, pleading, despite our infidelities and ingratitude. Virgin of Reconciliation, do not reject our prayers, but intercede for us, obtain for us the grace to love Jesus above all else. May we console you by living a holy life and so come to share the eternal life Christ gained by his cross. Amen.

Dear Lady of La Salette, speak to me in my own language. Signs and warnings of dire calamities may have been meaningful to a previous age, but such talk does little to convince me to love God. Certainly, the consequences of my errors desolate me, and I embrace the need to repent my sins and amend my foolish ways. But I must admit that threats don't motivate me—indeed, and perhaps irrationally, they only harden my heart. So speak to me, I implore you, in a language of spirituality that I can understand, that I may embrace the underlying truth of your message and live my life according to the Spirit of Love. Amen.

🌿 *Our Lady of La-Vang*

Her Story

*A*t the end of a century marked by power struggles between warlords, peasant uprisings and recurring insurgencies, King Canh Thinh ascended to the throne of a united Viet-Nam in 1792. Because the king knew that the deposed Nguyen Anh was receiving support from French missionaries, Canh Thinh outlawed Roman Catholicism in 1798 and ordered all Catholic churches and seminaries destroyed. Thus began the first persecution of Catholics in Vietnam.

To escape the violence, many Catholics from Quang Tri, which is in central Vietnam, fled to a deep jungle area. The place was called La-Vang, perhaps after the name of a plant that grew there, perhaps after the indigenous word that means "crying out." Cold, hungry, sick and afraid of the jungle beasts, they prepared themselves for martyrdom.

One night, while they were gathered together to pray, a lady surrounded by light appeared among them. She was wearing a long cape and holding a child. Two angels stood by her side. All of the people could see her, and they recognized her as the Blessed Mother. She offered them words of comfort and encouragement, told them to boil leaves from the nearby trees to use as medicine and promised to intercede on behalf of all who came to that spot to pray. She continued to appear periodically to the people during this first period of persecutions.

In 1802 Nguyen Anh succeeded in seizing the throne, and his reign as King Gia Long was one of tolerance for Catholics. But his successors returned to the previous king's policy of Catholic persecution, and from 1820 onward both missionary priests and indigenous Catholics were hunted down and exiled, branded or killed. More than one hundred thousand became martyrs. It is said that our Lady continued to appear at La-Vang during these violent years.

The persecutions ended in 1884 with the death of the last Nguyen emperor, though the chapel at La-Vang was destroyed in 1885. The local bishop ordered a new chapel built in 1886; it was consecrated in 1901, and the bishop proclaimed Our Lady of La-Vang as the Protectress of Catholics. When the number of pilgrims began to exceed the chapel's capacity, a new church was constructed and consecrated in 1928. In 1961 the Council of Vietnamese Bishops selected this church as the National Sacred Marian Center, and Pope John XXIII declared it a basilica.

Unfortunately, the church was destroyed during the most recent war in Vietnam, in 1972. It has not yet been rebuilt, but pilgrims still journey to the shrine to honor Our Lady of La-Vang.

In 1988 Pope John Paul II himself honored Our Lady of La-Vang during the canonizing ceremony of the Vietnamese martyrs, calling for the rebuilding of her church and invoking our Lady's intercession on behalf of peace and solidarity in Vietnam.

⌖ TRADITIONAL PRAYER

O Mary, give my dear ones true charity through which they may forgive with all their hearts and bear with resignation the crosses laid upon them by those they believe to be their enemies.

—*Pope John XXIII*

⌖ NEW PRAYER

Dear Lady of La-Vang, take away my terror of bullies and bigots, that I may dare to step forward as a protector of people who are insulted, assaulted and sometimes killed on account of their faith, their race, their gender, their age, their sexual orientation, their appearance or their mental capacity—just for being what God created them to be. Inspire me to speak out against prejudice. Enhearten me to follow the example of your son, who treated all persons with dignity and kindness, spoke out against discrimination and protected those who could not defend themselves. Amen.

🦋 Our Lady of Levoca
| OUR LADY OF LEVOCHA |

HER STORY

Our Lady of Levoca, sometimes called Levocha, is a depiction of Our Lady of the Visitation, and her shrine dates from the thirteenth century, when the people of Levoca, Slovakia, built a chapel to thank Mary for saving them from the Tartar invasions. Soon the chapel and shrine, located on Marian Hill (Mariánska Hora), became a well-known pilgrimage destination.

Franciscan friars founded a monastery at Levoca in the fourteenth century, encouraging the annual Marian pilgrimage. The chapel was enlarged in 1470 to accommodate the increasing numbers of pilgrims. At the same time, a sculpture of the Madonna was installed above the high altar.

During the Reformation Era the statue of our Lady was hidden away; she was venerated secretly for many years but eventually forgotten. In 1698 officials searching for a valuable document in the basement of the town hall discovered a secret room that concealed six statues. Five were deteriorated beyond recognition, but the sixth, an image of the Blessed Mother, was as if newly carved. It also gave off a warm glow. The statue was restored to the chapel, where it again became an object of veneration and a supposed source of healing. The bishop proclaimed the statue miraculous in 1761, and devotion to our Lady became the focal point of life in Levoca.

The chapel was expanded again in the eighteenth and nineteenth centuries, and a new church was completed in 1914. When the Communist takeover of Slovakia in 1949 led to the suppression of all forms of religious observance, Our Lady of Levoca had to be hidden away again, and devotions were kept secret.

After the passing of Communist rule, the church was designated a minor basilica in recognition of the millions of people who had made the sacred journey to the hilltop sanctuary. Our Lady of Levoca shrine is Slovakia's most cherished pilgrimage destination, and a Marian pilgrimage celebrating our Lady's feast on July 2 attracts up to a quarter of a million pilgrims. They come not only to implore our Lady's protection and intercession but also to meditate on the mystery of the Visitation and our Lady's indispensable role in redemption history.

Our Lady of Levoca, dearest Mother, for these many centuries you have been the protectress and mother of your people. Look down upon us with your eyes of mercy and hear our prayer. Give us consolation in our afflictions, strength in our trials and light in doubt and darkness. You can help us in our needs and even though it should require a miracle, Jesus will refuse you nothing.

It is true, we are unworthy of your favors because of our sins, but we are your children and you are our mother. You will not cast us away. We beg you to find in our misery and weakness the very motive for granting our petitions. We love you, dearest Mother of Levoca, and we promise to win others to your love.

Accept us as your children, and cover us with the mantle of your protection. Obtain for us, above all, the grace of a holy life and a happy death. Forsake us not, dear Mother of Levoca, until we are safe in heaven to bless God with you, and sing your praises for all eternity. Amen.

NEW PRAYER

Dearest Lady of Levoca, we pray for the victims of hate crimes, both those who suffer violence directly and those who suffer the fear of violence, especially *[mention names]*. Send your angels to guard them in their hour of desperate need, to save them from danger. Send us also to protect them, to heal them of their hurts, to surround them with love. Encourage us to overcome our own fear of reprisal, that we may dare to love publicly those who are persecuted, to speak openly on their behalf and to denounce all violence in our midst. Above all, make us instruments of your son's peace, inspiring us to teach our neighbors to accept and to love others' religious, spiritual, ethnic, racial, gender, age, ability and sexual differences. Amen.

Our Lady of Loreto

HER STORY

The Basilica of the Holy House in Loreto is one of the most famous Marian shrines in the world, for, according to legend, inside is Mary's actual home, transported miraculously from Nazareth to this spot.

As the story relates, on May 10, 1291, angels carried the house to the area of Trsat (page 172), Croatia, to preserve it from desecration when the Christian forces were defeated in the last Crusade. The house remained there until December 10, 1294, when some shepherds near Recanati, Italy, observed a structure moving across the sea and marked its resting spot nearby. There it remained for a short time before angels moved it twice more, to Lecanati, Italy, and then to Loreto, on the eastern coast.

The house that appeared on the hill in Loreto had a single door and one small window. Inside were an altar, a hearth and a statue of the Blessed Mother. There was no foundation. Immediately, large numbers of pilgrims came to venerate the house and offer prayers of intercession to Mary, who in 1296, as the story goes, identified the home as hers to a nearby hermit. That same year local officials dispatched to Palestine sixteen reputable citizens, who returned with the news that the Basilica of the Annunciation in Nazareth contained only a foundation: the home itself was missing. Further, the dimensions of the foundation were said to match exactly the size of the house in Loreto; the stones of the house appeared to be the same type as found in the foundation; and crosses carved into the foundation were described as identical to those marked in the house. The conclusion was that the house was indeed Mary's home, miraculously transported across the sea.

Thus identified, the Holy House of Loreto became one of Christianity's most sacred sanctuaries, venerated because Mary would have been conceived and born within its walls. She would have accepted God's invitation to become Mother of God in this house and would have raised Jesus here, too.

Whether the legend is true or not, over the centuries Our Lady of Loreto has provided both physical cures and spiritual assistance. Among those who have sought her aid are forty popes and two hundred saints or blesseds, including Saints Ignatius of Loyola, Francis Xavier, Alphonsus de' Liguori and Thérèse of Lisieux.

The Litany of Loreto, a long prayer of entreaty to several dozen of Mary's titles, first appeared in 1578. In 1587 Pope Sixtus V granted an indulgence for its recitation. Pope Paul V in 1613 ordered the litany sung on Saturdays and on our Lady's feasts and feast eves.

A church was constructed to enclose the Holy House in 1468; it was made a cathedral in 1586 and a basilica in 1728. A fire in 1921 destroyed the original statue of our Lady; Pope Pius XI crowned the new statue himself.

Modern research into contemporaneous documents has cast doubt upon the veracity of the stories recounting the house's origins. Many scholars now suspect that a miracle-working statue might have been brought from Trsat and housed in a chapel that already existed at Loreto and that a confusion of facts gave rise to the legend about the miraculous transportation. Yet even if the Holy House of Loreto is not actually the home of the Blessed Mother, pilgrims can still meditate upon her spirit of *fiat* there, for Our Lady of Loreto continues to inspire people to heed the Lord's call to holiness.

‿ TRADITIONAL PRAYER

O Mary, immaculate Virgin, for the sake of your blessed house, which the angels moved to the pleasant hills of Loreto, turn your benevolent eyes toward us. For the holy walls within which you were born and lived as a child, with prayers and the most sublime love; for the fortunate walls that listened to the greetings of the angel who called you "blessed among all women," and which remind us of the Incarnation of the Word in your purest bosom; for your blessed house, where you lived with Jesus and Joseph, and which became during the centuries the fervently longed-for destination of the saints, who considered themselves blessed to kiss fervently your sacred walls, bestow upon us the graces for which we humbly ask, and the fortune of coming to heaven after the exile, to repeat to you the greetings of the angel: Hail, Mary. Amen.

‿ NEW PRAYER

O dearest Lady of Loreto, how difficult it has been to become the person God created me to be. Family members, friends and neighbors, coworkers, public officials, even church authorities have tried to direct me to become who they want me to be, to follow the path they have chosen for me, to shape me in their image. How afraid I have been to follow your example! To risk losing the support of all whom I love, to face the unknown alone, to dare to be myself because it is who I must be—this continues to be excruciating, yet also utterly sweet. So when I falter along the way, remind me again of your *fiat*, that it may inspire me to heed God's call, to answer over and over, "Let it be done to me as you have willed!" Amen.

ℬ Our Lady of Lourdes

HER STORY

*I*n the foothills of the Pyrenees in southwestern France lies Lourdes, one of the world's greatest pilgrimage sites. But in 1858, when the Blessed Mother first appeared to the peasant girl Bernadette Soubirous, Lourdes was a small village of no import.

On February 11 of that year, Bernadette went with her sister and friend to look for firewood. Upon reaching a nearby river, Bernadette heard a rushing sound; she turned to the grotto behind her and saw a beautiful lady dressed in white beckoning to her. After Bernadette prayed the rosary, the vision disappeared.

Bernadette returned to the grotto three days later and fell into a rapture when the lady appeared again. None of the other children was able to see the vision.

On February 18 the lady asked Bernadette to continue to visit the grotto. And this she did, accompanied by more and more of the villagers, who were curious about what might be taking place there.

On February 25 the lady directed Bernadette to go and drink from and wash herself in the spring; she then indicated a dry spot of land. In the presence of about 350 jeering witnesses, Bernadette began to dig in the dirt and "drink" the mud; then becoming aware of what was happening, she retreated in humiliation.

The lady did not return the next day, but Bernadette noted that water was issuing from the place where she had been digging. Nevertheless, the authorities continued to order her not to visit the grotto; she disregarded their commands.

On March 1 a pregnant woman dipped her paralyzed arm into the waters now flowing from the spring Bernadette had uncovered. Her cure was immediate and complete, and news of the miraculous spring began to spread.

When Bernadette told her parish priest of the lady's desire to have a chapel built near the grotto, he told her to ask the lady for her name. This Bernadette did on March 25, and the lady replied, "I am the Immaculate Conception." Having never before heard these words, Bernadette repeated them to the priest, who finally believed that the Blessed Mother had been appearing to Bernadette at the grotto.

Since March 1, 1858, millions of people hoping for healing have traveled to Lourdes to bathe in the miraculous waters, and the church has recognized sixty-five miracles occurring there. About five thousand inexplicable cures have also taken place. But perhaps the greatest miracles are those untold numbers of moral and spiritual healings experienced by the five million pilgrims who pray at Lourdes each year.

◌ TRADITIONAL PRAYER

Mother of Compassion, you stooped to earth to make yourself visible to a humble child, and reveal to her your secrets, in spite of her great unworthiness. How great should be her humility! You, the Queen of Heaven and of Earth, deigned to use as your instrument the most feeble of creatures. O Mary, vouchsafe to her, who presumes to call herself your child, the priceless virtue of humility. Grant, Most Tender of Mothers, that your child may follow in your footsteps always and in all circumstances, and that she may be a child after your own heart and that of your Divine Son.

—*Saint Bernadette Soubirous*

◌ NEW PRAYER

Dear Lady of the Immaculate Conception, remind us that the need for healing recognizes none of the arbitrary requirements of ability to pay, life expectancy or other qualifications that society uses to separate the sick from adequate healthcare. Remind us often that all people deserve the opportunity to be healed, and help us to treat all whom we encounter with compassion, that we, too, may be conduits of healing. We pray especially for *[mention request]*, imploring your intercession for a complete cure. O Mary, Mother of Healing, please ask your son to heal this sickness. We ask this in his name, through your intercession. Amen.

🍃 *Our Lady of Mantara*

HER STORY

S idon (now Saida, Lebanon) is an ancient city mentioned in the Bible. Tradition relates that when Jesus visited Sidon, Mary waited overnight for him outside the city in a cave named Mantara atop a hill. In the fourth century the emperor Constantine had, upon his mother's request, made the cave into a sanctuary to honor the Blessed

Mother, but over the centuries the place had been all but forgotten.

By the beginning of the twentieth century, Mantara had developed into a small town, and a community of Copts had begun to worship in a nearby grotto. In 1908 members of the community began to notice that a glow would sometimes emanate from the grotto. An altar was erected outside the grotto, then moved inside, and the archimandrite, or superior, from Sidon began to celebrate Mass there.

On the evening of June 11, 1911, about fifty people went to the hilltop to share the evening meal. At about 7:00 P.M. seven women approached the grotto, and they were suddenly blinded by a burst of light coming from the altar. Their exclamations attracted the others nearby, who rushed to crowd into the grotto. All were likewise blinded by the brilliant light.

After a short time the light softened, and the people could see within the light the image of a woman whom they accepted as the Blessed Mother because she was holding a child in her arms. Neither the woman nor the child spoke, but both looked at the assembled crowd, and the woman nodded her head, reached out to the people and smiled. For this reason the appearance is often referred to as the Holy Apparition of Total Silence.

The area around the altar was quickly packed as more people rushed in from the surrounding villages, Archimandrite Nicola Halabi among them. Those outside urged those inside to move along so that everyone could have a turn, and since the apparition lasted for more than two hours, everyone who wanted to was able to view the Madonna and Child. The local newspapers reported that at least four hundred people had seen the apparition.

Mantara immediately became a popular pilgrimage destination, but World War I interrupted the devotions, and Our Lady of Mantara faded into obscurity. Since those who had seen the Madonna were Copts, many Roman Catholics did not consider the appearance authentic. Nevertheless, the apparition at Mantara indicates that our Lady, as did her son, embraces all people as her beloved children, regardless of denominational affiliations. It seems she calls her children to follow this example.

❧ TRADITIONAL PRAYER

Hail, O Tabernacle of God the Word;
  hail, Holy One, more holy than the saints.
Hail, O Ark that the spirit has gilded;
  hail, sacred Glory of reverent priests.

Hail, unshakable Tower of the Church;
   hail, unbreakable Wall of the Kingdom.
Hail, O you through whom the trophies are raised.
   hail, O you through whom the enemies are routed.
Hail, O Healing of my body;
   hail, O Salvation of my soul.
Hail, O Bride and Maiden ever-pure.
   —*Akathist Hymn: Twenty-third Chant*

❧ NEW PRAYER

Dearest Lady of Mantara, too often I speak just to fill up the silence, at best saying nothing of import and at worst offending others with platitudes and inanities. May your quietness remind me that silence can be a holy space for the true communion of souls. May your gestures remind me that my expressions and actions speak more effectively than any words I might say. And may your smiles remind me that my attitude is the most important part of my communications with others. Amen.

✥ *Our Lady of Marija Bistrica*

HER STORY

*L*ocated in the village of Marija Bistrica, Croatia, about twenty miles north of Zagreb, is a black Madonna statue that according to local belief has worked untold numbers of miracles over the centuries.

The first records of the statue date from the early 1500s, indicating that it was placed in a chapel on the hill of Vinski Vrh. Fear of Turkish invaders led a priest to hide the Madonna within the wall of the parish church in Bistrica in 1545. When he died, he took the secret of the statue's location with him to the grave, but in 1588 the statue emitted a supernatural light to reveal its hiding place. The Madonna was then exhibited for public veneration until 1650, when once again the statue was hidden, this time in the wall behind the main altar. Found on July 15, 1684, the Madonna immediately became a source of miraculous healings and supernatural occurrences.

In 1715 the Croatian National Parliament commissioned a great altar for the church and in 1731 had the church expanded and consecrated to Our Lady of the Snows (page 167). The shrine that exists today was built between 1879 and 1882, and Pope Pius XI designated the church a minor basilica in 1923. In 1984 celebrations honoring thirteen hundred years of Christianity in Croatia and the third centenary of the finding of the miraculous statue took place at the shrine. Most recently, on October 3, 1998, Pope John Paul II took advantage of a visit to the shrine to beatify Aloysius Stepinac, the cardinal archbishop of Zagreb.

Proclaimed Queen of the Croats, Our Lady of Marija Bistrica assumes the heartaches and joys of the people of Croatia, welcoming hundreds of thousands of pilgrims each year. Her feast is celebrated on September 9.

∾ TRADITIONAL PRAYER

Immaculate Mother of Jesus, we honor you as God's chosen one, beautiful, beloved and free from all sin. Keep watch over us, pray that we rise above our sins and failings and come to share the fullness of grace. Be a mother to us in the order of grace by assisting us to live in your obedience, your faith, your hope and your love. Amen.

∾ NEW PRAYER

O holy Madonna, Our Lady of Marija Bistrica, pray for all of us who are "in the closet" in any way, who shroud our God-given beauty because we fear others' prejudice, hatred or violence, or because we have been made to feel ashamed or sinful. Shine your light in the dark corners of our lives, that we may conquer our fear of the hidden and the secret. Help us to believe that we are lovable even as we are, imperfect as we are, and that God does not reject us but calls us to become the uniquely wonderful persons we were created to be. Teach us to see ourselves truly and to embrace our uniqueness joyfully, and bless us all, that we may finally hail our God-given differences with thanksgiving. Amen.

℞. Our Lady of Medjugorje
| QUEEN OF PEACE |

HER STORY

*P*erhaps the most famous apparitions of the late twentieth century are those of Our Lady at Medjugorje, Bosnia. The appearances began on the evening of June 24, 1981, when Mirjana Dragicevic and Ivanka Ivankovic were walking past the hill of Podbrdo outside their village of Bijakovici and Ivanka saw a luminous figure, which she took for the *Gospa* (Croatian for "our Lady"). The girls persuaded a friend, Milka Pavlovic, to return with them. Another friend, Vicka Ivankovic, followed, bringing two boys, Ivan Dragicevic and Ivan Ivankovic. Five of the teenagers, ranging in age from thirteen to twenty, saw the figure, whom they described as a beautiful woman with black hair, wearing a gray gown and holding a baby.

Four of the original seers and two others returned to Podbrdo the next evening. When they ascended the hill to converse with the woman, she told them to pray seven Our Fathers, Hail Marys and Glory Bes and the Creed daily.

During the apparition on June 26, one of the seers sprinkled the figure with holy water; she smiled and said, "I am the Blessed Virgin Mary." When they asked why she had come to Bosnia, she answered, "I have come to tell you that God exists, and He loves you. Let the others, who do not see me, believe as you do." She said also the words that were to become both her refrain and prophecy over the coming years: "Peace, peace, peace! Be reconciled! Make your peace with God among yourselves."

When he heard of the appearance of the Gospa, the parish priest, Father Jozo Zovko, was skeptical. On the other hand, the bishop was inclined to believe. They both changed their minds, however, when the Communist authorities interfered. Against the bishop's objections Father Zovko even allowed the teenagers to use the church to visit with Mary; the Communists eventually sent him to prison.

The Gospa appeared daily, and pilgrims began pouring into Medjugorje, bearing witness to strange lights and other phenomena that occurred during the apparitions. When the appearances attracted international attention, the bishop issued a negative report. However, people began disclosing cures and conversions; thousands have now been recorded. When the seers were tested psychologically and physiologically, no medical explanation was found for their ecstasies.

In July 1991 the Gospa urged, "Dear children, today I invite you to pray for peace. At this time, peace is threatened in a special way and I am seeking from you to renew fasting and prayer in your families....much of what will happen depends on your prayers...." Sadly, when Communism collapsed in Yugoslavia, the people of the region did not heed the Queen of Peace's plea. Old ethnic and religious enmities, held in check by totalitarian rule, burst into civil war in 1991. While Bosnia-Herzegovina became the center of savage violence, including "ethnic cleansing," Medjugorje remained untouched.

Coming as she has during the twilight of Communism, the Gospa has seemed a fulfillment of Mary's apparitions at Fátima (page 91). Indeed, on August 25, 1991, Mary said, "I invite you to renunciation for nine days so that with your help, everything I wanted to realize through the secrets I began in Fátima may be fulfilled."

The apparitions at Medjugorje continue to this day, the Gospa having indicated that they will cease only when each of the visionaries has received ten secrets. At that time, she has promised, a great sign will appear to convince all skeptics, and the apocalyptic events she has foretold will begin. So far, three of the seers have received all ten secrets; the others have received nine.

Whatever the secrets might eventually reveal, the Gospa has proved to be a truly effective evangelist, having already converted thousands to Christianity. The conversions are directly attributable to her messages, which over the years have coalesced into a complete program of Christian education. Our Lady of Medjugorje has emphasized the need for conversion, consecration and purification. She has promised her protection to those who sanctify themselves through prayer and the sacraments. And she has affirmed that human choices will determine each person's ultimate salvation and participation in God's plan.

Though the church does not rule on ongoing apparitions, the Vatican announced in 1998 that there was no objection to private pilgrimages to Medjugorje. And in 1999 the secretary of the Congregation for the Doctrine of the Faith asserted, "For the moment, one should consider Medjugorje as a sanctuary, a Marian shrine, in the same way as Czestochowa [page 80]."

The Gospa has often thanked the visionaries for responding to her call. And through them, Our Lady of Medjugorje speaks to people around the world: "Pray in order to understand that you all, through your life and your example, ought to collaborate in the work of salvation."

Calm, O maiden most pure, the wild storm of my soul, for you alone showed yourself on earth to be the port of all who set a course through the perils of life. You who gave birth to the Light, brighten, O Pure Lady, the eyes of my heart. You were given to us on earth as protection, bulwark and boast. You were given to us as a tower and sure salvation. O maiden, for this we no longer fear adversity, we who devoutly glorify you.

—*Joseph the Studite*

CV NEW PRAYER

O Gospa, call me to conversion as I discover the root causes
of sin in my life.
O Gospa, witness my consecration as I surrender all that
I am to God.
O Gospa, recognize my purification through the grace of
your son.
O Gospa, grant me the protection of your own fullness of
grace whenever I face further temptation.
O Gospa, pray for my sanctification in the unconditional
love of your son.
O Gospa, encourage me to seek salvation through the
redemption of your son.
O Gospa, show me how I might participate more fully, more
wholly, in God's divine plan for the universe. Amen.

🦢 Our Lady of Montichiari

HER STORY

Since at least the third century the Blessed Mother has been associated with roses (Mystical Rose, page 61), and roses have figured in a number of her apparitions (Our Lady of Betania, Our Lady of the Philippines, Our Lady of La Salette, pages 35, 159, 113), including those of Montichiari, Italy.

In the spring of 1947 Pierina Gilli was working as a nurse in the Montichiari hospital. One morning, while she was alone in the ward, a beautiful woman suddenly appeared before her. As Gilli reported, the woman, dressed in a violet dress with a white veil, was "very sad, and her eyes were filled with tears which fell to the floor. Her breast was pierced by three big swords." The woman spoke only this: "Prayer—Penitence—Expiation." After a few moments of silence, she vanished.

On the morning of June 13, the woman returned. This time she was dressed in white and carried three roses. When Gilli asked her name, the woman said, "I am the Mother of Jesus and the Mother of all of you." Then she indicated that the thirteenth of each month should be celebrated in honor of the Rosa Mystica (Mystical Rose).

Our Lady then explained that the three swords shown piercing her heart had been, first, a priest's or monk's loss of vocation; second, the sins of avowed religious; and third, the "treason of Judas"—that is, the enmity of those priests and monks who leave the church.

Then she told of the three roses: white, for the spirit of prayer; red, for the spirit of expiation and sacrifice; and gold, for the spirit of penitence.

Mary appeared to Gilli again on October 22, declaring that she had placed herself between her son and humankind as Mediatrix.

Unlike the first three apparitions, the fourth, witnessed by a few other people, took place in Gilli's parish church, on November 16. Mary warned of a coming punishment because people had turned away from God. But she also said that she would pour forth the grace of which she is custodian during an "hour of grace," noon on December 8.

News of the apparitions had spread, and families began bringing their ill sons and daughters to the church. A boy with polio, a woman with severe tuberculosis, and a girl with mental disabilities were all cured. These healings caught the attention of the bishop, who ordered Gilli to stop the visits and retreat to a convent in Brescia. She complied, but years later, in February 1966, our Lady appeared to Gilli again in her room.

Pierina Gilli saw Mary again in Fontanelle, her hometown, on April 17, 1966, where our Lady bestowed healing powers upon a well. When people heard about the well, they flocked to taste of its curative waters. The church gave unofficial approval to Gilli to continue to receive the Blessed Mother, who was to give two miraculous demonstrations of her presence.

The first occurred on April 20, 1969. In front of hundreds of people gathered outside the parish church in Fontanelle, Mary caused a spectacular dance of the sun and stars. A similar miracle occurred on December 8, 1969.

The apparitions to Gilli occurred intermittently at least through 1976, and Mary's messages were consistent: humankind, and particularly the religious, must repent for sins against faith and morals, and if they do, she will bless them superabundantly.

∾ TRADITIONAL PRAYER

> Mary, the Virgin, well the heart knows,
> She is the Mystery, she is the Rose.
> In the Gardens of God, in the daylight divine
> I shall come home to thee, Mother of mine.
> Is Mary that Rose, then? Mary, the Tree?
> But the Blossom, the Blossom there, who can it be?
> Who can her Rose be? It could be but One:
> Christ Jesus, our Lord—her God and her Son.
> . . . .
> In the Gardens of God, in the daylight divine
> Make me a leaf in thee, Mother of mine.
> Does it smell sweet, too, in that holy place?
> Sweet unto God, and the sweetness is grace;
> The breath of it bathes the great heaven above,
> In grace that is charity, grace that is love.
> To thy breast, to thy rest, to thy glory divine
> Draw me by charity, Mother of mine.
>
> —*Gerard Manley Hopkins, "Rosa Mystica"*

∾ NEW PRAYER

O Rosa Mystica, your name is precious to me, for just as Jesus came forth from you who are the Mystical Rose, so I came forth from my mother, who is also a Rose. And like your son, I also am a beloved child of God, blessed with your abundant graces and God's unconditional love. O blessed Lady, in moments of difficulty or sadness, remind me of this glorious heritage, that I may count my bountiful blessings and rejoice in the gifts with which God has showered my life. Amen.

BLACK MADONNA
Replica of Our Lady of Einsiedeln

ℬ Our Lady of Montserrat

HER STORY

Our Lady of Montserrat, along with Our Lady of Czestochowa (page 80) and Our Lady of Einsiedeln (page 85), is one of the highly venerated black Madonnas. Known as *La Moreneta* (the dark little one) and, in other times, as *La Jerosolimitana* (native of Jerusalem), Our Lady of Montserrat is a small statue, about three feet tall, that depicts our Lady seated on a throne. She is holding the world in her right hand. The Christ child is seated on her lap, and he is making a gesture of blessing the world.

According to legend, Saint Luke carved the statue sometime during the life of the Blessed Mother, and the image was brought to Spain during the first century. It was considered so holy that about 718 it was hidden at Montserrat when the Moors conquered Spain and was then forgotten. In 890 some shepherds observed a strange light coming from the mountain of Montserrat, which is about thirty-five miles northwest of present-day Barcelona. As the boys approached the cave from which the dazzling light radiated, they heard instrumental music and singing. They informed their local priest, who verified the story and told the bishop of Manresa. The bishop himself led the procession to the cave, within which the villagers found the statue. He ordered it installed in his cathedral at Manresa, but the bearers of the statue soon found themselves miraculously unable to move. The bishop interpreted this as a sign that our Lady wanted her sanctuary to be constructed at Montserrat.

Montserrat is an imposing chunk of rock, rising to over four thousand feet. The shrine is located in the *Santa Cova* (Holy Cave) near the top of the mountain. At some point, probably in the twelfth century, the original statue (if indeed the legend is true) was replaced by the Romanesque one that is in the shrine today. Our Lady and the Christ child have a certain Byzantine look to them, and both figures are black. Perhaps they were originally carved and painted that way—commentaries on the Song of Songs, which depicts the bride as black, were popular at the time the statue was made. Some have suggested that the statue is modeled on, or was mistaken for, an image of dark-featured Isis and her son Horus, or is a Christianization of the earth-goddess concept. Or perhaps the color is a symbolic reminder that in Aramaic, the language of Mary and Jesus, the word that means "black" can also mean "sorrowful." It's also possible the figures turned dark because of the effects of centuries of candle smoke or because of chemical changes in the original pigments.

Many people have appealed to La Moreneta for illumination. Saint Ignatius of Loyola, for example, wrote his famous *Spiritual Exercises* after spending a night praying at Montserrat. As well, the healings attributed to our Lady's intercession have drawn many pilgrims to the shrine, which still attracts about a million annual visitors. Some come for cures and signs, but most come for those miracles of grace that transform lives. Whether such miracles occur during the pilgrimage experience or afterward, Our Lady of Montserrat always shows herself a solicitous mother.

◌ TRADITIONAL PRAYER

O blessed Mother, heart of love, heart of mercy, ever listening, caring, consoling, hear our prayer. As your children, we implore your intercession with Jesus your son.

Receive with understanding and compassion the petitions we place before you today, especially *[mention request]*.

We are comforted in knowing your heart is ever open to those who ask for your prayer.

We entrust to your gentle care and intercession those whom we love and who are sick or lonely or hurting. Help all of us, holy Mother, to bear our burdens in this life until we may share eternal life and peace with God forever. Amen.

◌ NEW PRAYER

Dearest La Moreneta, teach me to walk softly upon the earth. Help me to cherish life, in all its forms, as a manifestation of the Divine. Remind me that I am a co-creator of the world around me, that my attitudes and actions help shape the universe. Most of all, infuse me with your spirit, that I may experience and enjoy the glories and wonders of God's creation. Amen.

ℬ Our Lady of Mount Carmel

*P*eople sometimes refer to Our Lady of Mount Carmel as Our Lady of the Brown Scapular, for she presented the great gift of the Brown Scapular to the church. A scapular was originally a sleeveless outer garment of a monk's habit that falls from the shoulders, and laypeople showed their affection for a particular religious order by wearing that congregation's scapular. As fashions changed, scapulars became smaller, until now they are two small pieces of cloth, colored or white, plain or with images, joined by cords or strings and worn over the shoulders or around the neck. Over the centuries the Roman Catholic Church has approved a number of scapulars for popular devotional use; those with a Marian character include the Blue Scapular of the Immaculate Conception (page 23), the Green Scapular of the Immaculate Heart of Mary (page 32) and the White Scapular of Our Lady of Ransom. The most famous is the scapular of Our Lady of Mount Carmel, or the Brown Scapular.

According to legend, in Aylesford, England, on the morning of July 16, 1251, after a night spent praying for the Virgin's assistance in resolving the conflicts that were destroying the Carmelite Order, Saint Simon Stock had a vision of Our Lady of Mount Carmel. She was holding the infant Jesus, and a host of angels surrounded her. Handing Simon the Brown Scapular, she proclaimed:

> My beloved son, receive this scapular for your Order. It is the special sign of a privilege which I have obtained for you and for all God's children who honor me as Our Lady of Mount Carmel. Those who die devotedly clothed with this scapular shall be preserved from eternal fire. The brown scapular is a badge of salvation. The brown scapular is a shield in time of danger. The brown scapular is a pledge of peace and special protection, until the end of time.

Simon had been chosen as the sixth general of the Carmelites in 1245 when the Order's government was officially transferred to England from Palestine. The Carmelites had lived on Mount Carmel, made famous by the Prophet Elijah (1 Kings 18:41–46). In the shadow of Mount Carmel lies Nazareth, where the blessed Virgin conceived the Son of God. The Carmelites were the first to build a church to the Blessed Mother, honoring her as Our Lady of Mount Carmel. The congregation was formalized in the thirteenth century, but persecution by the Saracens during the Crusades forced the Order to leave its ancient monastery.

Soon after our Lady's presentation of the Brown Scapular, the problems facing the Carmelites disappeared. Pope Innocent IV reaffirmed the Order's official sanction, and King Henry III granted the Carmelites royal protection.

The wearing of the Brown Scapular quickly spread throughout Christendom. Indeed, King Edward I of England and Saint Louis, king of France, both wore the brown woolen scapular. Symbolically, it recalls the parable of the Good Shepherd: just as Jesus will do anything to find the one lost sheep, so the scapular seeks the salvation of every lost soul. Over the centuries many saints, such as Saint Alphonsus de' Liguori, were buried in their brown scapulars, and when their remains were exhumed, the scapulars were found perfectly preserved, though the bodies and other clothing had decayed.

There is another chapter to the story. In 1322 Our Lady of Mount Carmel appeared to Pope John XXII and revealed that she would descend into purgatory on the Saturday after their deaths to free those who had faithfully worn the Brown Scapular.

Many miracles have been attributed to the scapular and Our Lady of Mount Carmel. She is said to have calmed storms, deflected bullets, stemmed floods, ended droughts, extinguished fires and cured blindness and other infirmities.

The Brown Scapular has also figured in two of our Lady's greatest modern-day apparitions: the last apparition at Lourdes (page 122) occurred on July 16, the feast of Our Lady of Mount Carmel; and when Our Lady of Fátima (page 91) made the sun dance, she was wearing the scapular of Our Lady of Mount Carmel.

❧ TRADITIONAL PRAYER

O beautiful Flower of Carmel, most fruitful vine, splendor of heaven, holy and singular, who brought forth the Son of God, still ever remaining a pure virgin, assist me in my necessities. O Star of the Sea, help and protect me. Show me that you are my Mother!

—*Saint Simon Stock*

❧ NEW PRAYER

Most Blessed Mother, Our Lady of Mount Carmel, in this skeptical age it is easy to look upon the scapular, and all such sacramentals, as pure superstition, lucky charms for those with an immature faith.

I admit that I myself do not understand the power of two small bits of cloth. But I do understand that following your example—of letting go of limited human desires, of opening up to the infinite potentialities of the Divine, of trusting God in all things—can free me from the sad human bondage of settling for good enough. I long for that freedom, that peace, that joy that you experienced, but I feel paralyzed, unable to take that first trusting step, sick within at the possibility of free fall. Dear Lady, pray for me, that I may be released. Help me to dare to trust in divine providence. Teach me to believe that I shall become the person God has created me to be. Amen.

Our Lady of Naju

HER STORY

Though little known, the apparitions occurring in the small town of Naju, at the southwestern tip of South Korea, are among the most remarkable ever observed.

The story begins sometime in the 1970s. Julia Kim, born in Naju in 1947, was dying of cancer. Though her family was not Roman Catholic, she felt drawn to visit the local Catholic church, where she was able to question the priest about her illness. He told her that her suffering would bring her blessing. Immediately, she noticed a change in her body. Shortly thereafter, she was completely cured of her cancer.

Julia and her husband were soon baptized as Roman Catholics, and Julia became devoted to the Blessed Mother, placing a statue of Mary in her house.

On June 30, 1985, the statue began to weep. Then on October 19, 1986, the statue started to cry tears of blood, which was tested and determined to be of human origin. The weeping continued intermittently until January 14, 1992, for a total of seven hundred days.

Then, on November 24, 1992, the statue began exuding a fragrant oil. This phenomenon continued for seven hundred consecutive days until October 23, 1994.

Meanwhile, in May 1988, while the statue was still weeping, the eucharistic bread and wine Julia received at Mass became transformed into visible flesh and blood. Twelve such eucharistic miracles were recorded, and witnesses included at least two foreign bishops and Pope John Paul II himself. The last transformation occurred in October 1996.

Additionally, beginning on November 24, 1994, over the course of three years the sacred host or hosts seven times descended from "above" into the chapel in Naju. Besides Julia, witnesses included the apostolic pro-nuncio in Korea as well as at least one bishop and a number of priests and laypeople. On several occasions, when Julia consumed a host that had appeared in this way, it was seen to change into flesh when commingled with the eucharistic wine. Some witnesses described the host as having become a tiny human heart. Laboratory tests confirmed the presence of human blood.

Finally, Julia exhibited the stigmata.

During these years Julia was receiving many messages from our Lady, who spoke of the need for unity and of her desire for people to entrust themselves to her immaculate heart (page 32). She particularly singled out Julia to be an example:

> Because I love you, my Son Jesus and I called you, when your body was about to cease functioning, to deliver you from many sins. You did not take the initiative to entrust yourself to me, but I called you so that you could entrust yourself to me—as an apostle of my Immaculate Heart. This is only the beginning. There will be many sufferings. But do not be discouraged. Entrust everything—without exception—to my Immaculate Heart. Entrust even all your sins to me.
>
> Together with those brothers and sisters whom I united with you spiritually, pray, do penance and sacrifices and approach me walking the way of a little person with humility. My spirit is flowing in you and in them. So, work together. (message of October 24, 1986)

Mary spoke out against abortion, saying that it caused her pain. She warned of a great chastisement to come if humankind does not turn aside from sin. At the same time, she offered encouragement to Julia, and through her to all people, proclaiming that "even the smallest thing can become a great good work, if it is done with love" (message of May 8, 1991). And she affirmed her role as Co-redemptrix (page 13): "Is there anyone who can lower me from the cross? Moment after moment, there are more people who crucify me. I am suffering on the cross together with my son Jesus" (message of November 5, 1986).

Julia also received a number of messages from Jesus, who urged her to make the real presence in the Eucharist more widely known. His words also honored his mother: "The greatest treasure in my Church is my most holy Mother Mary. My mother is the Queen of the Universe, the Mother of Heaven and also your mother. This is why my mother Mary loves you as I have loved you; and she can do any-thing that I can do, through me and by my grace" (message of September 22, 1995).

The events at Naju continue, so the church has not yet ruled on their authenticity, though many people believe, and a number of peo-ple have reported both spiritual and physical healings. Many others are skeptical. Yet the messages given at Naju have indeed brought many people closer to God—which has always been the Blessed Mother's primary objective.

∾ TRADITIONAL PRAYER

O weeping Virgin Mother, refuge of sinners, we call upon you to petition your divine son to obtain for us the forgiveness of our sins and an abundance of blessings for us and for those for whom we pray. Alleviate our sufferings, cure our ills, console us in our sorrows, help us to lead a virtuous life and guide us to eternal life.

O weeping Virgin, Mother of God, remember us before your son, our Lord Jesus Christ, now, and at the hour of our death. Amen.

∾ NEW PRAYER

Dear Lady of Naju, when I focus on the future, I skip over the present, and when I concentrate on big responsibilities, I ignore my little jobs. But the present is all I have, and the simple tasks may be all I'll be able to accomplish. Help me to shift my focus, then, that I may aim to do all things, even the smallest things, with great love, in the hope that love will transform those small, seemingly unimportant things into something beautiful for God. Amen.

ℬ Our Lady of Neocaesarea

HER STORY

*T*he Blessed Mother's apparition at Neocaesarea is her second recorded appearance. According to tradition, Saint Gregory Thaumaturgus ("the Wonder-Worker," c. 213-c. 270), probably some-time during his episcopate of Neocaesarea, had been unable to come to terms with the concept of the Trinity, given the theological debates swirling through the church at that time. So he was granted a vision.

Appearing with Saint John the Evangelist, the Virgin Mary instructed the apostle to explain the mystery of the Trinity to Gregory. Saint John the Evangelist said, "I will gladly comply with the wishes of the Mother of God" and presented a discourse that became the basis of Gregory's *Exposition of Faith.*

Gregory was famed for the wonders—such as moving enormous boulders—he performed in God's name. He was also a gifted preacher whose sermons converted almost the entire population of his city. Saint Macrina, who had heard Gregory preach and had known him personally, learned of the apparition and at Neocaesarea told the story to her brothers Saints Gregory of Nyssa and Basil. Gregory wrote an account of the vision, which has been handed down to this day.

In a time of theological conflict and great persecution (under Decius in 250), Our Lady of Neocaesarea came to the aid of her children. Her apparition motivated Gregory Thaumaturgus to continue his work of evangelization, to God's great glory. At the same time, she blessed the church with a fuller understanding of the Trinity. And for this she has also been called the Most Pure Temple of the Holy Trinity.

◌ﻌ TRADITIONAL PRAYER

Remember, most tender Mother, that we are thy children, purchased by the precious blood of thine only-begotten Son. Deign to pray for us without ceasing to the blessed Trinity, that we may have the grace to be ever victorious over the devil, the world and all our perverse passions; that grace whereby the just may sanctify themselves ever more and more, sinners may be converted, heresies destroyed, unbelievers enlightened.

—*The Raccolta*

◌ﻌ NEW PRAYER

Dear Lady of Neocaesarea, when we try to explain and understand God, we really limit who God can be for us. So we ask you for the peace of soul to just let God be. Quiet our interior questioning and calm our frantic seeking, that we may give up our desperate need for answers and accept the gift of being still and knowing simply and utterly that God is. Amen.

Our Lady of Pompeii

HER STORY

The story of New Pompeii begins with Bartolo Longo, a lawyer who had joined a sect and publicly ridiculed Christianity. Converted in 1871 through the intercession of a good friend, Longo chose Maria as his baptismal name, attributing his miraculous change of heart to the Blessed Mother's influence.

One evening while walking among the ruins of ancient Pompeii, Longo had a mystical experience, hearing repeated, "If you seek salvation, promulgate the rosary." He immediately promised not to leave the valley until he had made the rosary known to the people.

At that time, the town of Pompeii was not a thriving center, and the old church was filthy and dilapidated. Longo persuaded a few people to help him clean the place, then invited them to join in praying the rosary. When only a few curious children gathered, he formulated a plan to distribute rosaries to every household in the valley. In 1873 he sponsored a festival on the feast of the Holy Rosary; it failed, as did his effort the next year. Finally, in 1875, he completely restored the church in preparation for a two-week mission presented by the Redemptorists. The mission's success led the bishop to suggest building an enlarged sanctuary and shrine.

Longo eagerly agreed, and his first task was to find an image of our Lady suitable for the shrine. All he could turn up was a junk painting of Our Lady of the Rosary (page 165). He bought it, and it was delivered to the church in a wagon of manure. Longo had the painting restored and placed it in the rebuilt chapel.

Longo asked his neighbors to pledge a "penny" a month for Mary's work, collecting enough money to lay the cornerstone of the larger shrine in 1876. Within the month four miraculous healings were reported. By 1885 Longo had recorded more than 940 cures.

The most famous cure was that of Fortuna Agrelli in 1884. She received a visit from the Blessed Virgin, who taught her to pray the 54 Day Rosary Novena. Upon completing the novena, the girl was completely cured of her chronic ailment. News of the cure reached even Pope Leo XIII and helped establish the cult of Our Lady of Pompeii.

Longo founded the Daughters of the Holy Rosary of Pompeii to care for the shrine and established the Dominican Tertiaries near the shrine, having himself become a Third Order Dominican when he was baptized. In 1885 he married the woman who had been helping him in his charitable work, Countess Marianna de Fusco.

The church was completed in 1894, and Longo and his wife presented it to Leo XIII. The church and shrine have remained in the care of the papacy ever since. In modern times more than three million pilgrims visit the Shrine of Our Lady of the Rosary annually—evidence that the spirit of devotion Longo sparked among the people of Pompeii continues to spread to the rest of the world.

In recognition of Longo's influence, Pope John Paul II beatified the lawyer on October 26, 1980, praising him as "the man of Mary," the "Herald of the Blessed Virgin Mary's Rosary" and "a layman who had lived his ecclesial pledge to the full" in recognition of his great love for Our Lady of Pompeii.

❧ TRADITIONAL PRAYER

Queen of the Most Holy Rosary, in these secular times of indifference, show your power with the signs of your ancient victories, and from your throne, from which you dispense pardon and graces, mercifully regard the Church of your Son. Hasten the hour of mercy, and for me, who am the least among human beings, kneeling before you in prayer, obtain the grace I need to live righteously upon the earth. In company of all the faithful Christians throughout the world, I salute you and acclaim you as Queen of the Most Holy Rosary. Amen.

—*Mother Teresa of Calcutta*

❧ NEW PRAYER

Most holy Lady of Pompeii, you urge me to pray, but all I can do is listen. Is my attentive silence a prayer? Please accept it as such. And help quiet my thoughts and emotions so that I might hear when the Spirit speaks to me. Amen.

🦋 Our Lady of San Juan de los Lagos

| Nuestra Señora de San Juan de los Lagos;
"Our Lady of Saint John of the Lakes" |

Her Story

*O*ur Lady of San Juan de los Lagos is a small statue, about a foot high, made of *pasta de Michoacan*—glue and cornstalks. And her first miracle is her self-preservation, for she is almost four hundred years old. She was first venerated by the Nochixlecas under the title *Cichaupilli*, which means "Lady," brought to the town of San Juan Bautista Mezquetitlan (now San Juan de los Lagos), Mexico, by the Spanish Franciscan missionary Fray Antonio of Segovia.

The statue is a black Madonna of the Immaculate Conception, and the Virgin's hands are pressed together in an attitude of prayer. She is standing on a crescent moon with a star at each end, and above her crown two angels hold a scroll with the inscription *"Mater Immaculata ora pro nobis."*

In 1623 the statue was very ragged looking, so the parish curate took it from the main church and placed it in the sacristy. But Ana Lucia, a native woman who cleaned the church, found the statue back in the main sanctuary each morning, despite having returned it daily to the side room.

In the same year a family of trapeze artists was passing through the village. During a practice session one of the daughters fell off the high wire and impaled herself on the swords and daggers that added the thrill of danger to the act. She died, and the family brought her body to the church for burial. When Ana Lucia saw the family's grief, she laid the old statue of our Lady on the dead girl's breast. Immediately, the girl sat up, alive and completely unharmed, her wounds having disappeared without a single scar. The subsequent investigation and interviews convinced church authorities that the miracle was real.

To thank our Lady the father of the family found a sculptor in Guadalajara who expertly restored the statue. Mysteriously, the sculptor simply vanished without accepting payment, and his disappearance added to the statue's glamour.

Since that distant year many other miracles have been attributed to the intercession of Our Lady of San Juan de los Lagos, and her shrine is one of Mexico's favorite places of pilgrimage. She is also carried around the countryside to visit those who cannot come to her. In this she shows her great compassion for all of her children, bringing them comfort and aid wherever they might be.

⌇ TRADITIONAL PRAYER

Holy Mary, Virgin of Virgins, Mother of God, Queen of Heaven, Mistress of the world, perfect Temple of the Holy Spirit, Lily of Purity, Rose of Patience, Paradise of Spiritual Pleasure, Mirror of Chastity, Treasure of Innocence: intercede for me, a poor, needy exile and wanderer, and grant me some little share of the full store of thy love!

—*Saint Peter of Alcantara*

⌇ NEW PRAYER

O Cichaupilli, Nuestra Señora de San Juan de los Lagos, we pray to you for those of little means, those marginalized members of our society who do not have enough to eat nor sufficient clothing to wear nor even proper shelter to protect them. They certainly cannot themselves travel on pilgrimage to appeal to you, so we bring you their supplications. Be a bountiful mother to them, that they might not suffer from lack of the basic necessities of life. And be an urgent mother to us, moving us to become your instruments of succor in providing them with all that they require. Amen.

⌇ Our Lady of Šiluva

HER STORY

*E*stablished in 1457, the small village of Šiluva, Lithuania, located about 120 miles northwest of Vilnius, grew up around the Roman Catholic church built by Peter Gedgaudas, a wealthy nobleman. Gedgaudas was a diplomat, and during one of his trips to Rome, he obtained a painting of the Madonna and Child. This he placed in the sanctuary of the new church.

Not many years afterward, the passions of the Reformation reached Lithuania. Lutheranism and Calvinism attracted a number of converts, including the authorities, who confiscated many Roman Catholic properties. When Father John Halubka, the priest of

Gedgaudas's church, learned in 1570 that his parish had become a target of plunder, he hid the church's documents with the treasured image of the Madonna and Child in a chest and buried it beneath a large rock nearby. The church was subsequently appropriated.

Passions cooled within two decades, and a new law gave Roman Catholics the right to repossess stolen properties. But to make a valid claim, they had to present documents to prove their ownership. Unfortunately, no one could find the record of Gedgaudas's transfer of land to the church, and the property remained in the hands of the local authorities.

More years passed. Then, unexpectedly, during the summer of 1608, a beautiful lady holding a baby appeared to a group of children playing in the fields. The children noticed that the lady was weeping bitterly. They also marked her location, which was atop a large rock.

Some of the townspeople who were Calvinists thought the vision the work of the devil, but the news spread quickly, and soon the entire village had assembled at the rock. Suddenly, the lady appeared again—to the entire assembly. A respected Calvinist pastor demanded to know why the lady was crying. She answered sadly, "Formerly my Son was adored and honored in this place. Now, they sow seed and cultivate the land." Then she and her child vanished.

The local bishop, hearing of the remarkable occurrence at Šiluva, immediately began an investigation, which turned up an old, blind man who remembered that Father Halubka had buried an oak chest under a large rock. When led to the site of the lady's apparition, the blind man miraculously recovered his sight. He indicated a spot, and there the chest was uncovered. Inside, undamaged, were all the church documents as well as the portrait of the Madonna and Child.

After a series of court battles, the land was returned to the Roman Catholic Church. A local priest built a small chapel on the site of the apparition, and in 1663 the local bishop commissioned a larger church to enshrine the rock and the painting. Devotion to our Lady spread when those who appealed to her began to receive miracles in reply. With the approval of Pope Pius VI, the bishop formally sanctioned devotion to Our Lady of Šiluva.

In 1770 someone placed a statue of the Madonna and Child near the church's altar. The cures attributed to the statue's intercession were so numerous that it was named Our Lady Health of the Sick and placed atop the apparition rock. Larger churches were built in 1818 and 1924 to accommodate the crowds, but in 1940, when the Soviet Union took control of Lithuania, devotion to Our Lady of Šiluva was forced underground. Not until Lithuania declared its independence in 1989 were the Catholic faithful able to practice their religion openly. Pilgrims once again flocked to Šiluva.

The sanctuary of Our Lady of Šiluva is now a thriving center of Marian devotion, receiving several hundred thousand pilgrims annually, who testify to Our Lady of Šiluva's efficacy as intercessor and healer.

∾ TRADITIONAL PRAYER

O most Holy Virgin Mary, you who appeared to the shepherds in the fields at Šiluva, you whose tears bathed the rock where once an altar stood, you who with plaintive voice said, "You plow and seed here where formerly my son was honored," grant that we, moved by your tears, may once, as our forefathers did, revive the spirit of adoration of your son in our hearts, strengthen the tottering structure of the shrine that is the family and seek forgiveness for the negligences and sins of our nation.

O Mother of God, we desire to raise up the glory of your revelation from forgotten ruins, that we may all the more honor you the patroness of our country and, with your help, obtain for our nation the spirit of a living faith. Through Christ our Lord. Amen.

∾ NEW PRAYER

Dear Lady of Šiluva, like many of your children, I, too, have strayed far from my youthful devotion to you. Yet how patient you have been in awaiting my return. And how determined you have been to recall me, sending me many reminders and invitations over the years. I thank you for your persistence, and I pray that, should I again wander, you will not forget my sometime devotion and will call me again into full communion with you and your son. Amen.

ℬ Our Lady of Sinj

HER STORY

Our Lady of Sinj is the title given to the miraculous icon of the Virgin Mary that is found in a shrine at Sinj, Croatia. Probably painted toward the end of the sixteenth century, the icon has, according to local tradition, saved the people of the area from war and invasion, famine and sickness many times.

The Franciscans brought the icon with them in 1687 when they fled from the expanding Turkish Empire, and Pavao Vuckovic, leader of the Croats, began construction of a church to house the icon in 1705. Just as the church was being finished in 1714, the War of Sinj broke out between Turkey and Croatia.

While a handful of Croatian soldiers bravely fought the assaulting Turkish army, the Franciscans and other citizens prayed unceasingly to Our Lady of Sinj. The presence of the icon inside the tiny fortress at Sinj, brought up from the church when the situation seemed desperate, encouraged the defenders. After a few days of inconclusive fighting, on the eve of the feast of the Assumption, the Turkish forces decided to storm the fortress. Though they half-destroyed it, they were soon forced to retreat.

The icon was returned to the rebuilt church in 1721, and before long devotion to Our Lady of Sinj had spread throughout the country. Her popularity has increased greatly over the centuries, and the Croatian year is filled with celebrations, processions, festivities and special ceremonies in her honor. Today the shrine at Sinj is an important spiritual site, annually receiving thousands of pilgrims who come to view the miraculous icon and to venerate Our Lady of Sinj, Mother of Mercy.

᥅ TRADITIONAL PRAYER

O Virgin Mary, Our Lady of Sinj, we dedicate ourselves to your service. We consecrate our minds, hearts and bodies and promise to work always for the glory of God and the salvation of all people. We pray for the church throughout the world. Protect the young and help the aged, save sinners and console the dying. You are our hope, Mary, Mother of Croatia and the whole world. Pray to your son for us so that we may be filled with selfless charity and deep faith. Ask Jesus for those things that we cannot obtain through our own actions, and help us in this, our present necessity. May we always see the will of the Father in our lives. We ask you this, sweet Spouse of the Holy Spirit, so that we may come to your son in grace. Amen.

᥅ NEW PRAYER

Most holy Lady of Sinj, instill the spirit of peace in our hearts. Teach us to trust that God's providence, through your motherly love, will take care of all our needs, that in so believing we may put aside all selfish strife—and attaining true peace within, that we may become peacemakers in our war-torn world. Amen.

🦋 Our Lady of Soufanieh

HER STORY

*J*ust a few blocks away from the house of Ananias, with whom Saint Paul spent three days after being blinded on the road to Damascus, is the home of Myrna Nazzour, a visionary with a remarkable message of unity for the world.

Myrna's supernatural experiences began in November 1982. Praying at the bedside of her ailing sister-in-law, Layla, Myrna noticed her own fingers beginning to ooze oil. When she touched Layla with the oil, the sick woman was immediately cured.

The Nazzours had an image of Our Lady of Soufanieh in their home, and on November 27 it also began to exude oil. The oils from Myrna—whose name means Mary—and the picture, tested and found to be pure olive oil, are known to have restored sight to a Muslim woman and the use of his limbs to a paralyzed boy.

On December 15 an invisible escort led Myrna to her roof garden, where she saw the Blessed Mother. But Myrna fled, terrified. Three days later, her husband, Nicholas, and some friends accompanied her to the garden, where she again saw the beautiful Virgin crossing to her on a bridge of light. Our Lady's message was simple: announce Christ, love one another and "remember God, because God is with us." The third apparition occurred on January 8, 1983. During the fourth, on February 21, our Lady taught Myrna this prayer: "God saves me, Jesus enlightens me, the Holy Spirit is my life; thus I fear nothing." During the fifth visit, on March 24, our Lady gave Myrna her commission: "Do not be divided as the great ones are. You, yourselves, will teach the generations *the Word* of unity, love and faith."

Myrna was Melkite Catholic and her husband was Eastern Orthodox. Nicholas's patriarch, Ignatius IV Hazim, investigated the phenomena, approving their authenticity on December 31, 1982. But the Roman Catholic bishop of Damascus, the Most Reverend Paulus Barkash, also opened an investigation. As a personal witness, he verified the phenomena himself.

Myrna began to experience ecstasies in October 1983. They would recur intermittently, even during Myrna's foreign travels, usually lasting for five to seventy-five minutes, though the longest recorded was seventy-two hours.

On November 25, 1983, she received the stigmata in her hands and side; they opened in the afternoon and disappeared, untreated, that night. Her second experience of the stigmata occurred on April 19, 1984; though deeper than the first wounds, these, too, disappeared the evening after appearing. Her later stigmata (1987 and 1990) also included the wounds from the crown of thorns.

Then on May 31, 1984, after oil exuded painfully from her eyes, Myrna had her first apparition of Jesus. On September 7, 1985, Jesus spoke with Myrna about his mother: "I am the Creator. I created her, so that she could create me. Rejoice from the joy of heaven, because the Daughter of the Father and the Mother of God and the Spouse of the Spirit is born." Again, on August 14, 1987, Jesus said, "She is my mother from whom I was born. He who honors her, honors me. He who denies her, denies me. And he who asks something from her, obtains because she is my mother."

Jesus commissioned Myrna on November 26, 1987: "Go and preach to the whole world and tell them without fear to work for unity." The visits from Mary had continued since 1983, and our Lady underscored the words of her son on November 26, 1990: "We are with you and with everyone who wishes the feast [Easter] to be one."

Aside from the first instance, Myrna's stigmata opened only when the Roman Catholic and Eastern Orthodox churches celebrated Easter together (1984, 1987, 1990). And perhaps because of Myrna's prayers and those of her family and friends and others who came to know her story, in 1997 representatives of the World Council of Churches and the Middle East Council of Churches agreed upon recommendations for determining a common date for the celebration of Easter, having reached this accord in Syria, Myrna's homeland. The various churches have been considering these recommendations, with the hope that sometime soon Christians throughout the world will celebrate Easter on the same day.

ᗯ TRADITIONAL PRAYER

Spouse of the Holy Spirit and Seat of Wisdom, help us in the great endeavor that we are carrying out to meet in a more and more mature way our brothers and sisters in the faith, with whom so many things unite us, although there is still something dividing us. Through all the means of knowledge, of mutual respect, of love, shared collaboration in various fields, may we be able to rediscover gradually the divine plan for the unity in which we should enter. Mother of unity, teach us constantly the ways that lead to unity....

—*Pope John Paul II*

◌∾ NEW PRAYER

Dear Lady of Soufanieh, I rejoice that the Spirit, your spouse, has led me away from the church of my youth and into another church that is more welcoming of all people and more accepting of my personal revelations. Yet my natal church's rejection of me still hurts, and I harbor resentments because of the wounds it has inflicted. Help me to forgive. Help me to heal. Help me to move forward. And one day, help me to become a bridge, to encourage the people of these churches to accept one another's faith and learn from one another in the spirit of truth and love. Amen.

ℬ. *Our Lady of the Green Scapular*

HER STORY

*T*he story of the Green Scapular begins on January 28, 1840, when Justine Bisqueyburu, a young woman from the French Pyrenees, was making her entrance retreat with the Sisters of Charity of Saint Vincent de Paul in Paris. While she was silently praying in the convent's chapel—the very same chapel where ten years earlier Catherine Labouré had received a vision of the Miraculous Medal (page 155)—the Blessed Mother appeared. Dressed in a gown of white covered by a blue mantle, Mary was holding her flaming immaculate heart over her breast in her folded hands. She spoke not a word, then disappeared. Justine received the same vision again at the end of her retreat and afterward on five more occasions.

Justine made her first profession of vows, then went to the convent in Blangy. There, on the feast of the Nativity of the Blessed Virgin, September 8, 1840, Mary again appeared to Justine. This time, our Lady held in her left hand a square of cloth strung on green cords. Upon one side of the cloth was an image of the Blessed Mother as she had previously appeared to Justine. The other side of the cloth presented an image of the Immaculate Heart, "all ablaze with rays more dazzling than the sun and as transparent as crystal." Pierced by a sword, the Immaculate Heart was also surrounded by these words: "Immaculate Heart of Mary, pray for us, now and at the hour of our death." Above the words was a golden cross.

As she beheld this vision, Justine heard within her soul the explanation of this "scapular": it was to help convert souls and would help Mary obtain for them the grace of a happy death.

When Justine prudently kept the experience to herself, mistrusting her senses, Mary repeated the vision—twice. Finally, Justine told her spiritual director, Father Aladel, who by chance was actively involved in spreading the devotion of the Miraculous Medal. After a period of discernment, during which the Blessed Mother complained of delays, the distribution of the Green Scapular, as it came to be called, was approved. Pope Pius IX gave his own blessing to the scapular in 1863 and 1870.

Because it consists of a single piece of cloth hung from a green cord, the Green Scapular is not a traditional scapular, which is made up of two small double squares of cloth. Despite the misnomer, the Green Scapular is one of the eight Marian scapulars approved by the church. The rest are the White Scapular of the Hearts of Jesus and Mary, the White Scapular of the Immaculate Heart of Mary (page 32), the White Scapular of Our Lady of Good Counsel (page 46), the White Scapular of Our Lady of Ransom, the Blue Scapular of the Immaculate Conception (page 23), the Brown Scapular of Our Lady of Mount Carmel (page 135) and the Black Scapular of Our Lady of Sorrows (page 54). The Green Scapular is unique because it does not require investiture in a confraternity; a simple blessing by a priest suffices. Another difference is that the Green Scapular does not have to be worn or carried directly on one's person. However, the prayer of the Green Scapular should be recited at least once daily—if not by the person for whom the scapular is intended, then by those who have presented the scapular to that person.

The Green Scapular has brought about countless conversions as well as bestowing a great many cures and other graces on its devotees. As Our Lady of the Green Scapular promised, this scapular has the power to change hearts and souls, and those who pray the prayer inscribed on it know firsthand that Mary has kept her promise.

ᴄᴖ TRADITIONAL PRAYER

Immaculate Heart of Mary, pray for us, now and at the hour of our death. Amen.

Dear Lady of the Green Scapular, we ask that you bless us at the moment of death—whenever it greets us—with the certainty of knowing that we are God's beloved children. Help us become children of the Resurrection, that we may completely embrace life now and enjoy Christ's promise both in this time and in the time to come. Amen.

ℬ Our Lady of the Highways

HER STORY

Many people around the world honor Mary as Our Lady of the Highways in memory of the dangerous travels that she undertook. The Gospel of Luke relates that Mary, newly pregnant, rushed out to the hill country to help her cousin Elizabeth during the older woman's pregnancy. Luke also recounts the hazardous journey Mary undertook with her husband, Joseph, when they went to Bethlehem to register for the census. Not only did they travel alone, easy prey for potential thieves or worse, Mary was almost ready to deliver—and could very easily have had her baby on the way. Luke tells of Mary and Joseph's bringing the baby to the Temple and of the Holy Family's later trip to Jerusalem for Passover. The Gospel of Matthew does not mention these journeys but does report the precipitous flight of the Holy Family across the desert wastes into Egypt to escape Herod's wrath. And it also mentions the family's return from Egypt to Nazareth. When Mary's son entered his active ministry, she would follow him all over the countryside, accompanying even his final trek up the hill of Calvary. And tradition relates that she then went with Saint John to Ephesus. For her time, she was one well-traveled woman.

Given the journeys she undertook, it is natural that Christians appeal to her experience and invoke her aid during their own traveling. And indeed, devotion to Our Lady of the Highways dates from the earliest days of Christianity and may have originated in Rome with the Shrine of *Santa Maria della Strada*, or Saint Mary of the Wayside (page 25). Saint Ignatius of Loyola honored Mary under this title.

Because of today's increasingly hazardous driving conditions, more and more travelers have begun to invoke the aid of Our Lady of the Highways, particularly in the United States.

When a terrible traffic accident occurred on I-95 in 1968, just a few yards away from the residence of the Oblate Helpers' Guild in Childs, Maryland, the community's founder, Father John Fuqua, was moved to invoke Mary's protection upon travelers. His inspiration prompted the dedication of a new shrine to Our Lady of the Highways. The tall statue of Mary, visible to all traffic on the interstate, reminds all travelers to drive responsibly and to pray to our Lady for safe arrival.

Another shrine to Our Lady of the Highways has been established in Little Falls, New Jersey, as an invocation of Mary's protection upon local drivers.

Even if not passing by one shrine or another, the people of God are always under Our Lady of the Highways' protection and guidance, for she watches over all her children on their life journeys.

◌ Traditional Prayer

May my traveling be to the honor and glory of your divine son. Enlighten my way and protect me on this journey. Bring me back home safe in mind, body and soul. Through Christ, your son. Amen.

◌ New Prayer

Dear Lady of the Highways, the way I am to proceed is completely hidden from me, as if I were speeding through a thick fog along a curving expressway some dark night. I can't see if the road I'm following will bring me to my heaven or to my hell. And I'm desperately afraid—of ending up alone, unable to communicate with anyone, unable to find my way back.

O Mother! Dispel the fog, illuminate the darkness and straighten the road, that I may discern where I am heading. Show me my proper destination, my heaven. Guide me there—draw me a map, please! Help me adjust my "driving habits"—my actions, my words, my attitudes—so that I may enjoy the journey and arrive safely where I am supposed to be. Amen.

🦋 Our Lady of the Hudson

HER STORY

*T*hough the Boatmen's Shrine of Our Lady of the Hudson is relatively new, dating only from the last century, the men and women who have made their living from this great river have appealed to our Lady for protection and assistance ever since Christians settled these shores.

The Boatmen's Shrine was established in Port Ewen, New York, because the town was a center for the transportation of coal via the Delaware-Hudson Canal from Pennsylvania to its northern markets. Approximately one hundred miles north of New York City, Port Ewen is on the western shore of the river. The towing companies and the International Longshoremen's Association, in tandem with those families whose livelihood depended on the river, constructed the shrine to thank the Blessed Virgin for the safety of the hundreds of people who have spent their lives working the waterways from New York City to the Great Lakes.

The centerpiece of the shrine is the six-foot statue of Our Lady of the Hudson. Carved from bluestone native to the area by Thomas Penning, she is depicted with a tugboat in her arms. The shrine was consecrated on June 28, 1952.

This stretch of the Hudson has a rich history of devotion to our Lady under her many titles. Just a few miles from the Boatmen's Shrine is Mount Saint Alphonsus, the former theologate of the Redemptorist Community, where special devotion to the Mother of Perpetual Help (page 51) is still observed. On the same stretch of road are found houses for the Marianists, the Christian Brothers and the Cabrini Sisters, all of whom honor Mary according to the unique charisms of their orders.

With the cleanup of the Hudson well advanced, more and more people are coming to the water for recreation. Our Lady of the Hudson looks out for their welfare while continuing to watch over those whose work takes them on the river, as well as safeguarding the Hudson's natural beauty for future generations to enjoy.

ᑲ TRADITIONAL PRAYER

Here are my prayers, Mary, use them where they are needed, you will know best. Don't bother saving a merit or two, use them all, Mary, I give them to you. It's the only way that I can repay my thanks for the grace you gave me. I give them to you without any strings, pass them to Jesus as your offerings; so take my prayers, Mary, with all my heart, I give them to you. Amen.

∾ New Prayer

O Lady of the Hudson, we thank you for guarding the beautiful Hudson River and all the beautiful rivers and waterways, lakes and seas that God has created. You remind us that water is sacred, the very essence of life. Keep us mindful of our role in protecting these waters of life, that we may become enlightened stewards, learning to participate wisely in God's ongoing creation. Amen.

Our Lady of the Miraculous Medal

Her Story

The era of modern Marian apparitions began in 1830, when the Blessed Mother gave the world, through Catherine Labouré, both the gift of the Miraculous Medal and one of the first revelations of the Immaculate Conception (page 23).

Born in 1806, Catherine entered the convent of the Sisters of Charity in the Rue de Bac, Paris, in 1830. On the night of July 18 of that year, the eve of Saint Vincent de Paul's feast, a voice awakened Catherine at around 11:00. A beautiful child beckoned her to the chapel, which was ablaze with light. After Catherine had knelt at the communion rail, the child announced the Mother of God (page 44). With a rustle as of silk, a lady appeared and seated herself in a chair by the altar. Dressed in a white robe and blue mantle, the lady gathered Catherine's hands in her lap. Catherine experienced what she described as the sweetest joy of her life.

The Blessed Mother told Catherine she would receive a mission from God. She also predicted misfortunes for France: the overthrow of the throne, the death of the archbishop, the trampling of the cross, violence in the streets. But Mary promised to protect the convent. Then she asked Catherine not to reveal the vision to anyone except her confessor, Father Aladel.

He was skeptical of her story. But within days antireligious rioting seized Paris. Churches were pillaged, and the archbishop was forced into hiding. On July 31 the revolt deposed King Charles X and installed Louis Philippe as king. As Mary had promised, the convent remained untouched.

On November 27, during evening prayers in the chapel, Catherine again beheld our Lady, who was dressed in dazzling white and was standing upon a globe.

After a moment Mary stretched out her hands. Myriad rays of light extended from the bejeweled rings on her fingers, and she said, "These rays symbolize the graces I will bestow upon all who ask of me."

Then an oval surrounded our Lady, and on it was written in golden letters "O Mary, conceived without sin, pray for us who have recourse to you."

Suddenly, Catherine saw the letter *M* surmounted by a cross, with a bar beneath, and beneath this monogram the hearts of Jesus, surrounded with a crown of thorns, and of Mary, transpierced with a sword. A voice charged Catherine to have a medal struck with these images, promising, "Persons who wear it with piety will receive great graces."

A few days later, as well as in March and September of 1831, our Lady appeared again and repeated her message. The last time, when she expressed disappointment that her request had not been carried out, Catherine's confessor finally went to Archbishop de Quelen. Though incredulous, he nevertheless had a small number of the medals created, since the images reflected Roman Catholic doctrine and encouraged devotion to Mary Immaculate.

The archbishop took one of the medals to the deathbed of the archbishop of Malines, Monsignor de Pradt, who had fallen away from the church. Immediately, Monsignor de Pradt repented. Hearing of other miraculous favors associated with the medal, Archbishop de Quelen gave permission for an unlimited number to be struck. He called it the Medal of the Immaculate Conception, but because of the number of miracles it seemed to engender, it quickly became known as the Miraculous Medal.

In 1870 Mary's other prophecies came to pass: the Franco-Prussian War and the murder of the archbishop.

Catherine subsequently hid her identity as the visionary until 1876, when she came out to the mother superior to fulfill Mary's request for a statue of Our Lady of the Globe. Pope Leo XIII approved the statue just before Catherine's death, on December 31, 1876.

Exhumed after her beatification in 1933, Catherine's incorrupt body was placed in a glass reliquary in the Chapel of Apparitions in the Rue de Bac, where it remains. She was canonized in 1947.

Many people consider the Miraculous Medal visions as the first of the modern Marian apparitions of warning. The words inscribed on the medal itself sparked requests for the definition of the Dogma of the Immaculate Conception, and this was promulgated in 1854.

The feast of Our Lady of the Miraculous Medal is celebrated on November 27, the anniversary of the first vision of the medal. Over the years our Lady has granted many favors to those who are devoted to the medal, which itself has no intrinsic power. It is not a good luck charm. Rather, it is a prayer, invoking the intercession of our Lady, and those who pray it regularly come to know the grace of being in close communion with the Mother of God.

❧ TRADITIONAL PRAYER

O virgin Mother of God, Mary Immaculate, we dedicate and consecrate ourselves to you under the title of Our Lady of the Miraculous Medal. May this medal be for each one of us a sure sign of your affection for us and a constant reminder of our duties toward you. Ever while wearing it, may we be blessed by your loving protection and preserved in the grace of your son. O most powerful Virgin, mother of our Savior, keep us close to you every moment of our lives. Obtain for us, your children, the grace of a happy death; so that, in union with you, we may enjoy the bliss of heaven forever. Amen.

❧ NEW PRAYER

Dear Lady of the Miraculous Medal, be with my [child/children] now as [she/he/they] enter(s) this day, which to these fearful parental eyes seems filled with so many perils. Protect [————] from bullies and gang members and others who might bring harm. Strengthen, and help me bolster, [————]'s self-esteem, that [————] might resist peer pressure. Warn [————] if necessary, and give [————] the grace to seek assistance when threatened. And if the threat becomes real, work a miracle if necessary to bring [————] safely through the danger and home again to my loving arms. I ask this in the name of your beloved son. Amen.

Our Lady of the Most Blessed Sacrament

HER STORY

When Mary stood at the foot of her son's cross (John 19:25–27), she was, in a sense, among the first to honor his sacrifice, among the first to participate in his most blessed sacrament of redemption. And although the Gospels do not indicate that she was present at the Last Supper, when Jesus instituted the Eucharist in commemoration of his forthcoming sacrifice, tradition strongly indicates that Mary participated in eucharistic services with the disciples. Some early church historians believed that Mary spent most of her time in adoration of her son in the Eucharist.

Mary's entire life centered around making her son known to others. From the moment of the Incarnation until her own Assumption, she fulfilled God's will of bearing Christ to the world. This mission included spreading devotion to the Most Blessed Sacrament. In the words of Saint Peter Julian Eymard:

> Mary devoted herself exclusively to the Eucharistic Glory of Jesus. She knew that it was the desire of the Eternal Father to make the Eucharist known, loved and served by all men....
>
> Ever since Calvary, all men were her children. She loved them with a Mother's tenderness and longed for their supreme good as for her own; therefore, she was consumed with the desire to make Jesus in the Blessed Sacrament known to all, to inflame all hearts with His love, to see them enchained to His loving service.
>
> To obtain this favor, Mary passed her time at the foot of the Most Adorable Sacrament, in prayer and penance.

A Marist father from Grenoble, Eymard (1811–1868) is known as the Apostle of the Eucharist, and he founded the Congregation of the Priests of the Most Blessed Sacrament, the Servants of the Blessed Sacrament for women and the Confraternity of the Blessed Sacrament for laypeople.

Eymard gave Mary the title Our Lady of the Most Blessed Sacrament, adopting her as mother for his eucharistic family. Establishing her feast on May 13, Eymard urged all the faithful to follow Mary's example.

The Blessed Mother herself seems to have taken note of Eymard's work, appearing as Our Lady of Fátima (page 91) on May 13, 1917, after the Guardian Angel of Portugal had brought the Most Blessed Sacrament to Lúcia, Francisco and Jacinta.

In encouraging frequent reception of the Eucharist, our Lady emphasizes the true presence of Jesus in the Most Blessed Sacrament. Mary's faith and love for her son have made her a channel of grace by which Christ comes into the hearts of God's people.

◑ TRADITIONAL PRAYER

Virgin Immaculate, Mother of Jesus and our Mother, we invoke you under the title of Our Lady of the Most Blessed Sacrament, because you are the Mother of the Savior who lives in the Eucharist. It was from you he took the Flesh and Blood which he feeds us in the Sacred Host.

We also invoke you under that title because the grace of the Eucharist comes to us through you, since you are the channel through which God's graces reach us.

And, finally, we call you Our Lady of the Most Blessed Sacrament because you were the first to live the Eucharistic life. Teach us to pray the Mass as you did, to receive holy Communion worthily and frequently, and to visit devoutly with our Lord in the Blessed Sacrament.

—John Cardinal Carberry

◑ NEW PRAYER

O holy Lady of the Most Blessed Sacrament, teach me to make of every moment of my life a sacrament, in commemoration of your son's sacrifice. Show me his presence in every person, in every event, in my every experience, that I may, like you, recognize his spirit incarnate. And help me, like you, to incarnate the Word through my words and actions, my thoughts and attitudes, my very joy, that this day I might reveal your son to the rest of the world. Amen.

❧ Our Lady of the Philippines

HER STORY

The first reports about Our Lady of the Philippines come from the town of Lipa, about sixty miles southeast of Manila. On September 12, 1948, Sister Teresita was meditating in her convent's courtyard when she heard a voice calling her. Turning to see who it was, she noticed a small, white, shining cloud in front of a vine-covered wall. The voice told her, "For fifteen consecutive days come to visit me here in this spot."

The next day Sister Teresita saw a figure in the cloud, identifying her as the Blessed Virgin because of her words: "People believe not my words. Pray, child, pray much because of persecution. What I ask here is exactly what I asked at Fátima. Tell this to the people." Suddenly, a shower of rose petals fell from the clear sky into the courtyard and beyond. The petals were so abundant that they were like snow drifts, with an extraordinary fragrance.

During Sister Teresita's last vision the apparition identified herself: "I am the Mediatrix of All Grace." She asked that a shrine be built in her honor at this spot.

The rose petals fell again in October and November, and when people dried and preserved them, the petals were found to be inexplicably imprinted with images of our Lady, her son and the Holy Family. People who mixed the petals with water and consumed them reported miraculous cures.

In March of 1949 the people of Lipa saw the Blessed Virgin in the sky on two occasions, once on the face of the sun and then among the clouds.

But church authorities forbade Sister Teresita and the other nuns of her community to talk of these events. The convent was eventually closed, and Sister Teresita's diary and all other written reports of the apparitions were ordered burned. The convent's Mediatrix of All Grace statue was to be destroyed also, but the nuns hid it away.

Years later, in February 1990, a luminous outline of a praying woman appeared on the leaves of a coconut tree in Lipa. Then the sisters received permission to display their statue again. On January 24, 1991, rose petals fell from the sky upon the convent. The next day six children playing in the garden saw the statue come to life. As a result, the church has reopened investigations of the events at Lipa.

Just a year before these latest occurrences at Lipa, in the small town of Agoo north of Manila, Judiel Nieva reportedly began receiving visits from the Blessed Virgin on the first Saturday of every month and on special religious feasts. In February 1993 his family's statue of Mary began to weep tears of blood. Thousands of people witnessed this phenomenon, which was said to have curative powers. On March 5, 1993, and again the next morning, a vast crowd of people saw the sun dance in the sky. And on March 6 this crowd, including many upper-level government officials, saw a silhouette of the Blessed Virgin appear in the air above a guava tree. Then the sky was filled with colored lights. Nieva reported that during these phenomena our Lady told him to ask people to pray for the children of famine-stricken Somalia.

Perhaps the most dramatic of the Philippine apparitions occurred in 1986, when President Ferdinand Marcos sent the Philippine army to crush the supporters of Corazon Aquino, who had defeated him in the general election. As the soldiers drove their tanks down the streets of Manila, intending to turn their weapons on their fellow citizens, they saw a cross in the sky. Then a beautiful lady reportedly appeared to them and said, "Dear soldiers, stop! Do not proceed! Do not harm my children!" Immediately, the soldiers left their tanks and joined the people in the streets. Eventually, Marcos handed over power to Aquino.

Though these events in the Philippines have not yet received church approval, our Lady has filled the hearts of the Philippine people with her love, and in times of turmoil they do not hesitate to appeal to her, invoking her intercession and asking for her gift of grace. The results—physical and spiritual cures and even political improvements—have been truly remarkable, attesting to the power of Our Lady of the Philippines to change hearts and move souls.

❧ TRADITIONAL PRAYER

We fly to your protection, O holy Mother of God; despise not our petitions in our necessities, but deliver us always from all danger, O glorious and blessed Virgin. Amen.

—*Sub tuum praesidium*

❧ NEW PRAYER

Dearest Lady of the Philippines, fill our souls with the beauty of your spirit, the beauty of a soul completely devoted to the will of God. Help us to discern the way we are to go, and when we are confused, send us a sign, like rose petals from the sky, to mark the path God has chosen for us. Amen.

💫 Our Lady of the Pillar
| Nuestra Señora del Pilar |

Her Story

*T*he appearance of Our Lady of the Pillar at Zaragoza, Spain, is the first recorded apparition of the Blessed Mother. What's even more remarkable is that it may have been the first recorded instance of bilocation, having perhaps occurred while she was still alive.

After Christ's resurrection, Saint James traveled as far west as the Iberian Peninsula, to bring the gospel to the borders of the Roman Empire. While he was evangelizing in the region of Zaragoza, which is about one hundred miles west of Barcelona, he became disheartened because of his lack of success. According to tradition, one evening in the year 40, while resting and praying alongside the Ebro River, he was stunned to hear angels singing, "Hail, Mary, full of grace" and to recognize the mother of his Lord descending from on high. She was seated on a "pillar," or throne, of light.

Her message was one of encouragement and instruction. According to one account, she explained,

> My son James, the Most High and Mighty God of Heaven has chosen this place that you may consecrate and dedicate here a church and house of prayer where, under the invocation of my name, He wishes to be adored and served, and all the faithful who seek my intercession will receive the graces they ask if they have true faith and devotion, and in the name of my Son I promise them great favors and blessings, for this will be my chapel and my house, my own inheritance and possession, and in testimony of my promise, this pillar will remain here, and on it my own image, which, in this place where you will build my church, will last and endure with the holy faith....On this spot the Most High will work miracles through my intercession for those who implore my protection in their need. And this pillar will remain in this place until the end of the world.

Other accounts have her saying simply, "This place is to be my house, and this image and column shall be the title and altar of the temple that you shall build." And with that, the Blessed Mother gave James a small wooden statue of herself holding the child Jesus and a column of jasper wood.

Saint James had a tiny chapel—just sixteen feet by eight feet—built on the spot and installed there the statue and column. According to tradition, this was the first church dedicated to the Blessed Mother. Many miracles and healings have been attributed to Our Lady of the Pillar over the centuries. The most remarkable concerns Michael Juan Pellicer Blasco, whose right leg was amputated. He often visited the shrine at Zaragoza to pray, anointing his stump with oil from one of the lamps burning before our Lady's statue. On March 29, 1640, he dreamed that he was in the basilica, and when he awoke, he found that his amputated leg had been regenerated. After a careful investigation, which included examining the records of surgery and interrogating witnesses to the burial of the amputated leg, Archbishop P. Apolaza formally declared the regeneration a miracle.

Many churches have been built on the site of the apparition, and today a huge basilica dominates the skyline. The statue, fifteen inches tall and carved in the Gothic style, still stands on the pillar and is usually decorated in a heavy dress. Thousands of pilgrims visit the Basilica of Our Lady of the Pillar daily, bringing their cares to Mary and, on special occasions, kissing her statue, thus honoring the great love she has demonstrated for her children from the very earliest declaration of the Christian message.

ೋ TRADITIONAL PRAYER

Glorious Virgin of the Pillar, your compassion for the Hispanic people encouraged the Apostle James and encourages us in all adversities and dangers that surround us. Pour upon us the abundance of your mercy and give us the spiritual and temporal graces that we need to serve God and you in this life and the life to come. Amen.

ೋ NEW PRAYER

Nuestra Señora del Pilar, sometimes I get so discouraged that I can't even find the will to pray. At such times when I can't even ask for your assistance, I need your singular help. Send me your spirit, that I may step outside of my discouragement. Give me a greater perspective, that I may see particular events in the context of my ongoing journey of faith. And remind me, dearest Mother, to be joyful in all of life's moments, for no matter how difficult they might be, they bring me to the place I am going and contribute to the person I am becoming. Amen.

🜂 Our Lady of the Rockies

HER STORY

*I*n 1979 Bob O'Bill, a mine worker for the Anaconda corporation, promised the Blessed Mother that he would erect a statue in her honor if his wife, Joyce, recovered from her illness. She did, and O'Bill began to enlist his friends and colleagues for his project.

O'Bill's vision inspired many people in his community of Butte, Montana, and Our Lady of the Rockies became a labor of love. As Joe Roberts, one of the volunteers, recalled, the statue was constructed out of "love of wives and mothers everywhere." But the statue was more than a love letter; it was also a way for the community to remember the answers they had received to their prayers and to rededicate themselves to the promises they had made and perhaps forgotten. In Roberts's words, "Many of us realized that we were bankrupt with unfilled pledges and promises made but not paid."

The community formed the nonprofit Our Lady of the Rockies Foundation and set to work collecting donations and soliciting help. To secure the site on the mountain, some people donated mining claims. Anaconda donated road-building machinery; Ideal Basic Industries, the cement base; and local businesses, supplies and other equipment. Even the U.S. government pitched in, allowing the foundation to "rent" an Army helicopter to carry the statue to its location on the Continental Divide, eighty-five hundred feet above sea level.

The statue itself is the largest piece of art in Montana. Standing ninety feet tall, it is made of six tiers of variously sized pipes welded together and weighs fifty-one tons. Construction began in 1983, and the shrine of Our Lady of the Rockies was completed and dedicated on December 20, 1985.

Not simply a product of promises kept, Our Lady of the Rockies is also a monument to cooperation among people. From her mountaintop perch she draws all people together in the spirit of service and love.

ᘉ TRADITIONAL PRAYER

Bless us, Our Lady of the Rockies, and this land, those peaks divine. May our hearts be like your arms, full of love and open wide.

—*Mark Staples*

Dear Lady of the Rockies, guide us in our efforts to work with others. Help us subdue our propensity to self-promotion, our selfish desire for individual recognition, our me-first attitudes that alienate and distance. Remind us that we are relational beings. And pray for us, that we may finally dare to connect with our fellow pilgrims. Amen.

ⵌ Our Lady of the Rosary

Her Story

The word *rosary* comes from the Latin word *rosarium*, which means "a garden of roses," and this derivation helps explain the origins of this Marian prayer. In the thirteenth century nobles customarily crowned their beloved with a garland of roses. At the same time, one of the customs of chivalry was for knights to pledge their honor to the Blessed Virgin Mary. From these two customs developed the practice of "crowning" the Blessed Mother, either by placing a wreath of roses upon one of her images or by offering a spiritual "garland of roses" to her through the rosary prayer.

During this period Domingo de Guzman, who became known as Saint Dominic, came to southern France to preach among the Albigenses. While he was praying in a chapel in Prouille in 1208, our Lady appeared and taught him the complete rosary prayer, urging him to preach it to the rest of the world as a remedy against heresy and sin.

The great power of the rosary soon became known throughout Christendom. Saint Thomas Aquinas (c. 1225–1274) preached on the rosary, and Saints Francis de Sales (1567–1622) and John Vianney (1786–1859) were both great devotees. Saint Louis Marie Grignion de Montfort (1673–1716) wrote, "The rosary is the most powerful weapon to touch the Heart of Jesus, Our Redeemer, who loves His Mother." In modern times Blessed Padre Pio (1887–1968) spoke often about the efficacy of the rosary prayer, asserting, "The rosary is my weapon."

The first rosary crusade occurred in 1571, launched by Pope Pius V to protect Christian Europe from invading Islamic forces. When the opposing navies finally met, many rosaries had been offered for victory, and the Christian armada did vanquish the Turkish fleet at the Battle of Lepanto on October 7. In the official words of the Venetian Senate, it was neither "generals nor battalions nor arms that brought us victory; but it was Our Lady of the Rosary." In thanksgiving, the pope established the feast of Our Lady of Victory (page 175) on October 7, attributing the victory to her intercession.

Just two years later, Pope Gregory XIII moved the celebration to the first Sunday of October, renamed it the feast of the Holy Rosary and allowed those churches with a rosary altar to observe the feast. Christian forces defeated the Turks again in Hungary in 1716, at which time Pope Clement XI extended the privilege of celebrating the feast to the entire church. Pope Pius X moved the feast back to October 7. The name was changed in 1960 to the feast of the Blessed Virgin Mary of the Rosary and again in 1969 to Our Lady of the Rosary. It is now a mandatory memorial, and the month of October has been dedicated to the rosary.

In the nineteenth century devotions to Our Lady of Pompeii (page 141) became popular, and these devotions helped spread the rosary prayer. The apparitions of our Lady at Fátima (page 91) in the twentieth century extended the devotions even further. On October 13, 1917, Our Lady of Fátima told the children, "I am the Lady of the Rosary. I have come to warn the faithful to amend their lives and to ask pardon for their sins....People must say the Rosary. Let them continue to say it every day."

Over the centuries countless numbers of people have become devoted pray-ers of the rosary, meditating on the fifteen sacred mysteries and appealing to Mary's motherly heart for help and healing. And Mary has consistently fulfilled the fifteen promises of the rosary, as given to Saint Dominic, dispensing special graces, protection and a number of other blessings to all those who serve her by faithfully reciting her prayer.

∾ TRADITIONAL PRAYER

Behold me at thy knees, immaculate Mother of Jesus, who dost rejoice at being invoked as Queen of the Rosary in the Vale of Pompeii. With joy in my heart, and my mind filled with the most lively gratitude, I return to thee who art my most generous benefactor, my dearest Lady, the Queen of my heart, to thee who hast shown thyself my true Mother, the Mother who loves me exceedingly. I was filled with groanings and thou didst hear my cry; I was in affliction and thou didst comfort me; I was in the valley of the shadow of death and thou didst bring me peace. The sorrows and pains of death laid siege to my soul, and thou, dear Mother, from thy throne in Pompeii with one look of pity didst make me serene. Who hath ever turned to thee with confidence and hath not been heard? If only the whole world knew thy great goodness, thy tender compassion for those who suffer, how all creation would have recourse to thee! Mayest thou be ever blessed, O Virgin and Queen of Pompeii, by me and by all others, both men and Angels, on earth and in heaven.

—*The Raccolta*

∾ NEW PRAYER

With the white rose in remembrance of your purity, the yellow rose in remembrance of your joy, the purple rose in remembrance of your queenship, the blue rose in remembrance of your sorrow and the red rose in remembrance of your martyrdom, I crown you, dear Mother, with this garland of my meditations on your sacred life. Through this special "rosary," inspire me to honor your living memory, to learn from your example and to embody your spirit, that my life, as yours, may be one of complete integrity and utter joy. Amen.

Our Lady of the Snows

HER STORY

According to legend, on August 4, 352—a sultry night in Rome— our Lady appeared in a dream to a childless, elderly, wealthy couple, who had prayed that the Blessed Mother might identify who should inherit their fortune. However, Mary expressed her wish that a church be constructed in her honor and told the couple that the church site would be covered with snow. Mary also appeared that night in Pope Liberius's dream, telling him of her desire.

The next morning, Rome awoke to the astonishing sight of a snow-covered Esquiline Hill—remarkably, the snowfall was arranged in the outline of a church. The summer snow was deemed a miracle indeed, and the childless wife and husband took the snow as a sign and donated the money to build the church. It was completed in two years and became the most important church in Rome dedicated to the Blessed Mother. It was also known as the Basilica Liberiana, having been consecrated by Pope Liberius. But it came to be called the

SALUS POPULI ROMANI

Madonna and Child attributed to Saint Luke
Basilica of St. Mary Major
Rome, Italy

Basilica of St. Mary Major in the seventh century.

Within the basilica, in the Borghese Chapel, is an ancient Byzantine painting, attributed to Saint Luke, of the Madonna and Child. Known as the *Salus Populi Romani,* or the Protectress of the People of Rome, this is the most venerated image of our Lady in Rome and is said to have ended an attack of the plague in 604 and an epidemic of cholera in 1837.

Renovated several times, the Basilica of St. Mary Major is known as the first shrine of Our Lady of the Snows. To commemorate the miraculous snowfall, the celebration of her feast on August 5 includes a shower of white rose petals from the dome of the Chapel of Our Lady during the solemn Mass.

Our Lady of the Snows has a worldwide reputation, and the largest outdoor shrine in the United States is the National Shrine of Our Lady of the Snows, located in Belleville, Illinois. Its meditation gardens, meeting centers and programs are all designed to bring pilgrims to a greater awareness of the presence of Christ in their lives.

❧ TRADITIONAL PRAYER

Remember, O most gracious Virgin Mary, that never was it known that anyone who fled to thy protection, implored thy help or sought thy intercession, was left unaided. Inspired with this confidence, I fly unto thee, O Virgin of virgins and Mother; to thee do I come, before thee I stand, sinful and sorrowful; O Mother of the Word Incarnate, despise not my petitions, but in thy mercy hear and answer me. Amen.

—*Memorare*

❧ NEW PRAYER

Holy Lady of the Snows, the forces of creation are often destructive and disruptive and terrify us, because we are powerless in the face of the thunderous sea or the raging storm. But through your miraculous intervention of summer snow, you have shown that these very forces of nature conform to God's will. Be our protector, therefore, in times of dangerous weather. And intercede with our Lord to stay the flood, to calm the hurricane, to subdue the tornado, to soften the blizzard and to wet the drought. We ask this in the name of your son, who stilled the towering sea so that his friends might not be harmed. Amen.

𝕭 Our Lady of Tínos

HER STORY

On the Greek island of Tínos, located about eighty-five miles southeast of Piraeus, in the church of Panayía Evangelístria, is found the *Megalokhari,* a miraculous icon of the Annunciation that, according to legend, was originally painted by Saint Luke.

The actual origin of the icon is inexplicable—perhaps miraculous. In 1822 a nun named Pelagia, during one of a number of visions, received an order from the Blessed Mother to tell the town officials where to dig to find a holy icon that had been buried many years previously. Our Lady described the abandoned field and asked that a church be built in her honor in the place where the icon was located.

Sister Pelagia eventually told her bishop about her visions. Knowing of an old man who had had similar visions, the bishop called the people of the island together and explained the Blessed Mother's request. Thus the excavations began, in September 1822.

This was a time of great difficulty for the Greek people, as the Greek War of Liberation against the Ottoman Empire had begun in 1821. Besides sending young men off to become soldiers, the people of Tínos were also caring for thousands of refugees. Everyone was busy; still, the islanders found the energy to search for the promised icon.

The excavations quickly turned up the foundations of a ruined church. But since further digging uncovered nothing else, the people became discouraged. Soon after the excavations stopped, an epidemic ravaged the island, killing many. When the bishop suggested an appeal to the Lady of Tínos for protection and a return to the search for the icon, the people assented.

The digging became more systematic. One month later, on January 30, 1823, someone struck a wooden object with his pickax. Ecstatically, the worker uncovered part of an icon showing an angel holding a lily. The diggers congregated around the spot and soon found the other part of the icon, which depicted the Virgin kneeling. The pieces were cleaned and joined and installed in a temporary shrine outside the new church of Panayía Evangelístria, which was being constructed simultaneously with the excavations.

Records indicate that the icon of Tínos had been installed in the Church of St. John the Precursor during the early years of Byzantium, but the style is much older. Some experts believe the icon to have been painted by Saint Luke. Its presence in Tínos is inexplicable. When the Saracens destroyed the Church of St. John in the tenth century, the icon was buried in the rubble, thus escaping total destruction. What is remarkable is that aside from being broken in two, after 850 years in the ground it was nearly undamaged.

The Megalokhari depicts the Annunciation. Both Mary and Gabriel are clothed in golden-yellow-green attire. Mary is kneeling, her head bent in prayer, while Gabriel holds the lily of purity. On a stand is a book, opened to the words of the Virgin's response to the angel's invitation.

The Megalokhari is known to have miraculous powers, and a number of cures have been documented. One case involved a man whose sight was restored. Another case was that of King Constantine, deathly ill in 1915, who asked to kiss the Megalokhari and immediately afterward began to get well. Indeed, the cures are so numerous that the shrine is often referred to as the Lourdes of Greece and still receives thousands of pilgrims annually who come to Tínos not only to pray for healing but also to deepen their relationship with their Blessed Mother.

ꙮ Traditional Prayer

O people of Tínos and all faithful, come and acclaim with hymns our Protectress; the all-venerable icon of the pure Mother of God is found to be a source of healing for us. Let us cry to her: Rejoice, O our glory and boast. Rejoice, thou who hast delivered humankind from the ancient curse. Amen.

ꙮ New Prayer

O most holy Megalokhari, is my day filled with annunciations of which I am unaware? Am I blind and deaf to God's call? Am I expecting God to speak in earth-quaking voices or blinding visions instead of through the words and actions of the people around me or the ordinary events of my day-to-day life? Open my heart to the possibility that God is inviting me to join in something unimaginably wonderful. Open my ears that I may hear and my mind that I may understand. And fill me with your grace, the grace of your *fiat*, that my soul might joyfully undertake whatever great or small thing God has planned for me. Amen.

—*Inspired by Denise Levertov's poem "Annunciation"*

ℬ Our Lady of Trsat
| QUEEN OF THE ADRIATIC |

HER STORY

*I*n the city of Rijeka, Croatia, about one hundred miles southwest of Zagreb, is the shrine of Our Lady of Trsat, also invoked as Queen of the Adriatic because of her proximity to that sea. According to legend, on May 10, 1291, angels moved Mary's home from Nazareth to Trsat. The Holy House remained there for three years until the night of December 12, 1294, when the dwelling disappeared. That night, shepherds near Recanati, Italy, observed a house moving across the sea and saw it settle on the land nearby. Then angels moved it again, to Loreto, Italy (page 119).

That same year, Count Nicola I (Frankopan) sent a delegation to Nazareth to investigate the transportation of the dwelling. In the early 1300s he had a chapel built on the site in Trsat where the Holy House was supposed to have rested. In 1367, to compensate the people of Croatia for their loss of the house, Pope Urban V presented the shrine with a miraculous painting of the Blessed Mother, which soon came to be known as Our Lady of Trsat.

Over the centuries this shrine has become a pilgrimage destination for Croats, Italians and other people from around the world. Hundreds of thousands now visit the icon annually, invoking the blessings and intercessions of Our Lady of Trsat, whose feast day is celebrated on May 10.

ᐍ TRADITIONAL PRAYER

O glorious Mother, Queen of the Adriatic, I come to you today as your child, as your devoted pilgrim. I kneel before you in your shrine with joy and gratitude for the gift of being here before your lovely image, so revered, so wonderful.

Mary, kind and gentle mother, I bring you today my heart, filled with love for your divine son, my spirit, filled with the hope of all Christians, and my mind, filled with desire for a deeper knowledge of my most loving Father.

When I consider those many pilgrims who have prayed here in your shrine, the many before me who have experienced your help and consolation, I feel much peace and joy.

Bless me, dear Mary, and bless and pray for all my dear ones and their intentions. Pray also for the intentions of those around me here in the shrine. Be to all of us, for all our lives, a source of love and consolation. Amen.

↬ NEW PRAYER

Dearest Lady of Trsat, I am afraid to trust in permanence, for so much of my life up to now has been conditional: relationships, jobs, homes, even church affiliations. So I ask you to inspire me with your spirit of trust, that I may begin to believe in permanence again. Teach me to trust in those blessings that are permanent: the commitment and support of my [spouse/partner], the joy of my [child/children/grand-children], the beauty of creation, the love of God. Help me participate wholly in these permanencies. Through you, O Lady of Permanence, I thank God for them.

But also bless my transiencies: my transient relationships, that they may honor all who are involved; my transient labors, that they may help others; my transient encounters, that they may reflect God's realm among us; my transient habitations, that they may offer a sanctuary of God's love. Help me participate wholly in these transiencies. Through you, O Lady of Transience, I thank God for them, too. Amen.

✍. *Our Lady of Vailankanni*
| OUR LADY OF GOOD HEALTH |

HER STORY

Our Lady of Vailankanni is the popular name of Our Lady of Good Health, who attracts Christian, Hindu and Muslim pilgrims from throughout India to this small town 150 miles south of Madras on the Bay of Bengal. The devotion dates from the sixteenth century and is based on three separate miracles attributed to the Blessed Mother.

The first miracle involved a shepherd boy who was carrying milk to his master's house in Nagapattinam. As he passed by a small pond, he stopped under a banyan tree to quench his thirst. Suddenly, a lady holding a child appeared. Awed by their beauty, the boy bowed reverently. When the lady then asked for some milk for her child, he gratified her request and noted the child's smile of pleasure. Rushing to his master, the shepherd enthusiastically related the reason for his delay and for the shortage of milk. But when the master found the pot filled to the brim, he went to the pond with the boy to prostrate himself on the ground where the lady had appeared. As the story spread throughout the neighborhood, the people became certain that Mary had been among them and so called the pond *Matha Kulam*, meaning "Our Lady's Pond."

A number of years later, a boy who was lame was selling buttermilk to passersby. One day he noticed standing before him a beautiful woman holding an exquisite child, both attired spotlessly. When the woman requested a cup of milk for her baby, the boy provided it instantly. Then the woman bid the boy go to Nagapattinam to tell a rich Catholic gentleman to build a chapel in her honor there beneath the banyan tree. Puzzled, the boy explained that he could not run her errand because he was lame. At that the woman told him to stand up and walk because he had been cured. Overjoyed, the boy raced to deliver the woman's message. Providentially, the gentleman had had a vision of our Lady the previous night, so he soon had a small thatched chapel built in Vailankanni and enshrined there a statue of our Lady holding the Christ child. As news of the boy's cure spread throughout the region, people came to the chapel to appeal to Mary. So many cures resulted that she became known as *Vailankanni Arokia Matha* (Our Lady of Health Vailankanni).

The statue itself depicts the Madonna and Child. Both are attired in gorgeous golden saris, and both are crowned. Our Lady holds her son in her left hand and a scepter in her right. She is shown standing on a crescent moon.

Years later, in the seventeenth century, a Portuguese merchant vessel was caught in a terrible storm in the Bay of Bengal. The sailors prayed for Mary's help, promising to build her a chapel wherever they might come ashore. When the sea calmed and the ship beached at Vailankanni, the sailors attributed their good fortune to Mary's intercession. To fulfill their vow they helped build a brick and mortar chapel in place of the thatched chapel already there. On subsequent voyages they furnished the chapel, which they dedicated to the nativity of our Lady, with rich decorations.

After 1660 devotion to Our Lady of Vailankanni spread slowly, limited mostly to the immediate region by the subcontinent's one hundred years of Dutch Reformed Protestant control and thereafter the centuries of British Anglican hegemony. But in 1933 a modern and spacious church replaced the Portuguese chapel, and in 1962 Pope John XXIII elevated the shrine to the rank of minor basilica, in recognition of Our Lady of Vailankanni's love for the people of India.

A number of shrines to our Lady have subsequently been established throughout the country, but millions of people come to Vailankanni annually to greet their heavenly mother. Next to the shrine, a Museum of Offerings filled with thousands of gold and silver gifts donated by grateful pilgrims attests to the miraculous healings that Our Lady of Vailankanni continues to obtain for her people.

Ꮽ Traditional Prayer

Dear Lady of Good Remedy, source of unfailing help, thy compassionate heart knows a remedy for every affliction and misery we encounter in life. Help me with thy prayers and intercession to find a remedy for my problems and needs, especially for *[mention request]*.

Dear Lady of Good Remedy, be ever present to me, and through thy intercession, may I enjoy health of body and peace of mind, and grow stronger in the faith and in the love of thy son, Jesus. Amen.

Ꮽ New Prayer

O Vailankanni Arokia Matha, when we pray for wellness or healing, do we expect that we must be fully healthy in order to do God's work on earth? Remind us that each of us has a purpose to fulfill in God's plan, no matter our individual capabilities or disabilities. Inspire in us the wisdom to perceive what we can do, and grant us the grace and courage to embrace our possibilities joyfully and lovingly. Amen.

ℬ Our Lady of Victory

Her Story

*P*ope Pius V first established the feast of Our Lady of Victory in 1571, in thanksgiving for the Christian armada's defeat of the Turkish fleet at the Battle of Lepanto on October 7 of that year, attributing the victory to Mary's intercession.

Just two years later, however, his successor, Pope Gregory XIII, moved the celebration to the first Sunday of October, renamed it the feast of the Holy Rosary, and allowed those churches with a rosary altar to observe the feast. When Christian forces defeated the Turks again on August 5, 1716, near Peterwaradin, Hungary, and liberated the island of Corcyra, Pope Clement XI extended the privilege of celebrating the feast of the Holy Rosary to the entire church. Pope Pius X moved the feast back to October 7. The name was changed in 1960 to the feast of the Blessed Virgin Mary of the Rosary and again in 1969 to the feast of Our Lady of the Rosary (page 165). It is now a mandatory memorial.

Despite the renamings, the church still honors Our Lady of Victory. The reason is threefold. First, by virtue of her immaculate conception, Mary was chosen of God as the only human being to "vanquish" fallen human nature: by the grace of God, she was all-holy and ever free of both original and personal sin; and as a virgin, she conceived and bore a child. Second, Mary was the mother of Christ, whose resurrection was a victory over death; thus, Mary is the mother of Victory. Third, Mary was the mother of Christ/Truth's victory over falsehood.

Churches throughout the world have retained the name Our Lady of Victory, and one of the most famous is Notre Dame des Victoires in Paris. And Christians still invoke the name in times of conflict or hardship because Our Lady of Victory is such a powerful intercessor on behalf of those who need her aid.

❧ TRADITIONAL PRAYER

Victorious Lady, you who have ever such powerful influence with your divine son, in conquering the hardest of hearts, intercede for those for whom we pray, that their hearts being softened by the rays of divine grace, they may return to the unity of the true faith, through Christ, our Lord. Amen.

❧ NEW PRAYER

O most powerful Lady of Victory, please ask Our Lord of Victory to strengthen my faith, for when the day's setbacks threaten to overwhelm me, I forget that Christ has already won the victory, and I fall into despair. Dearest Mother, catch me before I crash, and fill me with your faith in God's plan. Remind me to look beyond the failure of the moment to the life of eternity. Teach me to trust in God's providence, to believe that all will be well. Inspire me to hope again, that I may believe in Christ's ability to overcome all obstacles and bring to fruition God's design for my life. Amen.

🎬 Our Lady of Walsingham

*T*hough little known today, the shrine of Our Lady of Walsingham was once among the holiest places in the world, ranking as one of the four great shrines along with Rome, Jerusalem and Santiago de Compostela. It is the only one of the four dedicated to Our Lady.

Walsingham is a village in Norfolk, England, about one hundred miles northeast of London, and in 1061 a devout widow of the village, the noblewoman Richeldis de Faverches, prayed to discern how she might honor the Blessed Mother. One night, in a dream or vision or actual spiritual transportation, our Lady brought Richeldis to the Holy Land, to the house of the Annunciation. Providing the exact dimensions, Mary asked Richeldis to build a replica of this house in Walsingham. Richeldis experienced this apparition three times, thrice hearing Mary encourage, "Let all who are in any way distressed or in need seek me there in that small house that you maintain for me at Walsingham. To all that seek me there shall be given succor. The small house at Walsingham shall be a remembrance of the great joy of my Salvation, when Saint Gabriel the Archangel announced that I should become the Mother of God's Son through humility and obedience to his will."

Richeldis was unclear about where the carpenters should put the building. One night a heavy frost completely covered the ground except for two dry spots, which were both the exact dimensions of the house. The carpenters chose one spot but could not get the house to lie square on the foundation. Richeldis spent a night in prayer. The next morning, the carpenters found that the house had been moved to the alternate site, two hundred feet away. Moreover, it was completed with a skill surpassing theirs. They believed that angels had finished the work.

Pilgrims came from all over Christendom to honor the Blessed Mother at Walsingham. Pynson memorialized the shrine in a ballad circa 1470. Almost every English king visited the shrine, and it was said that even the Milky Way pointed to the house. Many miracles were reported, and the nearby spring was said to be curative.

For protection, a chapel was constructed above the house. A statue of our Lady eventually became part of the shrine. A mile away the Slipper Chapel was built for pilgrims who left their shoes to travel barefoot to the Holy House. Henry VIII himself made this barefoot journey, but probably in 1537 the king had the Holy House razed, the miraculous well filled with trash and the Walsingham martyrs executed. In 1538 the statue of Mary was burned. Devotions to Our Lady of Walsingham were outlawed.

In 1896 Charlotte Boyd, an Anglican who converted to Roman Catholicism, purchased and restored the Slipper Chapel, then donated it to the Roman Catholic Church. Simultaneously, Father George Wrigglesworth, a local priest, built a shrine to Our Lady of Walsingham in the new Roman Catholic Church of the Annunciation at King's Lynn, and in 1897 he organized the first Marian pilgrimage to the Slipper Chapel since the Reformation. The devotion was slow to catch on, and the Slipper Chapel became the National Roman Catholic Shrine to Our Lady of Walsingham in 1934.

In 1921, however, Alfred Hope-Patten had become Anglican vicar at Walsingham. He researched the village's history, had the statue of Our Lady of Walsingham reproduced and commissioned the reconstruction of the Holy House. During the reconstruction workers uncovered the foundations of the original shrine, along with the filled-in well. In 1938 the church in Walsingham was enlarged and proclaimed the Anglican Shrine of Our Lady of Walsingham.

Although English Roman Catholics had been allowed to practice their religion since 1829, relations between the Roman Catholic and Anglican shrines remained somewhat strained until the 1980s when Pope John Paul II celebrated Mass at Walsingham.

The reconstructed statues of Our Lady of Walsingham depict our Lady enthroned and crowned, with a lily scepter. The child Jesus is seated on her knee, and he is holding the Book of the Gospels. His right hand is stretched out in a gesture of blessing. The statue embodies the message of Walsingham, for as promised to Richeldis, our Lady and her son will bless all who seek her in the house of the Incarnation.

ᏨᏇ Traditional Prayer

Alone of all women, Mother and Virgin, Mother most blessed, Virgin most pure, we salute you, we honor you as best we can with our humble offerings. May your son grant us that by imitating your most holy manners, we also, by the grace of the Holy Spirit, may deserve to conceive the Lord Jesus spiritually in our inmost souls, and once conceived, never to lose him. Amen.

O Lady of Walsingham, denominational conflicts disturb me deeply because my background includes two Christian traditions. So I pray for your aid in overcoming religious divisions. Help me become a bearer of your message of welcome, that I also may extend my home's hospitality to people of all faiths. And teach me to be an example of religious tolerance, that others might learn not only to coexist but also to accept the truth and good inherent in other religious traditions. Amen.

꩜ Our Lady of Wambierzyce

Her Story

*I*n the southwestern corner of Poland is one of that nation's oldest places of pilgrimage, the shrine of Our Lady of Wambierzyce. Devotion to Our Lady of Wambierzyce dates from 1218, when, according to legend, a blind man miraculously recovered his sight after praying before a statue of the Blessed Mother placed in a hollow tree trunk by the side of the road. When news of the miracle became known, the people of the region built a small chapel at the site.

As the statue became well known for granting favors, a bigger church was built. This was replaced with a basilica in 1695. All except the Renaissance façade collapsed, so another basilica was constructed. This is the church now present in Wambierzyce. The basilica features a giant entry staircase of thirty-three steps, built in remembrance of Jesus' assumed age at the time of his death. Located outside are more than eighty stations depicting events in the lives of Mary and Jesus.

But the jewel is the miraculous statue of Our Lady of Wambierzyce, enshrined in a special chapel inside the basilica. To her the faithful come, imploring her intercession for physical and spiritual needs and bearing gifts of thanksgiving for graces received.

꩜ Traditional Prayer

O generous and merciful Mother of God and all people, you have been honored for ages in Wambierzyce shrine! Trustfully looking at your image known for numerous graces, we beseech you to lovingly protect the pope and the entire church with your maternal care. Protect the world from wars, bless our nation and defend it from disasters and kindle faith and love in our families. Obtain the grace of conversion for sinners, health for the sick and joy for the sad. Show the right path to the young, and pray for the grace of numerous vocations to the priesthood and consecrated life. Child of God, carried at the hands of the most holy Mother Mary, have mercy on us and bless us. Amen.

ᴐᴠ New Prayer

Dear Lady of Wambierzyce, I come before you in desperation, for I am in need of healing *[mention request]*. Hear me in my exigency, I implore you, and be my Advocate before your son, securing from him for me all that I ask in your name. Amen.

Our Lady of Zhyrovytsi

Her Story

According to legend, at the end of the fifteenth century, outside the tiny village of Zhyrovytsi, in northeastern Ukraine, four shepherd boys were tending their flocks when they saw brilliant rays of light proceeding from a wild pear tree. When they approached, they found a beautiful icon of the Madonna in the tree's branches. They removed it and entrusted it to their landlord, who was a relative of the archbishop-metropolitan of Kiev.

The landlord locked the icon in a wooden chest for safekeeping. When he opened the chest the next day, the icon was gone. At the same time, the shepherd boys noticed that the painting had reappeared in the pear tree. The local religious authorities interpreted these events as meaning that the Blessed Mother wished to remain on that spot, so there they built a church to enshrine the icon, which became known as Our Lady of Zhyrovytsi.

The icon is of the Virgin of Tenderness type (page 200), depicting the Madonna and Child in a loving embrace. Our Lady wears a red gown covered by a blue tunic, and the infant Jesus wears a white robe. Both are wearing golden crowns with a cross on top. The Greek letters for "Jesus Christ" and "Mary, Mother of God" appear beside the figures.

The icon's fame spread throughout the region and even reached Rome, where Our Lady of Zhyrovytsi was venerated in the Church of

Sts. Sergius and Bacchus, which was assigned to the metropolitan of Kiev in 1639. In 1718, to everyone's surprise, some workers discovered an icon embedded in the plaster in one of that church's walls. The icon was recognized as that of Our Lady of Zhyrovytsi, but its discovery in Rome has remained a mystery to this day.

Devotion to Our Lady of Zhyrovytsi has spread even to the United States, and a shrine has been established in Olyphant, Pennsylvania, on the grounds of Sts. Cyril and Methodius Ukrainian Catholic Church. There, as well as in all the places where she is venerated, pilgrims appeal to Our Lady of Zhyrovytsi for her loving intercession and miraculous cures.

◌ TRADITIONAL PRAYER

Hail, O blessed Virgin Mary, Mother of God, who deigned to appear to a group of poor shepherd boys in the form of an icon in a pear tree in Zhyrovytsi. Most holy Immaculate Virgin, Our Lady of Zhyrovytsi, who art the mother of my Lord, the Queen of Heaven and Earth, Mother of divine grace, Virgin most merciful, to you I come both sinful and sorrowful. To you I render humble homage and thanks, O Mother most admirable. I promise to serve you always and do all in my power to make others love you.

I place in you all my hope; I confide my salvation to your care. Through intercession with your divine son enlighten my mind, purify my heart and fill my soul with the graces I stand in most need of now. Accept me for your servant, and protect me under your blue mantle, O Mother of Mercy. I humbly beseech you, O Mother most powerful, to obtain for me the graces and favors I now seek, if they be beneficial to my immortal soul, and the souls for whom I pray [mention request]. By your power obtain for me the strength of will to resist all temptations until death. Dear Lady of Zhyrovytsi, by the love which you did bear to God, I beseech you always to help me, especially at the hour of my death. Do not abandon me, I implore you, until you see me safe in heaven, blessing you and singing your praises for all eternity. Amen.

◌ NEW PRAYER

Dearest Lady of Zhyrovytsi, I must admit that these stories of heavenly appearances and miraculous images really test my credulity. But there must be a truth in the inexplicable, some message you wish to convey, some lesson I must learn. So I ask you to teach me to look beyond the incredible details of the legends and perceive the transcendent meaning. Make yourself known to me in my doubting, that I might come to trust in your power as Advocate, to seek your assistance as Mediatrix and to believe in your role as Co-redemptrix. Amen.

 Panagia
|"The All-Holy"|

Her Story

*T*he fathers of the Eastern tradition called Mary *Panagia*, the All-Holy, celebrating her as free from all sin, and this recognition has spread throughout the church. The understanding of Mary as all-holy is founded on the idea of her complete sanctity, a concept so important that Saint Thomas Aquinas, the Universal Teacher, systematically clarified how Mary came to be Panagia: Since God chose Mary as Jesus' mother, God doubtless made her worthy of that role. No one who had sinned would have been worthy to be Mother of God (page 44); thus, God kept Mary free from all personal sin. Because she is the only human so graced, she is the All-Holy.

Panagia is a favorite title for the Blessed Mother among Eastern Catholics, who venerate her as All-Holy in many famous icons. The Kiev Panagia, for example, depicts her with arms upraised in an attitude of praise or supplication, while the child Jesus rests in a roundel within her breast, to symbolize his presence in her womb. This particular icon signifies her position as intercessor. Indeed, the title Panagia implies Advocate (page 2), for her position as the only all-holy human places her directly between God and humankind. While Catholics believe that all the saints can advocate before the Lord, the understanding of the Blessed Mother as Panagia has made her the most popular intercessor of all.

❦ Traditional Prayer

> I supplicate you, Lady,
> now do I call upon you,
> And I beseech you, Queen of all.
> I beg of you your favor,
> Majestic maiden, spotless one,

O Lady Panagia.
I call upon you fervently,
O sacred, hallowed temple,
Assist me and deliver me
protect me from the enemy
And make me an inheritor
of blessed life eternal.

—*Saint Nectarios of Aigina, "O Virgin Pure"*

❧ NEW PRAYER

O Panagia, sometimes the shadows of the valley of death invade my soul and I can no longer see beyond myself. I lose all connectedness—I even lose God. The isolation paralyzes me, freezes my thoughts and feelings inside. I can't even pray because I don't know where—or if—God is. When my soul feels this petrifying isolation, please intercede for me, praying for me the prayers that are bound within. O dearest Mother, you know my needs and you understand the desires of my heart: please express them for me to God. Be my Advocate in the dark times, asking your son, the Light of the World, to dispel all shadows from my soul and reconnect me with his love. Amen.

🕮 *Queen of All Saints*

HER STORY

From the earliest days of the church, Christians have believed in Mary's sainthood, and the fact that her story is part of the canon of Scripture was held to constitute the ultimate form of canonization. Three additional considerations have supported belief in the saintliness of her life.

First, she was believed to have suffered a living martyrdom. During the time of the Roman persecutions, martyrdom and local veneration were sufficient for including someone in the canon of saints. Mary's widespread acclaim as Queen of Martyrs (page 186) meant that she was also considered a saint.

Second, she was believed ever-virgin (page 17). After the Roman persecutions, virginity—a complete self-dedication to Christ— became the new ideal of sanctity. According to Scripture, Mary remained a virgin though she was mother of Jesus, and belief in her ever-virginity became widespread.

Third, people of great wisdom and insight into the mysteries of Christianity were venerated as saints. Mary's intimate knowledge of God's will and her intimate association with Christ, the revealed Truth, have made her the Seat of Wisdom (page 195), the greatest human repository of understanding. If the title were to be conferred, she would be known as the greatest doctor of the church.

Mary is considered to possess these qualities of sainthood in superlative measure. As the foremost of all saints, she has inspired the people of God to strive to lead holy lives.

Mary also fulfills the role of queen by raising other souls to saint-hood. Many other saints have appealed to her for sanctity. Saint Thérèse of Lisieux, for example, prayed to Our Lady of Victory (page 175) for the grace to become a saint.

What the Queen of All Saints did for Saint Thérèse, who considered herself "little" and insignificant, she can do for anyone. All that is necessary is to approach her with ardor, humility, simplicity and faith.

ᐁ TRADITIONAL PRAYER

O most exalted creature in the world!...Since there is no one but God above thee, so that compared with thee the greatest saints of heaven are little; O Saint of Saints, O Mary! Abyss of charity, and full of grace, succor a miserable creature who by his own fault has lost the divine favor. I know that thou art so dear to God that He denies thee nothing. I know also that thy pleasure is to use thy greatness for the relief of miserable sinners. Ah, then, show how great is the favor that thou enjoyest with God, by obtaining for me a divine light and flame so powerful that I may be changed from a sinner into a saint; and detaching myself from every earthly affection, divine love may be enkindled in me. Do this, O Lady, for thou canst do it. Do it for the love of God, who has made thee so great, so powerful and so compassionate. This is my hope. Amen.

—*Saint Alphonsus de' Liguori,* The Glories of Mary, *II*

ᐁ NEW PRAYER

Holy Queen, Mother of All Saints, what other calling is there but to be a saint? But what does that mean? Inspire me to learn, that I may understand God's will for me. And in becoming the person God created me to be, to become a saint and to serve as encouragement to others. Amen.

𝕭 Queen of Apostles

HER STORY

𝕿he roots of this title are biblical, based on the Acts of the Apostles' account of the assembly of the disciples in the Upper Room:

> When they had entered the city, they went to the room upstairs where they were staying, Peter, and John, and James, and Andrew, Philip and Thomas, Bartholomew and Matthew, James son of Alphaeus, and Simon the Zealot, and Judas son of James. All these were constantly devoting themselves to prayer, together with certain women, including Mary the mother of Jesus, as well as his brothers. (1:13–14)

The Blessed Mother's presence among the disciples after the Ascension is an indication of her preeminent role as first and chief disciple of Christ. From Gabriel, Mary was the first to know of Christ's coming into the world. With her *fiat* she was the first to believe in the fulfillment of the divine promise. And with her request to Jesus during the wedding at Cana, she was the first to proclaim his saving presence to the rest of the world.

The title Queen of Apostles appeared in the oldest version of the Litany of Loreto (page 119), that of Paris at the end of the twelfth century. The feast of our Lady as Queen of Apostles, May 17, was approved in 1890. Many congregations with missionary and apostolic orientations, including the Salvatorians, Claretians and Pallotines, venerate Mary under this title.

Having brought forth the Light of the World, Mary leads every person to her son, but as Queen of Apostles, she leads the apostles and all who proclaim Christ resurrected in announcing Christ's redemption to the world.

∾ TRADITIONAL PRAYER

Mother Mary, lead me to the grotto of Bethlehem, so that I may indulge in the contemplation of the great and sublime event that is about to take place in the silence of the greatest and most beautiful night that the world has ever seen.

—*Padre Pio*, Time of Birth

Most holy Queen of Apostles, many of us do not feel called to go door to door proclaiming Christ, though it is perhaps the most direct way to introduce people to the Lord. But in our time, is it the most effective? Support us rather in living our day-to-day lives in happiness and truth, that our outward demeanor and inner peace in the Lord may attract others to seek us out. And then give us the courage of our convictions and the wisdom to explain the source of our joy, our relationship with the resurrected Christ. Amen.

Queen of Martyrs

Her Story

This passage from the Gospel of Luke's account of the presentation of Jesus in the Temple indicates that the very earliest Christians identified Mary as a martyr: "Then Simeon blessed them and said to his mother Mary, 'This child is destined for the falling and the rising of many in Israel, and to be a sign that will be opposed so that the inner thoughts of so many will be revealed—and a sword will pierce your own soul too'" (2:34–35). Though, as some would believe, Mary may have experienced a painless childbirth, her life was destined for martyrdom from the very beginning.

Perhaps the best explication of Mary's martyrdom is found in *The Glories of Mary* by Saint Alphonsus de' Liguori. Mary did not die to witness to the faith as other martyrs did, but Alphonsus held that "suffering sufficient to cause death is martyrdom, even though death does not ensue from it." And he drew from the prayerful meditations of other saints to prove that Mary endured such suffering. Saint Bernard (1090–1153), for example, said, "Mary was a martyr not by the sword of the executioner, but by bitter sorrow of heart." Saint Anselm (c. 1033–1109), for another, asserted that had not God miraculously preserved Mary's life, her grief at Jesus' Passion would have caused her death, not once, but a thousand times.

Alphonsus insisted that Mary's martyrdom was longer than that of all other martyrs; indeed, her entire life may be seen as a prolonged dying. Enlightened by the Spirit, she understood her son's destiny from the moment of the Annunciation. And time would not mitigate her sorrow at the thought of losing her beloved son, for the older

Jesus grew, the closer was the moment of his death. So Mary's grief was always increasing.

Alphonsus maintained that Mary's martyrdom was also the greatest of all because she endured hers in her soul while other martyrs suffer principally in the body. He quoted Saint Antoninus (1389–1459), who wrote that the Blessed Mother herself suffered all the tortures of her son's innocent flesh. As Saint Lawrence Justiniani (1381–1456) explained, "The heart of Mary became, as it were, a mirror of the Passion of the Son, in which might be seen, faithfully reflected, the spitting, the blows and wounds, and all that Jesus suffered." Saint Bonaventure (1221–1274) added, "Those wounds—which were scattered over the body of our Lord—were all united in the single heart of Mary."

Finally, Alphonsus continued, Mary suffered without the least alleviation. The martyrs' love of Jesus turned their pain to sweetness, but Mary's love of Jesus was the very cause of her grief. The greater her love for him, the more bitter and inconsolable her sorrow.

As Saint Anselm summarized, "The most cruel tortures inflicted on the holy martyrs were trifling, or as nothing in comparison with the martyrdom of Mary."

Her sufferings having exceeded those of all the martyrs, Mary, Queen of Martyrs, has served as an example and inspiration to all people who have faced martyrdom since the earliest days of Christianity.

ᴄᴡ TRADITIONAL PRAYER

Mary, most holy Virgin and Queen of Martyrs, accept the sincere homage of my filial affection. Into thy heart, pierced by so many swords, do thou welcome my poor soul. Receive it as the companion of thy sorrows at the foot of the Cross, on which Jesus died for the redemption of the world. With thee, O sorrowful Virgin, I will gladly suffer all the trials, contradictions and infirmities which it shall please our Lord to send me. I offer them all to thee in memory of thy sorrows, so that every thought of my mind, and every beat of my heart may be an act of compassion and of love for thee. And do thou, sweet Mother, have pity on me, reconcile me to thy divine Son Jesus, keep me in His grace and assist me in my last agony, so that I may be able to meet thee in heaven and sing thy glories. Amen.

—*The Raccolta*

Holy Queen, it's hard to imagine wanting to be a martyr. But sometimes the Lord's call to martyrdom is irresistible. So I ask you, when God calls me to bear witness to what I believe in, stand with me so that I may heed the call. Encourage me to act and speak in such a manner that I bear honor to the truth as I know it. Inspire me to respond with love to those who criticize or ridicule, even to those who inflict harm or torture. And protect me from fear, that I may strive for the ultimate good of all people. Amen.

🐝 Queen of Peace

HER STORY

Our Lady is known as Queen of Peace because she is the mother of Jesus, the Prince of Peace. The scriptural foundation for his title is extensive. During his ministry Jesus often explained his purpose to his disciples: "Peace I leave with you; my peace I give to you" (John 14:27); "I have said this to you, so that in me you may have peace" (John 16:33). He would not have been able to give peace without being master of it himself. And when Jesus appeared to his disciples after his resurrection, his first words of greeting were words that emphasized this authority: "Peace be with you" (Luke 24:36 and John 20:21)—as if to say, "Be at peace, for I, peace, am here with you still."

Because Mary is Queen of Peace, in every war and conflict she has made the grace of peace available in abundance. A remarkable example comes from El Salvador, where in 1682 some merchants found a box abandoned on the beach. Unable to open it, they tied it on a donkey's back and brought it to the city. When they passed by the church in San Miguel, the donkey stopped, and the men were able to open the box. Inside was a statue of the Madonna and Child. At that time the region was experiencing civil warfare, but when the combatants heard about the statue, they abandoned their weapons and made peace. The statue again brought peace to this region in 1833 and, consequently, was named Our Lady of Peace.

Surprisingly, it was not until World War I that the title Queen of Peace was officially recognized, when Pope Benedict XV inserted it into the Litany of Loreto (page 119) as a plea for peace among nations. He also issued a pastoral letter asking people to petition Mary for peace. Almost immediately, on May 13, Our Lady appeared to three children at Fátima (page 91) and during her third apparition promised that she would bring peace soon and end the current war if the faithful would do penance and pray the rosary. But she also predicted that the hardness of people's hearts would cause a greater war to begin not long thereafter. Her predictions proved true.

During Mary's more recent apparitions at Medjugorje (page 127), she has introduced herself as the Queen of Peace, and peace has been one of her constant themes. On June 26, 1981, for example, she said, "Peace, Peace, Peace! Be reconciled! Only Peace. Make your peace with God among yourselves." Through her messages to the children of Bosnia, she has invited the world to peace in four ways: peace in human hearts through reconciliation with God, peace in human families through God-centered living, peace in human communities through forgiveness and peace in the world through union with God.

The world has yet to embrace Mary's message of peace, but the Queen of Peace has shown that she will never give up on her children, hoping that humankind will finally accept her gifts of reconciliation, forgiveness and peace.

ᘒ Traditional Prayer

Most loving Mother, you who by your motherhood earned a share in your divine son's kingship, we, your devoted children, are comforted by the thought that our redeemer was proclaimed by the prophets and by the angels at Bethlehem as King of Peace. Thus, it must be pleasing and acceptable to you to hear yourself greeted as Queen of Peace, a title that comes from the very depths of our being.

May your powerful intercession keep your people from hatred and discord and turn their hearts into the ways of peace and brotherhood, which Jesus came to teach and establish for the prosperity and safety of all.

Glorious Queen, be pleased to crown with success the fatherly care with which the supreme pontiff, vicar on earth of your divine son, strives to bring nations together and keep them united around the one and only center, the living Father. Enlighten us and our leaders so that we may not thwart his saving purposes. Revive and maintain harmony in our families, peace in our hearts and charity throughout the world. Amen.

O Queen of Peace, war still fractures our world, still tears societies apart, still sets neighbor against neighbor. Even more prevalent and destructive is the strife within families that sets spouse against spouse, sister against brother, parent against child. Send the grace of your peace into these conflicts, dear Lady, that people may let go of their hate and embrace love, that people may finally let go of their righteousness and embrace the need for relationship. As we know so well that we cannot have peace in the world until we have peace in our hearts, bless each of us with the personal gift of your peace, that we may rest tranquilly and trust completely in the knowledge of God's love for each of us, a love that knows no bounds, that in its infiniteness embraces each of us equally and completely, that has room for all of us no matter our differences. Amen.

🦚 Queen of Prophets

HER STORY

*L*ike many girls of her time, Mary was probably named for Moses' sister, Miriam, one of the great prophets. Many Christians don't realize that Mary was also a prophet—indeed, the first among prophets. Though the Israelite prophets had been predicting the coming of a messiah for many centuries, Mary was the greatest of these because she could and did proclaim that her own pregnancy fulfilled the prophecies.

Her prophetic words, which have come to be known as the Canticle of Mary or the Magnificat, appear in the Gospel of Luke (1:46–55), spoken upon her visit to her cousin Elizabeth. In her song of praise Mary proclaimed that through her son, still to be born, God would scatter the proud, bring down the powerful, lift up the lowly, feed the hungry, turn the rich away and fulfill all the promises made to Abraham and his descendants. She revealed the wonderful work that Christ would accomplish for and through the mystical body of the church.

Mary would witness in her son's life the fulfillment of all that she and the other prophets had foretold. But she was not just a witness; she was also the instrument leading to the prophecies' fulfillment. She understood this distinction and even foretold the honor that would consequently accrue to herself: "Surely, from now on all generations will call me blessed; for the Mighty One has done great things for me" (Luke 1:48–49). What she prophesied certainly came to be, for all generations since have called her Blessed Mother (page 6) and have honored her gift of prophecy by acclaiming her Queen of Prophets.

◌ TRADITIONAL PRAYER

Queen of Prophets, help me to imitate the prophets and your own example. They never sought the world with its pleasures, but God alone. They were willing to suffer for him in their zeal to save souls. Teach me to be zealous for the honor of God and for the salvation of my soul and that of my neighbor. Help me to realize that the most divine of all divine things is to labor with God for the salvation of souls. Amen.

◌ NEW PRAYER

Most holy Queen of Prophets, I worry so much about what the future has in store for me that it might be comforting to have your gift of insight. But I don't ask for that gift. Rather, gift me with your trust that divine providence will care for all my needs. Give me a share in your faith that all will be well. Inspire me with your hope that God will answer the true desires of my heart. And help me believe in a future filled with the glory of God. Amen.

🦋 Queen of the Universe

HER STORY

The concept of Mary's queenship has a strong foundation in Scripture, for as Christ is referred to as King in the Gospel of Luke (1:32 and 1:43), so his mother is logically accorded the title Queen. And the titles referring to the Blessed Mother's queenship are numerous: Queen of All Hearts, Queen of All Nature, Queen of All Saints (page 183), Queen of Angels, Queen of Apostles (page 185), Queen of an Army of Virgins, Queen of the Church, Queen of Confessors, Queen of Families, Queen of Heaven (Paradise), Queen of the Holy Rosary, Queen of Martyrs (page 186), Queen of Patriarchs, Queen of Peace (page 188), Queen of Prophets (page 190), and Queen of Purgatory, as well as Queen of innumerable countries and peoples (for example, Ireland, Poland, Vietnam).

However, the one title of queenship that encompasses all the others is Queen of the Universe, and this title, too, has a scriptural foundation in the book of Revelation:

> A great portent appeared in heaven: a woman clothed with the sun, with the moon under her feet, and on her head a *crown* of twelve stars. (12:1; emphasis added)
>
> And she gave birth to a son, a male child, who is to *rule* all the nations with a rod of iron. But her child was snatched away and taken to God and to his *throne*....(12:5; emphasis added)
>
> "...they will make war on the Lamb, and the Lamb will conquer them, for he is Lord of lords and *King of kings*, and those with him are called and chosen and faithful." (17:14; emphasis added)
>
> On his robe and on his thigh he has a name inscribed, "*King of kings* and Lord of lords." (19:16; emphasis added)

While the emphasis is on the kingship of the Lord Jesus Christ, it is clear that his distinction as king accords his mother her recognition as queen. Over the centuries the church fathers and mothers and theologians have made many references to Mary's queenship. Saint Alphonsus de' Liguori, for example, wrote, "We may thank our most loving Queen for all, since all comes to us from her hands and by her powerful intercession" (*The Glories of Mary*, II). The Litany of Loreto (page 119) invokes the intercession of Mary as queen nine times, and based on Revelation 12, the final mystery of the rosary is a meditation on the coronation of the Blessed Virgin Mary—her crowning as queen. The concept has become so generally accepted that Pope Pius XII instituted the liturgical feast of the Queenship of Mary in 1954, issuing that same year an encyclical about Mary's queenship, *Ad Coeli Reginam*.

Mary's queenship is one of love and service, in which she gives of herself for the good of humankind. Indeed, she gave her son, accepting his sacrifice for the salvation of all of creation. For this gift—the ultimate gift a mother can bestow—God has crowned her Queen of the Universe.

❧ TRADITIONAL PRAYER

Queen of heaven, rejoice, alleluia.
For he whom you merited to bear, alleluia.

Has risen as he said, alleluia.
Pray for us to God, alleluia.
Rejoice and be glad, O Virgin Mary, alleluia.
Because the Lord is truly risen, alleluia.

—*Regina Coeli*

ᘏ NEW PRAYER

We praise you, Holy Mary, Queen of the Universe, for your wonderful gift of intercession on our behalf.

> Queen of All Hearts, we thank you.
> Queen of All Nature, we thank you.
> Queen of All Saints, we thank you.
> Queen of Angels, we thank you.
> Queen of Apostles, we thank you.
> Queen of an Army of Virgins, we thank you.
> Queen of the Church, we thank you.
> Queen of Confessors, we thank you.
> Queen of Families, we thank you.
> Queen of Heaven, we thank you.
> Queen of the Holy Rosary, we thank you.
> Queen of Martyrs, we thank you.
> Queen of Peace, we thank you.
> Queen of Patriarchs, we thank you.
> Queen of Prophets, we thank you.
> Queen of Purgatory, we thank you.
> Queen of the Universe, we thank you.

O Queen of Our Hearts, we thank you for your maternal concern for us, your devoted children. Pray for us, that we may always seek to do God's will. Amen.

ᘏ Refuge of Sinners

HER STORY

The reference to Mary as Refuge of Sinners is related to her identity as Mother of Mercy (page 49). Those who have sinned must throw themselves on the mercy of the Lord of Mercy, yet they also fly to Mary, Mother of Mercy, so that she may advocate for them with the

Lord. She herself also shows mercy to sinners by carrying their appeals forward. Thus she has become known as the Refuge of Sinners, gathering all who have sinned to herself so that she might speak on their behalf.

The tradition is as ancient as the Sub tuum praesidium, one of the oldest prayers of Marian intercession, which reads in part, "Under your mercy, O holy Mother of God, we take refuge." And throughout the ages, saints and popes have confirmed what the voice of the people has spoken: that Mary is a sure refuge in all circumstances, but she particularly welcomes those who have done wrong and carries them back to Jesus.

This title is somewhat controversial because many Christians would say that Jesus is the only refuge of sinners, that appealing to Mary as such erroneously and dangerously places her on the same level as her son. But Mary's role as Refuge of Sinners is only that of Advocate (page 2). Loving and merciful as she might be, she herself cannot grant remission of sins. Only Jesus can do that. But when asked, she appeals to his sacred heart on behalf of sinners in order to obtain his mercy. For that Christians honor and praise her.

❧ Traditional Prayer

O Mary, Mother of God, as you are above all creatures in heaven and on earth, more glorious than the cherubim, more noble than any here below, Christ has given you to his people, firm bulwark and protectress, to shield and save sinners who fly to you. Therefore, O Lady, all-embracing refuge, we solemnly recall your sweet protection and beg the Christ forever for his mercy. Amen.

❧ New Prayer

O holy Mother, Refuge of Sinners, my wrongs weigh heavily on my soul, for I have not treated others well at all. Grant me the refuge of your loving-kindness, and let me unburden myself to you, for you are my loving mother and will not refuse to hear me. Not only have I been impatient, intolerant and irritable with my loved ones, I have tested and angered them. I have pushed them away and have not allowed them to love me. And I fear I have done the same with your son.

O Refuge of Sinners, hear me in my remorse. Fill me with your loving spirit, that I may put aside my negativity and begin to love again. Support me as I attempt to reconnect with my loved ones whom I have wronged. Teach me how to love them in positive, affirming ways, and help me learn from them the joy of loving intimacy. Finally, carry my repentance to your son, helping me dare to reestablish a holy relationship with him, too. Amen.

Seat of Wisdom
| SEDES SAPIENTIAE; OUR LADY OF THE CHAIR |

HER STORY

Seat of Wisdom, or *Sedes Sapientiae*, is one of the oldest of the Blessed Mother's mystical titles. Our Lady Seat of Wisdom, also known as Our Lady of the Chair, is a representation of the enthroned Madonna—that is, though seated on a throne as if to receive honor herself, she is rather presenting the Christ child to the world so that all can honor him. And this she did in actual fact by carrying him in her womb and bringing him forth into the world.

The earliest Christians understood Christ to be incarnate Wisdom, and Saint Paul calls Christ "the wisdom of God" in 1 Corinthians (1:24). Thus, as the mother of Jesus, Mary herself became the throne, or seat, of wisdom.

∾ TRADITIONAL PRAYER

Most amiable Queen of heaven and earth, favored Daughter of the Father, sublime Mother of the divine Son, illustrious Spouse of the Holy Spirit, I venerate and praise that privilege, unique in the world, whereby—pleasing God in your humility and faith, and preserving your spotless virginity—you became the great Mother of the divine Savior, our Master, true Light of the world, uncreated Wisdom, Source of all truth and first Apostle of truth. You gave the world the book to read: the eternal Word. For the ineffable joy you felt and for that privilege so sublime, I bless the august Trinity and I ask you to obtain for me the grace of heavenly wisdom, to be a humble and fervent disciple of Jesus, a devoted child of the Church, the pillar of truth. Make the light of the Gospel shine to the farthest bounds of the earth, overcome errors, gather everyone around the See of Peter. Enlighten doctors, preachers, and writers, O Mother of Good Counsel, Seat of Wisdom, Queen of All Saints. Amen.

O Sedes Sapientiae, I exclaim with elation to thank you for birthing Wisdom. O holy Seat of Wisdom, I sing with joy to thank you for mothering Wisdom. O most blessed Lady of the Chair, I raise my voice with gladness to thank you for sharing Wisdom with all of your children, for giving Christ to the world, for teaching Jesus the ways of humankind so that he might teach us the ways of God. O holy Madonna, I thank you. Amen.

ᘄ Star of the Ocean (Sea)

HER STORY

*T*he origins of this title, one that displays Mary's loving concern for her children, are indistinct. Perhaps it comes from 1 Kings 18:41–45: After having shown the falseness of the prophets of Baal, Elijah sent his servant to the crest of Mount Carmel to look for the cloud that would bring the drought-ending rains; the little cloud, no bigger than a hand, is seen to be a symbol for Mary, the "star of the sea," and thus the sign of hope announcing renewal. The Carmelites built a church on Mount Carmel, calling it Stella Maris.

The use of the name Stella Maris is attributed to Saint Jerome (c. 342–420), but he called Mary *Stilla Maris,* meaning "a drop of the ocean"; perhaps a copyist mistranscribed the phrase.

Saint Paschasius Radbertus (c. 785–c. 860), French Benedictine abbot and theologian, used this title for Mary in his writing: "Mary Star of the Sea must be followed in faith and morals lest we capsize amidst the storm-tossed waves of the sea. She will illumine us to believe in Christ born of her for the salvation of the world." Archbishop Hincmar of Reims (c. 806–882) wrote of Mary as "a star of the sea assumed into the heavens." Two ancient Marian hymns refer to Mary by this title: "Ave Maria Stella" (eighth–ninth century) and Herman of Reschenau's "Alma Redemptoris Mater" (eleventh century).

Perhaps the most important use of this title comes from a prayer by Saint Bernard of Clairvaux (1090–1153), who was renowned for his mystical relationship with the Virgin Mary and his treatises on Mariology:

If the winds of temptation arise;
If you are driven upon the rocks of tribulation,
Look to the star, call on Mary;
If you are tossed upon the waves of pride, of ambition,
    of envy, of rivalry,
Look to the star, call on Mary.

∞ TRADITIONAL PRAYER

Hail thou star of ocean,
God's own mother blest,
Ever sinless Virgin,
Gate of heavenly rest.

Oh! by Gabriel's Ave,
Uttered long ago,
Eva's name reversing,
'Stablish peace below.

Break the captive's fetters,
Light on blindness pour;
All our ills expelling,
Every bliss implore.

Show thyself a Mother;
May the Word divine,
Born for us thine Infant,
Hear our prayers through thine.

Virgin all excelling,
Mildest of the mild;
Freed from guilt preserve us
Meek and undefiled.

Keep our life all spotless,
Make our way secure,
Till we find in Jesus,
Joy for evermore.

Through the highest Heaven
To the almighty Three,
Father, Son and Spirit,
One same glory be. Amen.

—*The Raccolta*

Holy Mother, you show your loving concern for your children at all times, in all places. And you lovingly deign to speak our particular and peculiar languages. So with confidence I approach you, our Star of the Ocean, and speak to you in the language of the sea and of seafarers:

Ahoy, Mary, Star of the Ocean, pray for all who go down to the sea in ships, whether they be merchants or fishers, naval personnel or recreational sailors; bless them with fair winds and following seas, and watch over their passage, guiding them safely back to port, to home and loved ones. Be their bright star of hope during the dark nights and the storm-tossed days. And by your light remind them that God loves them dearly, that they are precious in God's sight.

Ahoy, Mary, Star of the Ocean, pray for me also. Though I may not set forth across the waves, I nevertheless encounter tempestuous days and stormy nights during my earthly voyage. Be my beacon of hope when all seems hopeless. Remind me of the calm that follows the storm and of the dawn that follows the darkness. Illuminate the truths that I must embrace.

Ahoy, Mary, Star of the Ocean, my protection, my guide, ask your son to quiet the storms of my turmoil, as he stilled the stormy Sea of Galilee. And send him across the waters to me in my distress, that he may bring me to my safe haven and, once there, calm my anxiety with his boundless love.

O Stella Maris, star of the ocean of my life, pray for me now and always. Amen.

Theotokos
|"GOD-BEARER"|

HER STORY

*I*n the Russian Orthodox tradition, the Blessed Mother is known under three titles—*Theotokos* (Mother of God), *Aeiparthenos* (Ever-Virgin, page 17) and *Panagia* (All-Holy, page 182). The Orthodox Church proclaims these titles as a way of explaining the correct doctrine of the Incarnation, the conjoining of the divine and the human in Jesus Christ.

But the title Theotokos predates the East-West split, having been used by the Greek fathers from Origen, or perhaps Hippolytus, onward. The word *theotokos* derives from the Greek *theos*, which means "God," and *tiktein*, which means "to give birth." Thus Mary, as Theotokos, is the one who birthed or bore God into the world.

In the early fifth century Nestorius and his supporters attacked the title because they thought it incompatible with their understanding of the nature of Christ. So they proclaimed Mary *Christotokos*, meaning "Christ-bearer." But following the guidance of Saint Cyril of Alexandria, the Council of Ephesus in 431 rejected Nestorianism and sanctioned Theotokos. As the council explained, since Jesus, Mary's son born according to the flesh, is truly one of the divine persons of the Trinity, the title Theotokos affirms that God entered history, that Jesus was really "God is with us" (Matthew 1:23). So the council declared that Mary was truly Mother of God (page 44). The Council of Chalcedon in 451 referred to Theotokos in defining the hypostatic union (the substantial union of the divine and human natures in the one being ["hypostasis"] of Jesus Christ).

In the Orthodox icon of the Theotokos, Mary is shown holding the Christ in such a way that his body is completely contained within hers. Around them are seraphim, whose duty is to love and adore God; on either side of the throne are griffins, creatures that symbolize Christ the Savior. The entire depiction emphasizes Mary's role as God-Bearer.

❧ TRADITIONAL PRAYER

It is truly right to bless you, O *Theotokos*, ever blessed and most pure, and the Mother of our God. More honorable than the cherubim, and beyond compare more glorious than the seraphim, without defilement you gave birth to God the Word. True *Theotokos*, we magnify you.

—*Divine Liturgy of Saint John Chrysostom*

❧ NEW PRAYER

O Theotokos, I am often overcome by human limitations. My words seem to mutilate my thoughts. My expressions seem to disguise my feelings. My actions seem to contradict my very best intentions.

Grant me your strength of belief, that I may come to trust the power of God to do all things in me, even those that seem impossible to my very imagination. Infuse me with your faith, that I may come to believe God can help me transcend human fears and worries, human anger and vindictiveness, human sadness and suffering. And bless me with your fertility, that I, too, may birth God in my soul and rejoice in God's loving-kindness. O Theotokos, pray for me. Amen.

Virgin of Tenderness

HER STORY

*A*ccording to Russian Orthodox tradition, Saint Luke painted the very first icon of the Blessed Mother. Because iconographic technique requires the iconographer to replicate the original as perfectly as possible, the known icons should be close copies—or close copies of copies—of Luke's painting. However, variations in the positions and postures of the Madonna and Child are possible, the first two variations being *Theotokos* (page 198) and *Hodegetria* (page 22). The Virgin of Tenderness (*Eleousa* in Greek; *Umileniye* in Russian) is the third. The famous icon of Our Lady of Vladimir may have been the first depiction of the Virgin of Tenderness variation.

In the representation of the Virgin of Tenderness, Mary and Jesus are shown with their cheeks pressed together, with Jesus nestled in his mother's right arm, embracing her about the neck, gazing at her and even breathing on her. This icon thus emphasizes the close emotional ties between this mother and her child. But it also expresses the concept that the Blessed Mother is mother of all human relationships with God, for she is gazing at the viewer as well as upon her own child. Additionally, the icon reveals the child's destiny, for Jesus' bare, crossed feet symbolize the death he suffered on the cross.

As are all icons, the Virgin of Tenderness is simple yet symbolic, urging the viewer to meditate upon the theological truths that it depicts.

ᴏᴠ TRADITIONAL PRAYER

Rejoice, Mary, Mother of God, Virgin, full of grace, the Lord is with thee: Blessed art thou among women and blessed is the fruit of thy womb, for thou hast borne the Savior of our souls. Meet it is in truth, to glorify thee, O Birth-giver of God, ever blessed, and all undefiled, the Mother of our God. More honorable than the cherubim, and beyond compare more glorious than the seraphim, thou who without stain didst bear God the Word, true Birth-giver of God, we magnify thee. Amen.

◌◡ NEW PRAYER

O Virgin of Tenderness, be with those children who have lost their mothers. Be a mother to them, comforting them in their loss, protecting them in their aloneness, cheering them in their sadness. Provide them with the loving-kindness and tenderness they so desperately need at the moment of their loss and at every moment thereafter. Most of all, in the name of the love you bore for your own son, bring them together with loving people who will be able to nurture them and encourage them and love them unconditionally. Amen.

ANNUNCIATION

Sculpture by F. Schiavina
Church of the Annunciation
Nazareth, Galilee

A New Litany of Mary

Hail, Mary! O Full of Grace, the Spirit is with you!
We bless you and honor you and exalt your very name.

Hail, Blessed Mother, we thank you for your
unconditional love.
Hail, Mother of All People, we thank you for your
unconditional love.
Hail, Mother of the Church, we thank you for your
unconditional love.
Hail, Mother of the Unborn, we thank you for your
unconditional love.

Hail, Ever-Virgin, we extol your spirit.
Hail, Immaculate Conception, we extol your spirit.
Hail, Mary of the Immaculate Heart, we extol
your spirit.
Hail, Mystical Rose, we extol your spirit.
Hail, New Eve, we extol your spirit.
Hail, *Panagia,* we extol your spirit.

Hail, Cause of Our Joy, we honor your *fiat*.
Hail, Cedar of Lebanon, we honor your *fiat*.
Hail, Mary of the Annunciation, we honor your *fiat*.
Hail, Lady of Loreto, we honor your *fiat*.
Hail, Lady of Trsat, we honor your *fiat*.
Hail, Lady of Walsingham, we honor your *fiat*.

Hail, Queen of All Saints, we praise your example.
Hail, Queen of Apostles, we praise your example.
Hail, Queen of Martyrs, we praise your example.
Hail, Queen of Prophets, we praise your example.

Graciously hear us, O Spouse of the Spirit, as we beseech your aid.

O Comforter of the Afflicted, pray for us.
O Help of Christians, pray for us.
O Mother of Perpetual Help, pray for us.
O Lady of Csíksomlyó, pray for us.
O Lady of Kevelaer, pray for us.

O Lady of Gietrzwald, heal us.
O Lady of Lourdes, heal us.
O Lady of San Juan de los Lagos, heal us.
O Lady of the Pillar, heal us.
O Lady of Tínos, heal us.
O Lady of Vailankanni, heal us.
O Lady of Wambierzyce, heal us.

O Mother of Sorrows, comfort us in our sorrowing.
O Lady of Akita, comfort us in our sorrowing.
O Lady of Gyor, comfort us in our sorrowing.
O Lady of Kalwaria Zebrzydowska, comfort us in
   our sorrowing.
O Lady of La Salette, comfort us in our sorrowing.
O Lady of Naju, comfort us in our sorrowing.

O Lady of Einsiedeln, protect us from all harm.
O Lady of Marija Bistrica, protect us from all harm.
O Lady of Sinj, protect us from all harm.

O Lady of China, protect us from all oppression.
O Lady of Czestochowa, protect us from all oppression.
O Lady of Kazan, protect us from all oppression.
O Lady of La-Vang, protect us from all oppression.
O Lady of Levoca, protect us from all oppression.
O Lady of Šiluva, protect us from all oppression.

Hail, Lady of El-Zeitoun, teach us to pray.
Hail, Lady of Knock, teach us to pray.
Hail, Lady of Mount Carmel, teach us to pray.
Hail, Lady of Pompeii, teach us to pray.
Hail, Lady of the Green Scapular, teach us to pray.
Hail, Lady of the Miraculous Medal, teach us to pray.
Hail, Lady of the Rosary, teach us to pray.

Hail, Mother of Mercy, teach us compassion.
Hail, Refuge of Sinners, teach us compassion.
Hail, Mary, Reconciler of People and Nations, teach us to love
one another.
Hail, Lady of Kibeho, teach us to love one another.
Hail, Lady of Soufanieh, teach us to love one another.
Hail, Lady of Medjugorje, teach us the way of peace.
Hail, Queen of Peace, teach us the way of peace.

O Mary of the Assumption, help us to persevere.
O Mother of Grace, help us to persevere.
O Lady of Aparecida, help us to persevere.
O Lady of Ephesus, help us to persevere.
O Lady of Hope of Pontmain, help us to persevere.
O Lady of Montserrat, help us to persevere.

O Lady of Fátima, give us the spirit of repentance.
O Lady of Montichiari, give us the spirit of repentance.

Hail, Lady of Banneux, teach us to trust God's providence.
Hail, Lady of Beauraing, teach us to trust God's providence.
Hail, Lady of Divine Providence, teach us to trust God's
providence.
Hail, Lady of the Hudson, teach us to trust God's providence.
Hail, Lady of the Rockies, teach us to trust God's providence.

Hail, Lady of the Philippines, teach us to trust God's
omnipotence.
Hail, Lady of the Snows, teach us to trust God's omnipotence.

O *Nikopoia*, help us to triumph over what separates
us from God.
O Lady of Guadalupe, help us to triumph over what separates
us from God.
O Lady of Victory, help us to triumph over what separates
us from God.

Hail, *Madonna della Strada*, illuminate our way to God.
Hail, Mother of Good Counsel, illuminate our way to God.
Hail, Lady of Neocaesarea, illuminate our way to God.
Hail, Lady of the Highways, illuminate our way to God.

O Ark of the New Covenant, guide us to your son.
O *Hodegetria*, guide us to your son.
O Mary the Dawn, guide us to your son.
O Morning Star, guide us to your son.
O Mother of God, guide us to your son.
O Lady of Mantara, guide us to your son.
O Lady of the Most Blessed Sacrament, guide us
    to your son.
O Lady of Zhyrovytsi, guide us to your son.
O Seat of Wisdom, guide us to your son.
O Star of the Ocean, guide us to your son.
O *Theotokos*, guide us to your son.
O Virgin of Tenderness, guide us to your Son.

Hail, O admirable Advocate, save us by your intercession.
Hail, O Co-redemptrix, save us by your intercession.
Hail, O Mediatrix, save us by your intercession.

Hail, Lady of All Nations, we glorify your name.
Hail, Queen of the Universe, we glorify your name.

Holy Mary, Mother of God, pray for us now and always, that we may
in this moment find encouragement in your maternal care as you lead
us joyfully toward your son's eternal kingdom. Amen.

Other Sources

Alphonsus de' Liguori. *The Glories of Mary.*
www.cin.org/mardol00.html

Ball, Ann. *A Litany of Mary.* Huntington, Ind.: Our Sunday Visitor,
1988.

*Bernadette of Lourdes: The Only Complete Account of Her Life Ever
Published.* trans. J. H. Gregory. New York: Louché, Keane & Fitch,
1915.

Brown, Michael H. *Seven Days with Mary.* Milford, Ohio: Faith
Publishing Company, 1998.

Bunson, Matthew, Margaret Bunson, and Stephen Bunson. *John Paul
II's Book of Saints.* Huntington, Ind.: Our Sunday Visitor, 1999.

The Catholic Encyclopedia Vol. 7. Robert Appleton Company: 1910.
Online edition posted 1999 by Kevin Knight.

Christopher, Joseph P., Charles E. Spence, and John F. Rowan, eds.
The Raccolta. New York: Benziger Brothers, 1952.

Connor, Edward. *Recent Apparitions of Our Lady.* Fresno: Academy
Guild Press, 1960.

Cowan, Tom. *The Way of the Saints: Prayers, Practices, and Meditations.*
New York: G. P. Putnam's Sons, 1998.

Cross, F. L., ed. *The Oxford Dictionary of the Christian Church.* Oxford:
Oxford University Press, 1957, 1978, 1997.

Czarnopys, Theresa Santa, and Thomas M. Santa, C.SS.R. *Marian
Shrines of the United States: A Pilgrim's Travel Guide.* Liguori, Mo.:
Liguori, 1998.

Daughters of St. Paul, comp. *Queen of Apostles Prayerbook.* Boston:
St. Paul Books and Media, 1991.

Egan, Eileen. *At Prayer with Mother Teresa.* Liguori, Mo.: Liguori,
1999.

The Essential Catholic Prayer Book: A Collection of Private and Community Prayers. Liguori, Mo.: Liguori, 1999.

The Essential Mary Handbook: A Summary of Beliefs, Practices, and Prayers. Liguori, Mo.: Liguori, 1999.

Foley, Leonard, O.F.M., ed. *Saint of the Day: Lives, Lessons and Feasts.* Fourth Revised ed., Pat McCloskey, O.F.M. Cincinnati: St. Anthony Messenger Press, 2001.

Gallery, John Ireland. *Mary vs. Lucifer: The Apparitions of Our Lady, 1531–1933.* Milwaukee: The Bruce Publishing Company, 1960.

Hoever, Hugo, S.O.CIST. *Lives of the Saints: For Every Day of the Year.* N.p.: Catholic Book Publishing Company, 1999.

In Praise of Mary: Hymns from the First Millennium of the Eastern and Western Churches. Middlegreen, England: St. Paul Publications, 1981.

John XXIII, Pope. *Days of Devotion: Daily Meditations from the Good Shepherd.* Ed. John P. Donnelly. New York: Penguin Books, 1967.

———. *Journal of a Soul.* Trans. Dorothy White, New York: McGraw-Hill, 1964.

John Paul II, Pope. *Dives in Misericordia.* Città del Vaticano: Libreria Editrice Vaticana, 1980.

———. *Redemptoris Mater.* Città del Vaticano: Libreria Editrice Vaticana, 1987.

———. *Veritatis Splendor.* Città del Vaticano: Libreria Editrice Vaticana, 1993.

Larssen, Raymond E. F., comp. and ed. *Saints at Prayer.* New York: Coward-McCann, Inc., 1942.

Leaflet Missal Company Staff. *A Holy Card Prayer Book: A Compilation of Saints and Holy People.* Saint Paul, Minn.: The Leaflet Missal Company, 1992.

———. *A Holy Card Prayer Book II: A Compilation of Saints and Holy People.* Saint Paul, Minn.: The Leaflet Missal Company, n.d.

Libreria Editrice Vaticana. *Catechism of the Catholic Church.* Liguori, Mo.: Liguori, 1994.

The Lost Books of the Bible. Cleveland, Ohio: The World Publishing Company, 1926.

McClory, Robert. *Faithful Dissenters: Stories of Men and Women Who Loved and Changed the Church*. Maryknoll, N.Y.: Orbis Books, 2000.

McClure, Kevin. *The Evidence for Visions of the Virgin Mary*. Wellingborough, Northamptonshire: The Aquarian Press, 1983.

Myers, Michelle. "For Crying Out Loud." *Nation* (September 1999).

O'Connor, Edward D., C.S.C. *Marian Apparitions Today: Why So Many?* Santa Barbara: Queenship Publishing Company, 1996.

Pennington, M. Basil, O.C.S.O. *Through the Year with the Saints: A Daily Companion for Private or Liturgical Prayer*. New York: Image Books, 1988.

Power, Rev. Albert, S.J. *Our Lady's Titles*. New York: Frederick Pustet Company, 1928.

Ribordy, Chad, and Angel Mortel. "A Journey for Those Left Behind." *National Catholic Reporter* (December 11, 1998).

Scanlan, Michael, T.O.R. *Titles of Jesus: A Manual for Prayer and Praise Based on New Testament Titles of Our Lord, Jesus Christ*. Steubenville, Ohio: Franciscan University Press, 1985, 1989.

Stevens, Clifford. *The One Year Book of Saints*. Huntington, Ind.: Our Sunday Visitor Publishing Division, 1989.

Swann, Ingo. *The Great Apparitions of Mary: An Examination of Twenty-Two Supranormal Appearances*. New York: The Crossroad Publishing Company, 1996.

Varghese, Roy Abraham. *God-Sent: A History of the Accredited Apparitions of Mary*. New York: The Crossroad Publishing Company, 2000.

Wright, Kevin. *Catholic Shrines of Central and Eastern Europe: A Pilgrim's Travel Guide*. Liguori, Mo.: Liguori, 1999.

———. *Catholic Shrines of Western Europe: A Pilgrim's Travel Guide*. Liguori, Mo.: Liguori, 1997.

Zimdars-Schwarts, Sandra L. *Encountering Mary: Visions of Mary from La Salette to Medjugorje*. New York: Avon Books, 1991.

Helpful Web Sites

web.frontier.net/Apparitions
www.americancatholic.org/Messenger/Oct1997/Wiseman.asp
www.apparitions.org
www.britannica.com
www.catholic.com
www.catholic.net
www.catholic.org
www.catholicapologetics.org
www.catholic-church.org/barnabites
www.catholicdoors.com
www.catholic-forum.com
www.catholicism.org
www.catholicity.com
www.catholicpages.com
www.christusrex.org/www1/apparitions
www.dailycatholic.org
www.ewtn.com
www.kalwaria.ofm.pl
www.ladyofallnations.org
www.liguori.org
www.maria.org
www.marianland.com/thirdsecret-text.html
www.mariology.com
www.medjugorje.com
www.medjugorjeusa.org
www.ourladylebanon.com
www.sacramentals.com
www.saintmeinrad.edu
www.santuarioloreto.it
www.snows.org
www.theotokos.org.uk/pages/approved/appariti
www.theworkofgod.org/Aparitns
www.truecatholic.org
www.udayton.edu/mary
www.vatican.va
www.voxpopuli.org
www.walsingham.org.uk

Index